BLACKSTONE'S GUIDE

The Employment Tribunal and the Fees Order

BLACKSTONE'S GUIDE TO

The Employment Tribunals Rules 2013 and the Fees Order

John Macmillan

Employment Judge

OXFORD
UNIVERSITY PRESS

OXFORD
UNIVERSITY PRESS

Great Clarendon Street, Oxford, OX2 6DP,
United Kingdom

Oxford University Press is a department of the University of Oxford.
It furthers the University's objective of excellence in research, scholarship,
and education by publishing worldwide. Oxford is a registered trade mark of
Oxford University Press in the UK and in certain other countries

© John Macmillan 2013

The moral rights of the author have been asserted

First edition published 2013

Impression: 1

Published in the United States of America by Oxford University Press
198 Madison Avenue, New York, NY 10016, United States of America

British Library Cataloguing in Publication Data
Data available

ISBN 978-0-19-870498-0

Printed in Great Britain by
CPI Group (UK) Ltd, Croydon, CR0 4YY

Foreword

I am extremely pleased that John Macmillan has been commissioned to write the first guide to the 2013 Rules and the Fees Order. No one could be better qualified. As a long-serving and very highly regarded Regional Employment Judge, he has a complete understanding of every aspect of the Employment Tribunals. He has studied closely the drafting history of the Rules, including the helpful consultation responses, and has analysed their provisions carefully and thoroughly. He is kind enough to pay tribute to the drafting style adopted by the working party, but the compliment can be reciprocated: his own language is conspicuously clear and concise. His deep knowledge of the case law on the previous rules also provides valuable insights—although I would sound a note of caution here: applying the old cases to provisions which are deliberately differently worded, and sometimes differently structured, is an exercise to be performed with circumspection.

When I was first asked to chair the working party my optimistic aim was to produce Rules which were—in the equally optimistic words of the law reformers of the Interregnum—'easy, plain and short'. It was a much more difficult task than I had appreciated. Even when we had made a choice, itself often far from straightforward, about what course we wanted to take on a particular aspect, there were sometimes unexpected constraints—among them the provisions (and language) of the primary legislation. There is also a difficult balance to be struck between the advantages of a new structure, or new language, and the disadvantages of departing from provisions to which, whatever their defects, everyone had become accustomed. I was all the more fortunate therefore to be chairing a group with such wide skills and experience, and to be assisted by particularly able lawyers from BiS and MoJ. John Macmillan delicately draws attention to some areas in the Rules which may cause problems. I hope he is wrong, but it would be foolish to suppose that we (though, as he points out, not every word of the Rules is in fact our work) got everything right. When those, or other, problems arise, practitioners and tribunals alike will benefit greatly from the clear exposition and rigorous analysis in this very welcome work.

Sir Nicholas Underhill
September 2013

Preface

The Employment Tribunals Rules of Procedure like Topsy in 'Uncle Tom's Cabin' just grow! The 1993 Rules and its predecessors ran to a mere 20 rules which appeared to be quite adequate. The 2004 Rules contained 61 rules, yet through a regrettable combination of pedantry, poor draftsmanship and muddying judicial process with political policy, were much less adequate for the task of enabling the Tribunal to justly and fairly manage a caseload of ever growing size and complexity. The 2013 Rules have 106 rules, but much of that increase has been achieved by breaking up many of the formerly excessively long rules into digestible chunks. By rendering them into plain English, introducing much greater flexibility and making some radical changes, they give employment judges, practitioners and parties alike hope for a much better future. (The same cannot, alas, be said for the Fees Order!)

One of the most important new provisions is r. 7 which enables the territorial Presidents to give non-binding guidance on matters of practice and how powers in the Rules are to be exercised. This is a welcome response to recent complaints of inconsistency, albeit much of that stemmed from a lack of understanding of the concept of judicial independence. Litigation is a worrying business at the best of times and having Rules that are easy to read and understand coupled with explanations of how at least some of them can be expected to work in practice, can only help to ease the burden. It is very important that the Tribunal's judiciary embrace the concept with generosity and enthusiasm.

I am grateful to Judge David Latham, the President of the Tribunals in England and Wales, for his suggestion that I should write this book. As a member of a working group drafting the Tribunal's standard documentation to complement the new Rules, I have seen them evolve and been party to some suggestions for change. I have learned much from discussions with my colleagues in the group, Regional Employment Judges (REJ) Jonathan Parkin and Carol Taylor and Employment Judge Alison Lewzey, and I am grateful to them for being the grit in the oyster of my thought processes. The flaws in the end product exposed in the following chapters are however entirely mine.

I am also grateful to Judge Shona Simon, the President in Scotland, for offering me guidance on Scottish practice and the Rules and for answering my queries generally.

My special thanks to Lord Justice Underhill, the inspiration behind the new Rules, for agreeing to provide the Foreword and to Judge Liz Potter, the REJ at London Central for providing the material for Chapter 13 and scrutinizing my rendition of it into the style of the Guide as a whole.

My thanks to Amy Jones my Assistant Commissioning Editor at OUP for her help and guidance and for reassuring me that it didn't matter when Topsy-ism proved contagious and the book outgrew several estimates of length.

And lastly my thanks to my wife Polly, whose encouragement makes all things possible, for accepting with patience that in my case retirement doesn't do anything like what it says on the tin!

John Macmillan
July 2013

Complimentary eBook version

Oxford University Press is providing all customers of this title with a free electronic version of the book for quick and portable access to the material. In order to claim your eBook, please navigate to <http://global.oup.com/booksites/content/9780198704980/> and use the login details as follows: username Macmillan, password ETRules2013.

Contents

Contents

Table of Cases

Table of Legislation

1

INTRODUCTION

A. SCOPE OF THE GUIDE

The purpose of this Guide is to provide a thorough comparative analysis of **1.01**
the Employment Tribunals Rules of Procedure 2013 and their immediate predecessors, the 2004 Rules, with a commentary on the changes, together with a
commentary to the Fees Order 2013. The main Rules of Procedure are dealt
with sequentially in Chapters 3–12 except those for national security proceedings which are in Chapter 13, while the Rules themselves are at Appendix 1. The
Regulations (The Employment Tribunals (Constitution and Rules of Procedure)
Regulations 2013)[1] to the extent that they require individual commentary, are
dealt with in Chapter 2 but references to them are made where appropriate
throughout the text. In the following chapters a reference to a regulation (e.g.
reg. 11) is a reference to the 2013 Regulations and a reference to 'old reg.' is a
reference to a regulation in the Employment Tribunals (Constitution and Rules
of Procedure) Regulations 2004 unless stated otherwise.

The Rules of Procedure Regulations were laid before Parliament on 31 May **1.02**
2013 with three provisions coming into effect on the 1 July: reg. 1 ('Citation and
commencement'), reg. 3 ('Interpretation'), and reg. 11 ('Practice directions')
the latter provision having to be in effect far enough ahead of the main Rules
to enable a Presidential Practice Direction to be made supplementing r. 8(1)
which would be unable to function without it. The remaining provisions came
into effect on 29 July 2013. Schedule 1 to the Regulations is the Employment
Tribunals Rules of Procedure 2013; Schedule 2 is the Employment Tribunals

---

[1] SI 2013/1237.

(National Security) Rules of Procedure 2013; Schedule 3 is the Employment Tribunals (Equal Value) Rules of Procedure 2013. Although the Equal Value Rules represent perhaps the greatest drafting triumph of the new Rules in that both clarity and simplicity have rendered the procedure as understandable and as fit for purpose as it is ever likely to be, no commentary is offered on them as they are unchanged in effect from their predecessors in Schedule 6 to the 2004 Rules.

1.03 The Employment Tribunals and the Employment Appeal Tribunal Fees Order 2013[2] and the Added Tribunals (Employment Tribunals and Employment Appeal Tribunal) Order 2013[3] came into effect on 29 July 2013 and apply only to claims presented on or after that date. The Added Tribunals Order merely designates both employment tribunals and the Employment Appeal Tribunal as 'added tribunals' for the purposes of s. 42(1)(d) of the Tribunals, Courts and Enforcement Act 2007 thus enabling the Lord Chancellor to prescribe fees in respect of them. The Fees Order is the subject of challenge by way of judicial review proceedings in both Scotland and England. The petitioners in Scotland are Fox and Partners, solicitors of Edinburgh and in England the trade union UNISON. The full hearings will take place in October 2013. Although an interim interdict was refused by Lord Bannatyne in the Court of Session on 10 July on the basis of the balance of administrative convenience, he held that a prima facie case had been made out on all grounds advanced in the petition. The government announced during the hearing that if the petitioners were ultimately successful all fees paid after 29 July 2013 would be refunded with interest and they accepted that the outcome would be binding throughout Great Britain. However, if the Fees Order is overturned or is required to be substantially amended in terms of the level of fees payable in certain proceedings, there are likely to be a number of claims bought out of time by claimants seeking extensions of time on the grounds that the claim could not have been presented earlier because they were unable to pay the claim fee. The principal commentary on the Fees Order is at Chapter 14 but important sections of commentary appear throughout the Guide e.g. Chapter 4, paras. 4.18–4.20. The Fees Order itself is at Appendix 2.

1.04 The Rules mark a milestone in the history of the tribunal in that they are the first to be (largely) drafted by its senior judiciary—led by Sir Nicholas (now Lord Justice) Underhill in his then capacity as President of the Employment Appeal Tribunal—rather than civil servants. Unsurprisingly, despite the fact that the end result is undoubtedly a quantum improvement on its predecessors in terms of comprehensibility, some provisions are problematic (e.g. r. 19) and areas of ambiguity and uncertainty remain (e.g. rr. 21 and 52). These are explored in detail, with tentative, first attempt, suggestions at interpretation offered. Where appropriate, familiar cases on aspects of the Rules are examined with a view to

---

[2] SI 2013/1893.
[3] SI 2013/1892.

determining to what extent they might still be considered good law, and in some particularly contentious areas, for example costs, a more extensive guide to the case law is provided. Given the constraints of space and time the book is not, and is not intended to be, a comprehensive guide to the practice and procedure of the employment tribunals.

B. BACKGROUND TO THE 2013 RULES

Speculating upon the motives which led the Ministry of Justice (MoJ) to suggest to the Department for Business Innovation and Skills (DBIS), which, in its various incarnations, had always been the jealous guardian of the Rules, the rule-making authority being the Secretary of State,[4] that the Underhill group should be entrusted with the task of redrafting the Rules of Procedure, and which led to DBIS consenting, is both interesting and potentially informative. Following the Resolving Workplace Disputes consultation in 2011, the government received feedback that the rules had, over recent years, become over-elaborate and could sometimes act as a barrier to effective case management. They had also been the subject of much, sometimes scathing, judicial criticism for the poor quality of their drafting (see for example *Khan v. Heywood & Middleton Primary Care Trust* in both the EAT [2006] ICR 543; [2006] IRLR 345 and the Court of Appeal [2007] ICR 24; [2006] IRLR 793 on r. 25). Since s. 22 of and Schedule 5 to the Tribunals, Courts and Enforcement Act 2007 the employment tribunals are the only significant jurisdiction not to have its own rule-making committee and to be wholly dependent on a government department for its rules of procedure. Whilst this had the obvious difficulty that the Rules could be (and at times expressly were) used as vehicles for making economic and political statements, something which is wholly inappropriate in rules of procedure for a court or tribunal, there were also clear and worrying human rights implications. **1.05**

Article 6 of the European Convention on Human Rights, which forms Schedule 1 to the Human Rights Act 1998, at Art. 6.1 provides for the right to a fair trial: **1.06**

In the determination of his civil rights and obligations or of any criminal charge against him, everyone is entitled to a fair and public hearing . . . by an independent and impartial tribunal . . . .

The government is frequently directly or indirectly involved in litigation before the tribunal in its capacity as employer. Many of the long discrimination cases heard by the tribunal are against public sector employers who (apart, possibly, from Foundation NHS Trusts) are likely to be emanations of the state, while claims against the MoJ, DBIS and other government departments by civil

---

[4] Employment Tribunals Act 1996, ss. 1(1) and 7(1).

servants are by no means unknown. But it is also involved in its capacity as the Crown, whether in the context of guaranteeing payments to employees of insolvent employers or in a regulatory capacity as the (effective) respondent in appeals against certain notices e.g. of underpayment of the National Minimum Wage or of improvement or prohibition under the Health and Safety at Work etc Act 1974. It is also involved as applicant in the case of prohibition orders under s. 3A of the Employment Agencies Act 1973. It is therefore highly questionable, in consequence of its role as the rule-maker and sole author of the Rules, whether the employment tribunal could be accurately described as 'independent and impartial' in any case in which the government is directly or indirectly involved in any capacity.

1.07 A judicially led, and largely judicially constituted, working group would address some of these issues and also the vexed question of lack of clarity. As the consultation document[5] (hereinafter 'the Underhill Review') noted:

> The review sought to make recommendations in order to develop a new set of rules that ensure employment tribunal cases can be managed effectively, flexibly, proportionately and consistently in order to ensure a system that is fair to all parties.

The working group consisted of Sir Nicholas himself, Judge David Latham, the President of the employment tribunals in England and Wales, Judge Shona Simon, the President in Scotland, Brian Napier QC, and Angharad Harris, Chair of the Law Society (England and Wales) Employment Law Committee. The group was supported by officials from DBIS and the MoJ and an expert user group consisting of legal, business, and employee representatives such as the CBI and TUC who helped inform discussions. No greater tribute can be paid to the achievements of the Underhill group than the wholehearted approbation of the style and, generally speaking, content of the draft Rules when they were put out to consultation, the government's response to the Consultation[6] recording that:

> The majority of respondents (83%) welcomed Mr Justice Underhill's review and supported the moves towards stripping out complexity and over-elaboration in the tribunal rules. They particularly welcomed the plain English approach adopted, and the shortening of the rules. One response from the judiciary even described the review as 'the most conspicuous example of drafting simplification anywhere'....

1.08 The rest, regrettably, is not history. The original intention was that the Rules should come into effect on 6 April 2013 but they were delayed to enable them to be brought into effect at the same time as, and to include rules to accommodate, the Fees Order. This hiatus allowed DBIS lawyers to 'tinker' with the drafting introducing a plethora of seemingly unnecessary changes—some minor, some less so (e.g. rr. 39 and 70(1)) —largely, but not entirely, to detrimental effect, at

---

[5] Employment Tribunals Rules: Review by Mr Justice Underhill BIS/12/1039 September 2012.
[6] Employment Tribunals: Government Response to Mr Justice Underhill's Review of Employment Tribunals Rules of Procedure BIS/13/696, 14 March 2013.

least two sets of such changes not even being drawn to the Underhill group's attention. It also allowed the Rules once again to become instruments of policy with r. 66 (poorly drafted and of dubious legality: see para. 10.23) and the change to the costs rule in Health and Safety Act notice appeals (see paras. 12.30 and 12.31) being the most obvious examples. This latter change in particular gives rise once again to the question of whether the Rules are Art. 6 compliant, at least in this particular context. These changes and the issues which are the subject of commentary in the following pages notwithstanding, the 2013 Rules of Procedure remain a very considerable improvement on their immediate predecessors.

C. THE RULES AND APPEALS

The Rules of Procedure refer throughout to a claim and claimants. A 'claim' **1.09** means any proceedings before an employment tribunal making a 'complaint' (r. 1(1)). (In the Rules themselves the words are rendered as 'Employment Tribunal' contrary to the usual conventions. Hereafter the conventions used in the Rules will be adopted). A 'complaint' means 'anything that is referred to as a complaint, reference, application or appeal in any enactment which confers jurisdiction on the Tribunal'. The Rules in Schedule 1 therefore apply to all appeals which can be made to the Tribunal even where they are not expressly provided for in the Rules themselves. Those that are expressly provided for are levy appeals (r. 104), appeals against Health and Safety Act improvement and prohibition notices (r. 105), and unlawful act notice appeals (r. 106). The original intention was that, as in the 2004 Rules, certain provisions would be disapplied in the case of such appeals but ultimately this was not done. Among appeals not expressly provided for but which are nonetheless subject to the Rules by virtue of the definition of 'claim', are appeals against underpayment notices under s. 19C of the National Minimum Wage Act 1998. At least five other instances of the Tribunal's appellate jurisdiction to which the Rules will apply can be found in Table 2 of Schedule 1 to the Fees Order.

D. THE RULES AND THE CPR

Under the 2004 Rules a line of authorities developed which suggested that in **1.10** some circumstances, most notably when granting relief from sanction from an unless order, a Tribunal was making an error of law if it did not follow the Civil Procedure Rules where they covered an area not specifically provided for in the Tribunal's Rules of Procedure. Although in *Neary v. Governing Body of St Albans Girls School and anor* [2010] ICR 473 CA that solecism was expressly disavowed, its ghost seemed to linger on, it being held that the applicable provision of the CPR (CPR 3.9(1)) was merely a checklist or prompt, thus still giving it some, albeit much reduced, status vis-à-vis the Rules. In *Raggett v. John Lewis Plc* [2012] IRLR 906 EAT in allowing the claimant's appeal against the inclusion of VAT in a costs order where the respondent was registered for VAT but the claimant was not, the EAT, which cited *Neary* as its authority, observed that the Tribunal should exercise powers under the Rules in accordance with the same general principles which apply in the civil courts, but the Tribunal is not obliged to follow the letter of the CPR 'in all respects'.

1.11 There are dangers even in this 'watered down' approach to the difficult issue of the relationship, if any, between the Rules of Procedure and the CPR. It is respectfully suggested that it is wrong on the simple ground that there is no relationship. The Civil Procedure Rules have effect by virtue of s. 1 of the Civil Procedure Act 1997 (which only applies to England and Wales) and apply to the county court and superior civil courts in England and Wales. They do not apply to Employment Tribunals nor to civil courts in Scotland which are currently governed by the Sheriff Court—Civil Procedure Rules (Act of Sederunt (Sheriff Court Ordinary Causes Rules) 1993). The Employment Tribunals Rules of Procedure have effect by virtue of s. 7 of the Employment Tribunals Act 1996 and apply only to Employment Tribunals. Both the 1996 Act and the Rules apply to Scotland as well as England and Wales. There is no provision in the Rules, nor any historical precedent, for interpreting them differently in the two jurisdictions. The objections to any proposal that the Tribunal should follow let alone is obliged to follow, the CPR are therefore obvious: they occupy separate, self-contained, silos. Those objections would not be met by any claim that could be made that the CPR and the Sheriff Court Rules say the same thing in any given situation.

1.12 It seems possible that what prompted the approach rejected in *Neary* may have been (understandable) judicial dislike of the 2004 Rules both because of their poor drafting and their use as a vehicle for policymaking in the employment field. However, it is suggested that there was never any basis for turning to the CPR *as such* even as an aid to interpretation or as a checklist or prompt given the different statutory backgrounds to the CPR and the Rules of Procedure and the fact that the CPR has no application in an important part of the territory of Great Britain in which the Tribunal's Rules apply. But while it cannot be appropriate to attack a decision of an Employment Judge on the grounds that some provision of the CPR has been overlooked, the CPR simply having no application, direct or indirect in the Tribunal,[7] no objection could legitimately be taken if an Employment Judge, in seeking to cast light on some aspect of the Rules or to deal with a case management issue not covered by the Rules, were to turn to the CPR, or the Sheriff Court Rules, provided that in adopting or indeed adapting what they might find therein, they did so because it appears to be sensible guidance enabling the Judge to manage the case effectively in accordance with

---

[7] Unless expressly adopted, as in r. 31.

the overriding objective in r. 2 and not because 'the CPR says so'. The point is not blunted (indeed it is perhaps strengthened) in those cases where a rule borrows language from the CPR (e.g. r. 34 and CPR 19.2(2)(b) and r. 43 and CPR 32.5). The fact that only a small part of an equivalent rule in the CPR has found its way into the Rules of Procedure would seem to indicate that the Underhill Group was aware of the equivalent CPR provision and expressly did not adopt those parts not replicated in the Rules.

E. REDUNDANT PROVISIONS

Old rules 53 (Employment Agencies Act 1973) and 55 (Dismissals in connection **1.13** with industrial action) are not reproduced in the 2013 Rules, nor are most of the provisions in old Schedule 4 relating to Health and Safety at Work etc Act 1974 notice appeals. In the first and third cases they simply replicated provisions in the legislation and were therefore unnecessary. In the case of r. 55 the power which the rule provided for was available as an ordinary case management order.

2

THE REGULATIONS

A. OVERVIEW

The Regulations are reduced from twenty in number in 2004 to fifteen. Those **2.01** concerning the overriding objective, calculation of time-limits, and territorial jurisdiction become part of the Rules (rr. 2, 4, and 8 respectively). Other provisions are merged. Generally the substance of the Regulations is unchanged. Regulation 4 'Establishment of Tribunals' is a significantly weaker version of its predecessors which made it clear that it was for the territorial Presidents to determine the number of Tribunals to be established for the purposes of determining proceedings, but the final version stops short of transferring that power to the Lord Chancellor which earlier drafts had done. Such a transfer would have involved a serious interference with the role and responsibilities of the Presidents and may have infringed at least the spirit of s. 3 of the Constitutional Reform Act 2005. Most of the Regulations do not require commentary and are dealt with where appropriate in the following chapters. The few that do require comment are dealt with below.

B. ROLE OF THE PRESIDENT, REJs, AND THE VICE PRESIDENT

Regulation 7 defines the responsibilities of the territorial Presidents and the **2.02** Regional Employment Judges (REJs) and their equivalent in Scotland, the Vice President. Prior to the 2004 Regulations the REJs and the Vice President were 'responsible for the administration of justice by tribunals' in their regions. In the 2004 Regulations whilst adding the words 'and Employment Judges' after the word 'tribunals' the REJs and the Vice President became 'responsible to the President' for the administration of justice within their regions, introducing for the first time something approximating to a 'chain of command' structure. Nonetheless, in practice REJs and the Vice President enjoyed a considerable amount of autonomy.

2.03 No doubt in the name of achieving consistency across the regions, the 2013 Regulations go considerably further. The Presidents are enjoined by reg. 7(1) to use the resources made available to them to:

(a) secure, so far as practicable, the speedy and efficient disposal of proceedings;

(b) determine the allocation of proceedings between Tribunals; and

(c) determine where and when Tribunals shall sit.

REJs and the Vice President may be directed by their respective Presidents 'to take action in relation to the fulfilment of [these responsibilities] *and [they] shall follow such directions.'* The italicized words were included only in the final version of the Regulations. There are some worrying implications here, at least potentially. There is the implied hint of sanction should an REJ or the Vice President fail to follow such a direction, perhaps of judicial misconduct proceedings and although the three stipulated areas of responsibility are at first sight purely of an administrative nature, the dividing line between administrative and judicial matters (particularly in the case of reg. 7(1)(a)) can be indistinct. In the light of s. 3 of the Constitutional Reform Act, reg. 7 will have to be interpreted as though it gives the Presidents no power to interfere in matters of a purely judicial nature.

C. PRACTICE DIRECTIONS

2.04 The power for Employment Tribunal Rules to enable the Presidents to make practice directions derives from s. 7A of the Employment Tribunals Act 1996 and the power must therefore be interpreted in the light of that section. The power first appeared in the 2004 Regulations (reg. 13) and is reproduced in the 2013 Regulations (as reg. 11) without change of substance (other than the addition of a new provision concerning the making of practice directions for judicial mediation which includes the possibility of allowing a Judge allocated to hear a case to act as mediator in the case). The power has never been exercised in England and Wales. In Scotland three practice directions have been issued in respect of counterclaims (now redundant as a result of the changes in the 2013 Rules), exchange of documents, and sisting (staying) cases for private mediation.

2.05 In the county court the role of practice directions is, roughly, to supplement the CPR with further regulatory detail. It seems that practice directions in Employment Tribunals may be intended to go further. Section 7A(2C) ETA provides that the territorial Presidents may not make practice directions without the approval of the Senior President of Tribunals and the Lord Chancellor.

However, by subs. (2D) the approval of the Lord Chancellor is not required for practice directions 'to the extent that they consist of guidance about...the application or interpretation of the law [or] the making of decisions by members of an employment tribunal'. There are two problems here. The first is the risk of such a practice direction infringing judicial independence. The second is the use of the word 'guidance' both because the issuing of Presidential guidance is now the subject of its own rule (r. 7: see paras. 3.15–3.19) and because whereas practice directions are intended to be binding, guidance by its very nature cannot be, and r. 7 expressly so provides. There is a further complication. Section 7A(1)(b) provides that Rules of Procedure may include provisions 'for securing compliance with' practice directions. The 2013 Regulations and Rules of Procedure do not do so. Non-compliance with a practice direction by a party would therefore appear not be an irregularity for the purposes of r. 6 (see para. 3.13) which applies only to non-compliance with the Rules.

It seems likely that if the power to make practice directions as opposed to   **2.06** giving guidance under r. 7 is to be exercised at all in future (other than where the Rules expressly require it: rr. 8 and 88) it will be to provide procedural structure where none exists, as for judicial mediations, or to underpin with additional detail the Rules themselves. What a particular rule means and how it is to be applied in certain circumstances would seem to be more appropriately a subject for r. 7 guidance.

D. TRANSITIONAL PROVISIONS

Transitional provisions appear in reg. 15. The Rules apply to all claims already   **2.07** before the Tribunal on 29 July 2013 no matter what stage they have reached, subject to two exceptions. First, where a respondent receives a claim form from the Tribunal before 29 July which contains an employee's contract claim, rr. 23 to 25 do not apply. Instead r. 7 of the 2004 Rules applies. In such a case, there is no requirement for any employer's contract claim (counterclaim) to be included in the response (although for commentary on whether this is a requirement that can rigidly be enforced see paras. 5.32–5.34); no requirement for the claimant to enter a response to the counterclaim unless directed to do so; and no default judgment if they fail to do so. Second, where the proceedings before the Tribunal are an appeal against assessment to training levy, a Health and Safety Act improvement or prohibition notice, or an unlawful act notice under the Equality Act, if the appeal was presented to the Tribunal before 29 July the 2004 Rules continue to apply. In the case of levy appeals this appears to mean the date on which the notice of appeal is sent by the Industry Training Board to the Tribunal rather than the date on which it was received by the Training Board.

3

INTRODUCTORY AND GENERAL—RULES 1–7

A. INTERPRETATION

Rule 1 is the interpretation provision for the Rules, the Regulations having their own **3.01** interpretation provision at reg. 2. Most are uncontroversial and self-explanatory. Some are dealt with in the appropriate places in the following chapters. Only a few call for special comment here.

'"Employment Tribunal" or "Tribunal" means an Employment Tribunal estab- **3.02** lished in accordance with regulation 4, and in relation to any proceedings means the Tribunal responsible for the proceedings in question, whether performing administrative or judicial functions.' By virtue of r. 1(2) 'Tribunal' includes an Employment Judge sitting alone. The definition is problematic simply because it does not separate administrative functions from judicial and in some cases the Rules do not make it clear whether a decision is to be taken by the Tribunal staff or a Judge (e.g. rr. 10 and 11). In most, but not all, cases the problem is resolved by the context and by making the initial decision susceptible to reconsideration by a Judge.

'"Present" means deliver (by any means permitted under r. 85) to a tribunal **3.03** office.' Rule 85(2) limits the means by which a claim form can be presented to those prescribed in a Presidential practice direction. This is discussed in more detail at paras. 4.05–4.08.

'Tribunal office.' For the purposes of the Rules a Tribunal office is one which **3.04** carries out administrative functions in support of the Tribunal. Historically most of the premises where hearings were held also carried out administrative functions on behalf of the Tribunal but there is an increasing tendency to centralize administrative support to one office per region. The term 'Tribunal office' will in future apply only to such offices even though staff might be present at other offices within the region on a daily basis for the purpose of clerking hearings.

B. THE OVERRIDING OBJECTIVE

3.05 The overriding objective first appeared in the 2001 Regulations and re-appeared in the 2004 Regulations (reg. 3) in almost identical terms. The wording closely (but not exactly) followed the wording of CPR 1.1–1.3. In the 2013 Rules the overriding objective is brought into the Rules as r. 2 and some important changes are made which reflect the spirit in which the Underhill review was undertaken. There are two new elements of the objective to deal with cases fairly and justly which require the Tribunal, so far as practicable, to avoid unnecessary formality and seek flexibility in the proceedings (r. 2(c)) and to avoid delay, so far as compatible with proper consideration of the issues (r. 2(d)). Introduced into r. 2(b), which deals with proportionality, is a need to have regard to the importance as well as the complexity of the issues; 'importance' presumably being judged objectively rather than subjectively through the eyes of the parties. Although no express connection is made, the overriding objective now has teeth. By making it a rule rather than a regulation it is brought within the ambit of r. 6 ('Irregularities and non-compliance') meaning that a party who breaches the objective by failing to assist the Tribunal in its furtherance or by failing to co-operate with the other parties or the Tribunal, risks one of the sanctions discussed below at para. 3.13.

C. ALTERNATIVE DISPUTE RESOLUTION

3.06 Rule 3 is entirely new and reflects the growing importance in particular of judicial mediation. It requires the Tribunal wherever practicable and appropriate, to encourage the parties to 'use … the services of Acas, judicial or other mediation, or other means of resolving their disputes by agreement'. It may be largely symbolic as experienced Judges (and indeed newly appointed Judges who are used to using ADR in their practices) are already familiar with the advantages of mediation and conciliation in seemingly intractable cases. It seems very likely that this rule, together the new power to make practice directions for judicial mediation, which may include the power to permit an Employment Judge to act as mediator in a case even though they have been selected to decide matters in that case (reg. 11(1)(b)), will lead increasingly to the blurring of the distinction between the role of the Judge as judge and as mediator.

D. TIME

Another provision brought into the Rules from the Regulations is the calcula- **3.07** tion of time-limits for various purposes. Previously in reg. 15 (one of the better drafted provisions of the 2004 Rules) the provisions are now in r. 4. Several of them, including the examples, are repeated more or less verbatim. There are two important additions to the rule, one significant omission and one material change of wording.

The Rule creates a new provision about when acts must be done (r. 4(1)). It **3.08** provides that 'unless otherwise specified by the Tribunal' an act required by the Rules, an order, or a practice direction to be done on or by a particular day may be done at any time before midnight on that day. If there is an issue about compliance, the onus is on the party claiming to have complied.

Rule 4(2) is also new and provides that where the time specified by the Rules, a **3.09** practice direction or an order for doing any act ends on a day other than a working day as therein defined, the act is done in time if done on the next working day. It is important to note that this does not affect the expiration of statutory time-limits for presenting claims.

Rule 4(6) represents a change from old reg. 15(6) concerning the calculation of **3.10** time which runs from the date on which a document is sent to a party. Regulation 15(6) provided that, unless the contrary was proved, the date on which the document was deemed to have been sent to the party was to be regarded as the date on the letter from the Tribunal which accompanied the document. Rule 4(6) provides that it is to be regarded as (unless the contrary is proved) the date endorsed on the document or, 'if there is no such endorsement', the date on the letter accompanying the document. In consequence, if a date of sending is endorsed on the document then a different date on the accompanying letter is only available as evidence in support of an attempt to prove the contrary.

Old reg. 15(5) is omitted. This provided that the requirement in r. 14(4) to send **3.11** a notice of hearing to the parties not less than fourteen days before the date fixed for the hearing was only to be construed as a requirement to place the notice in the post not less than fourteen days prior to the hearing. This meant that in practice the parties might receive significantly less than fourteen days actual notice. Rule 54 (preliminary issue hearings under r. 53(1)(b)) and r. 58 (final hearings) now require the Tribunal to 'give the parties not less than 14 days notice' of the hearing. Thus there now seems to be a requirement that the notice is *received* not less than fourteen days prior to the hearing.

E. EXTENDING OR SHORTENING TIME

Rule 5 applies to time-limits but only to those 'specified by the Rules or in any **3.12** decision'. It would therefore not apply to any time-limit imposed for the payment of a fee under the Fees Order, nor to a time-limit imposed by a practice direction. It represents a welcome change from the 2004 Rules in that any time-limit can be extended whether or not it has already expired. The express exclusion in the 2004 Rules of a power to extend the time-limit for submitting a response after it had expired was widely regarded as one of its more repugnant features.

F. IRREGULARITIES AND NON-COMPLIANCE

3.13 Rule 6 is an entirely new and welcome provision. It enables the Tribunal to impose sanctions in the case of non-compliance with any provision of the Rules or an order which is not an unless order. Faced with such non-compliance 'the Tribunal may take such action as it considers just', which may include:

(a) waiving or varying the requirement (in the order);

(b) striking out the claim or the response;

(c) barring or restricting a party's participation in the proceedings; and

(d) awarding costs in accordance with rr. 74–84.

3.14   Note that the list of sanctions in the rule is illustrative not exhaustive. There is no requirement for the order in question to have been endorsed with a penal notice drawing the parties' attention to r. 6 nor for any warning of the consequences of non-compliance to have been given before a sanction is imposed. Issues of proportionality will loom large in determining what, if any, sanction to apply, as will the magnitude and frequency of and motive for the non-compliance. The authorities on relief from the sanction of strike out following non-compliance with an unless order discussed at paras. 7.67–7.69 will be of assistance when determining the level of sanction to impose under r. 6.

G. PRESIDENTIAL GUIDANCE

3.15 Rule 7 introduces a concept which is possibly unique and certainly new to the Tribunal, that of Presidential guidance 'as to matters of practice and as to how the powers conferred by these Rules may be exercised'. The nearest equivalent in other courts appears to be practice directions. There is clearly the potential for overlap and confusion with practice directions issued under reg. 11, particularly as such directions are also to be concerned with how the powers conferred by the Rules are to be exercised. Indeed the practice direction may now be largely redundant, not least because Presidential guidance does not require the consent of either the Senior President or the Lord Chancellor. For further discussion on this issue see para. 2.4. There are two differences in practical terms: while a practice direction must be published by the President 'in an appropriate manner to bring it to the attention of the persons to whom it is addressed', guidance is to be published 'to bring it to the attention of claimants, respondents and their advisors'. This suggests the possibility that the two are intended for different audiences, although the more likely explanation is merely that the two provisions have different authors, reg. 11 repeating the words of old reg. 13. The other difference is that guidance is expressly non-binding on Tribunals although they must have regard to it. There is no requirement in r. 7 for the Tribunal to give reasons for not following relevant guidance but, unless it was departed from by consent, r. 62(1) would require reasons to be given.

The requirements about publication have led some to speculate that guidance **3.16** is intended only for the parties and their advisors, but that is clearly wrong. Given the background to this rule as explained in the consultation documents and the need for Tribunals to have regard to any such guidance, the publication requirement is in addition to the publication to Judges and Tribunal members. It was expressly stated in the consultation that the intention was to provide illustrative guidance to all parties, *and Employment Judges*, through the Tribunal process.

The consultation documents suggest that the rule has its origins in two **3.17** concerns: that of the unrealistic expectations of some parties' about what a Tribunal can achieve and the perceived lack of consistency in case management and decision making by Tribunals and Judges across the country. Almost all respondents to the consultation (93 per cent) agreed with the principles behind the proposal. It was felt that guidance which sets out normal or likely practice will be important in supporting shorter rules, and make it easier for non-lawyers to understand what was required of them and would also help to ensure consistency in case management and decision making.

4

STARTING A CLAIM—RULES 8–14

A. OVERVIEW

This section of the 2013 Rules preserves the five components of the equiva- **4.01** lent provisions of the 2004 Rules (old rr. 1–3 and 34) namely presentation; the requirement to use a prescribed form; the requirement to provide certain basic information on the form; power for the Tribunal to reject non-compliant claim forms; and the right to have such decisions revisited. But there are important changes of detail and substance, at least potentially, in all components, in particular with regard to the places at and means by which a claim can be presented, the grounds on which a claim form can be rejected, and the introduction of a discrete reconsideration regime for rejected claims which appears to have the effect of making the prescribed form no longer sacrosanct. The language is simplified and much of the complex administrative detail removed.

Some troubling implications of the fees regime are discussed here rather than **4.02** in the chapter on the Fees Order itself (Chapter 14).

B. PRESENTING THE CLAIM

1. Claims, complaints, and appeals

4.03 By virtue of r. 1(1) 'claim' means any proceedings before an Employment Tribunal making a complaint. The claimant is the person bringing the claim. 'Complaint' means anything that is referred to in the relevant legislation as a claim, complaint, reference, application, or appeal. The Rules therefore apply, subject to one exception, to levy appeals under the Industrial Training Act 1982, appeals against improvement and prohibition notices under the Health and Safety at Work etc. Act 1974, appeals against unlawful act notices under s. 21 of the Equality Act 2010, and appeals against notices of underpayment issued under s. 19C of the National Minimum Wage Act 1998—plus several other very infrequently used appeal provisions. They also apply to applications under s. 3C of the Employment Agencies Act 1973 for the variation or revocation of a prohibition order. The exception is that in the case of an appeal it is 'not necessary' for either the appellant or the respondent to the appeal to use the prescribed forms (reg. 12(2)(b)).

4.04 A single claim form may include any number of complaints even if they are unrelated and there is no express requirement for all complaints on a claim form to be against one employer. However, including multiple complaints against multiple unconnected employers in the same claim form will almost inevitably result in the rejection of the claim on one of the grounds discussed below in Part C. It is possible for some complaints on a claim form to be rejected while the remainder are accepted in which case the reconsideration regime (see paras. 4.44–4.56) applies to the rejected complaints.

2. Presentation

4.05 The basics of commencing Employment Tribunal proceedings are not expressly changed but the places at which and the means by which presentation can be achieved is now the subject of Presidential practice directions. Rule 8(1) (read with r. 85(2)) has the effect that a claim can only be started by presenting a completed claim form using a prescribed form 'in accordance with the practice direction made under regulation 10 which supplements this rule'. The initial impetus for this change is that at the same time that the claim form is presented either a fee must be paid or remission application made, and so presentation by methods which makes this impossible is not permitted. Thus a claim can no longer be presented as an attachment to an email nor by fax. Words inserted into a late draft of r. 85(2) (but which did not appear in the final version of the Rules), would have prevented presentation of a claim form by hand delivery at a Tribunal office. This appears to remain a long-term ambition of the administration. As it is, the practice directions do not permit postal presentation at a Tribunal office. Claims may only be presented by post at one of two PO box addresses, those of the so-called central processing facilities for the handling of fees, currently Arnhem House in Leicester and The Eagle Building in Glasgow, to which claims presented via the Tribunal's website at http://www.justice.gov.uk/tribunals/employment/claims will also be routed.

In England and Wales claims may be presented by hand only at the regional **4.06** office for each region. In Scotland, in addition to Glasgow and Edinburgh, claims may also be presented by hand at the offices in Aberdeen and Dundee. All these offices will only accept claims during business hours defined as Monday to Friday (other than public holidays) 9.00 am to 4.00 pm. The full texts of the practice directions including the addresses of the Tribunal offices at which claims may be presented and the PO addresses are at Appendix 3.

The restrictions discussed above apply only to the presentation of the claim **4.07** form. By r. 1(1) 'present' means 'deliver by any means permitted under r. 85' namely by post, by direct delivery to the appropriate tribunal office or by electronic communication 'such as' fax or email. A response is also 'presented' (r. 16) but no limitations to the manner of presentation apply. The act of presentation stops time running for the purposes of the applicable limitation provisions. A claim is not presented until it is received at the Tribunal office which under all previous versions of the Rules included leaving it in the office's letter box after office hours as no clerical action, such as date stamping the claim form, is required (*Post Office v. Moore* [1981] ICR 623 EAT). Under the practice direction supplementing r. 8 this will no longer be possible. Although neither the Rules nor the Fees Order deal with the point, it must be presumed that where a claim is presented with the wrong fee or a remission application which fails and the claimant subsequently pays the correct fee pursuant to a notice under r. 11(2), the date of presentation for the purpose of r. 8(1) is the date on which the claim was originally received by the Tribunal.

Modern electronic methods of communication suggest that earlier cases such **4.08** as *Ford v. Stakis Hotels & Inns Ltd* [1987] ICR 943; [1988] IRLR 46 EAT which held that where the last day for presenting a claim was a day when the Tribunal office was closed and there was no external letter box, that day was a *dies non*, may no longer be good law. Subject to rr. 8(1) and 85(2), presentation may be achieved by any method which the Tribunal holds out as being one by which it will receive claim forms. If a technical fault prevents a claim or response which has been transmitted by one of these methods reaching the Tribunal office or entering its systems, the claim or response has still been presented. For a claim presented by completing the form available on the Tribunal's own website see *Tyne & Wear Autistic Society v. Smith* [2005] ICR 663; [2005] IRLR 336 EAT. For presentation by fax see *Yellow Pages Sales Ltd v. Davies* (UKEAT/0017/11).

3. Territorial jurisdiction

Rules 8(2) and (3) bring within the Rules old reg. 19 which delineated the territo- **4.09** rial jurisdiction of Employment Tribunals in England and Wales and Scotland respectively. There are significant changes of language and, ostensibly, one of substance.

4.10 Prior to the 2004 Regulations there were separate Rules of Procedure Regulations for England and Wales on the one hand and Scotland on the other, each defining, in terms of territoriality, the respective jurisdictions by reference to certain conditions relating, roughly, to where the cause of action arose. Regulation 19 of the 2004 Regulations combined those definitions but preserved the jurisdictional division by providing that Tribunals in England and Wales and Scotland respectively *'shall only have jurisdiction* to deal with' those types of proceedings described as English and Welsh proceedings or Scottish proceedings [emphasis added]. The division was clearly mandatory. Rule 8(2) of the 2013 Rules however provides that a claim 'may' be presented to a tribunal office in England and Wales' and r. 8(3) that a claim 'may' be presented in Scotland, if one of the redefined conditions, which are discussed below, is satisfied. This appears to be merely directory or permissive. But given the legislative and broader historical contexts it would be extremely surprising if that was the intention as it would have the effect in practice of treating Scotland simply as a region of a Great Britain-wide Tribunal and allow a purely English claim to be presented in Glasgow. In the absence of a clear statement in the Rules to the contrary, the phrase in r. 8(2) 'A claim may be presented to a tribunal office in England and Wales if . . .' should therefore be read as if the word 'only' appeared before the word 'if'. Similarly the phrase in r. 8(3) with regard to Scotland.

4.11 Rule 8(2) applies to England and Wales, r. 8(3) to Scotland. In each case paragraph (a) repeats old reg. 19(1)(a) and (2)(a) respectively and paras. (b) and (c) reproduce (although in much more accessible language) the effect of old regs. 19(1)(b) and (2)(b). Paragraphs (c) and (d) of old reg. 19(1) and (2) are not reproduced, no doubt because they are unnecessary. The redefined conditions therefore do not change the long-established territorial basis for presenting a claim.

4.12 Rules 8(2)(d) and (3)(d) are new but do no more than enshrine into the Rules in the context of the division of jurisdiction between England and Wales on the one hand and Scotland on the other, recent jurisprudence on the Employment Tribunal's jurisdiction to hear cases where the cause of action arises extra territorially but where there is a connection with Great Britain (*Lawson v. Serco Ltd* [2006] ICR 250; [2006] IRLR 289 HL(E) as developed in *Duncombe and ors v. Secretary of State for Children Schools and Families* [2011] ICR 495; [2011] IRLR 315 SC, *Ravat v. Haliburton Manufacturing & Services Ltd* [2012] ICR 389; [2012] IRLR 315 SC and *Bates van Winkelhof v. Clyde & Co LLP* [2012] IRLR 992 CA).

4. Multiple claimants

4.13 Rule 1(7) of the 2004 Rules allowed two or more claimants to present their claims on the same claim form only if 'their claims arise out of the same set of facts'.

Rule 9 of the 2013 Rules uses slightly different wording—if 'their claims are based on the same set of facts'. It is not clear whether the intention is to simplify the language or change the ambit of the previous rule. For example, following a large-scale redundancy exercise a group of claimants may have a range of claims from purely monetary through unfair dismissal to discrimination, depending on their length of service and personal circumstances. Whilst all such claims appear to 'arise' out of the same set of facts, namely the redundancy exercise, it is arguable that they are each 'based' on their own facts and so could not be brought together in the same claim form, particularly if the dismissals were on different dates. However, it seems unlikely that the intention is to narrow the ambit of old r. 1(7). Multiple claimants constitute a fees group for the purposes of the Fees Order (see para. 14.04).

4.14 While the Rule provides that where two or more claims are wrongly included on the same claim form it shall be treated as an irregularity under r. 6 (for the consequences of which see para. 3.13) there is no right for a respondent to object to the fact that inappropriately conjoined claims have not been thus treated. The only course open to a respondent in such circumstances is to enter separate responses as seems most appropriate (unless all the claims are resisted on the same grounds or not resisted (r. 15(3))) and to ask for an early preliminary hearing under r. 53(1)(a) so that case management orders can be made.

C. REJECTION

1. Grounds for rejection

(a) *Administrative defects*

4.15 A claim will be rejected by 'the Tribunal' in its entirety if either it was not made on a prescribed form (r. 10(1)(a)), or it does not contain all of the minimum information which under the 2013 Rules means simply the names and addresses of the parties (r. 10(1)(b)). Although r. 10(1)(a) is not expressed to be so, it is subject to reg. 12(2) which provides that it is 'not necessary' to use the prescribed form in 'proceedings in which a Tribunal will be exercising its appellate jurisdiction' (reg. 12(2)(b)) or in proceedings brought by an employer under s. 11 of the Employment Rights Act 1996 (reference concerning the particulars which should have been included in a statement under s. 1; reg. 12(2)(c)). There is potential for conflict between r. 10(1)(b) and reg. 12(1)(c) which provides that the Secretary of State may prescribed claim forms and that 'the provision of certain information on the prescribed forms is mandatory'. Existing versions of the prescribed form (and, it is understood, the next generation of prescribed forms) show that providing details of the claim is mandatory and that failure to provide it will lead to the rejection of the claim. But as the Rules no longer give the power to reject a claim form where this information is not provided this is not the case. However there is a substantial risk that claims will continue to be rejected administratively for this reason even though under the 2013 Rules a claim form with this information missing should be referred to a Judge for possible rejection under r. 12(1)(b)—see para. 4.21. While the Rule does not state that rejection under r. 10 is a matter for the Tribunal staff, a comparison with r. 12 which refers to the staff of the Tribunal Office referring a claim to a Judge if they consider that it should be rejected for a substantive defect, suggests that it is. Rule 11 also refers only to 'the Tribunal' and rejection for non-payment of the claim fee is clearly a matter for the administration only.

4.16   It is questionable whether the requirements to use a prescribed form and provide minimum information can be rigidly maintained in the light of previous case law (and see also the discussion below at paras. 4.49–4.53). For example in *Hamling v. Coxlease School* [2007] ICR 108; [2007] IRLR 8 EAT a decision not to accept a claim form because the claimant's address had not been given although her solicitor's full contact details were provided, was set aside on appeal on the ground that the omission was immaterial and irrelevant in the light of the overriding objective. Similarly in *Smith v. Automobile Proprietary Ltd* [1973] ICR 306; (1973) I.T.R. 247 NIRC it was said that 'to hold that a [claim form] should be considered bad merely because it does not give the address of an organisation as well known as the RAC, would be mere pedantry'.

(b) *Employment Agencies Act 1973*

4.17   Old r. 53 is not reproduced in the new Rules and it therefore seems that there is now a requirement to name the Secretary of State as the respondent to an application to vary or revoke a prohibition order, notwithstanding that he is, by virtue of s. 3C of the Act, the respondent to the application. A failure to do so could (subject to the comments made at paras. 4.49–4.53) lead to the rejection of the application.

(c) *Fees*

4.18   Rejection under r. 11 is an administrative, not a judicial decision. The rule provides that the Tribunal shall reject a claim if it is not accompanied by a Tribunal fee or a remission application[1] or, if the wrong fee is included or the remission application fails, if the claimant fails to pay the amount requested in a notice sent to her 'by the date specified'. The Fees Order and the rule are both silent about what date is to be specified but it is understood that Standard Operating Procedures (SOPs) issued to Tribunal staff will specify twenty-one days from the sending of the notice. As the time-limit is not one 'specified in these Rules' there is no power to extend it under r. 5. The Fees Order does not prescribe the form of the remission application and there seems no warrant for rejecting a claim form accompanied by a remission application which is not on the form which

---

[1] There is no express requirement either in the rule or para. 7 of Schedule 3 to the Fees Order for the documentary evidence required to support the application to be supplied with the application itself.

the administration prefers—which is understood to be the current county court remission application form.

Where a Type A fee (see Table 2 of Schedule 2 to the Fees Order for a list 4.19 of Type A claims) is paid with a claim form which the Tribunal staff believe includes a Type B claim (any claim which is not a Type A claim), the claimant will be given the opportunity to pay the difference. If the claimant objects on the grounds that there is no Type B claim, the claim will proceed as a Type A claim alone and a notice will be sent to the respondent to that effect. Otherwise the Type B claim will be rejected if the extra fee is not paid.

There must be significant doubt about the validity of r. 11. 'Access to the courts 4.20 is a Constitutional right: it could only be denied by the government if it persuaded parliament to pass legislation which specifically, in effect by express provision, permitted the executive to turn people away from the court door' (*R v. Lord Chancellor ex p. Witham* [1997] EWHC Admin 237, *per* Laws J). However, s. 42 of the Tribunals, Courts and Enforcement Act 2007 from which the right to charge fees in the Employment Tribunal is derived,[2] provides only that 'Fees payable under subsection (1) are recoverable summarily as a civil debt' (s. 42(8)). There is no power for a Judge to reconsider the rejection of a claim under rule 11 and nothing in either the Rules of Procedure or the Fees Order which enables a claimant to challenge the rejection of a remission application or the amount by which the fee is reduced as the result of a partially successful application. There are clear Art. 6 ECHR[3] implications here. Other implications are discussed in Chapter 14.

(d) *Substantive defects*

A claim or part of one will also be rejected if an Employment Judge considers that 4.21 it is one which the Tribunal has no jurisdiction to consider (r. 12(1)(a)); it is in a form which cannot sensibly be responded to (r. 12(1)(b)); or is otherwise an abuse of the Tribunal's process (r. 12(1)(b)), collectively described as substantive defects.

Whether the claim is rejected for an administrative defect or a substantive 4.22 defect, the claim form is to be returned to the claimant, in the former case explaining why it has been rejected and in the latter giving the Judge's reasons for rejection, together, in both cases, with information about how to apply for a reconsideration of the decision. For reconsideration see paras. 4.49–4.53 below.

2. Effect of rejection

Unlike the 2004 Rules, the effect of rejection (which is synonymous with the old 4.23 Rules concept of non-acceptance), is not expressly dealt with in the 2013 Rules,

---

[2] By virtue of the Added Tribunals (Employment Tribunals and Employment Appeal Tribunal) Order 2013, SI 2013/1892.

[3] European Convention on Human Rights which forms Schedule 1 to the Human Rights Act 1998, Art. 6 being the right to a fair trial.

no doubt because it was felt that it would be superfluous to do so. The 2004 Rules contained two provisions which seemed to be statements of the obvious and there is no reason to believe that their omission from the 2013 Rules signifies any intention to change the effect of rejection.

4.24   Old r. 2(1) expressly provided that where part of a claim was not accepted the Tribunal should not proceed to deal with that part and where no part of the claim was accepted it should not be copied to the respondent. The former point now appears by implication in rule 15 'Sending claim form to respondents'. The latter point is not dealt with in the 2013 Rules but in the absence of a provision to the contrary this must still be the case as it is a necessary consequence of rejection. The same is true of old r. 3(7) which provided that when a claim was not accepted it was to be treated as not having been received by the Tribunal. In consequence time was still running against the claimant for the purposes of the applicable limitation provision.

3. Rejection and fees

4.25   Surprisingly, the Fees Order and the Rules are silent about the fate of the fee if the claim is rejected. It is understood that as a matter of administrative discretion the fee will be returned if the claim is rejected for an administrative reason under r. 10 but not for a substantive reason under r. 12. This is most unsatisfactory to say the least and seems grossly unfair, particularly where the proceedings are to all intents and purposes a nullity as where the Tribunal clearly has no jurisdiction to entertain them or where it is clear on the face of the claim form that the Tribunal has no power to do so, for example because the claimant lacks the minimum qualifying service to bring the complaint. Not to return the fee in such circumstances smacks of obtaining money under false pretences. The process of presentation and acceptance will now be split as all claim forms, wherever originally presented, will be sent to one of the central processing facilities for the fees to be dealt with but decisions on rejection will still be a matter for the relevant Tribunal office. As those decisions will be taken after the processing of the fee (with the possible exception of a claim form presented initially to a Tribunal office and immediately rejected under r. 10) this will only serve to heighten the sense of injustice should the claim be ultimately rejected because of a substantive defect.

4.26   Where the original reason for rejection is rectifiable and a second, rectified, claim is presented and not rejected there may be an administrative concession that a second fee is not payable. But even if this is the case the concession has no legal force and could therefore be withdrawn at any time. It would seem that if a reconsideration application succeeds on the basis that the defect which lead to the rejection has been rectified, no further fee can be payable in any event as what is now being accepted is the original claim form as rectified.

4. Substantive defects

(a) *Absence of particulars*

There is an important difference between the 2013 Rules and its three immedi- **4.27**
ate predecessors in that there is no longer an express requirement for the claim
form to set out even the nature of the claim. Previous Rules have required that
at least some information about the claim be provided in the claim form in
order for it to be accepted. The 1993 and 2001 Rules both required the claimant
to set out 'the grounds, with particulars thereof, on which relief is sought'. In
Burns International Security Services Ltd v. Butt [1983] ICR 547; [1983] IRLR
438 EAT it was held that merely to state that the claim was one of unfair dismissal without providing any further information did not mean that the claim
should be rejected as the only requirement of the Rule which was mandatory
was that the claim be in writing: the rest was merely directory. The 2004 Rules
included in the concept of relevant required information 'details of the claim'.
In *Grimmer v. KLM Cityhopper UK Ltd* [2005] IRLR 596 EAT it was held that
the test was: '...whether it can be discerned from the claim as presented that the
complainant is complaining of an alleged breach of an employment right which
falls within the jurisdiction of the employment tribunal'.

Rule 12 introduces a new concept—rejection for substantive defects—and **4.28**
r. 12(1)(b) requires an Employment Judge to reject a claim or part of it if 'it
is in a form which cannot sensibly be responded to...'. This requirement is
clearly mandatory and in consequence *Burns International Security Services Ltd
v. Butt* is no longer good law. Any claim can of course be responded to simply
by presenting a response and it therefore seems likely that r. 12(1)(b) creates a
higher threshold for a claimant than a requirement merely to demonstrate that
the Tribunal has jurisdiction to hear the claim (a failure to do so being itself a
substantive defect). In consequence, cases which gave guidance on the meaning
of the 'details' or 'grounds' of the claim under previous Rules (e.g. *Grimmer*
and *Hamling v. Coxlease School* (above)) at best do no more than provide a very
basic starting point to interpreting the new Rules. In some, possibly most, cases
it seems very likely that at least some particulars of the claim must now be given.

When, then should a claim be rejected because it cannot sensibly be responded **4.29**
to? It must be remembered that the Rules do not allow for a claim to be accepted
but not sent to the respondent while the Tribunal attempts to elicit sufficient
information from the claimant to enable the claim to be understood, and it must
be presumed that it is not intended that the claim be sent to the respondent
but then stayed while the problem is addressed. The intention seems to be that
respondents should not be troubled with incoherent claims.

At one extreme, a claim form in which none of the boxes in section 5.1 of the **4.30**
old prescribed form or 8.1 of the new form are ticked and no narrative appears at
section 5.2 (8.2) clearly cannot be responded to unless at some other part of the
form the claimant gives at least a hint as to the nature of the claim. At the other,
although described in the conjoined appeals of *Fairbank v. Care Management*

Group/Evans v. Svenska Handelsbanken AB (UKEAT/0139/12) as 'the essentials to be pleaded', it would clearly be wrong to reject a claim simply because it did not set out (1) the legal basis for the claim: unfair dismissal, direct race discrimination, etc; (2) what the act or omission complained of was; (3) who carried out the act; (4) when the act or omission complained of occurred; (5) why the complaint is being made of the act/omission; (6) anything affecting remedy.

4.31 It is suggested that whether a failure to provide particulars of a claim is a substantive defect for this purpose depends on the nature of the claim, the materiality of the omission and proportionality, having regard to the overriding objective. Thus for example if the claimant has been dismissed but has only ticked the unfair dismissal box on the claim form and has given no narrative explanation of why the dismissal is unfair, the claim can sensibly be responded to because the essential facts—whether the claimant was dismissed and if so why—must be known to the respondent. This appears to be so even though the claim form makes no distinction between 'ordinary' unfair dismissal claims and constructive unfair dismissal, the same tick box applying to both. The issue of proportionality arises here and it is suggested that it would not be proportionate to reject a claim for failing to make this distinction by only ticking the unfair dismissal box and providing no narrative, as the claim can still sensibly be responded to by a bare denial of the fact of dismissal.

4.32 In *Dodd v. British Telecommunications Plc* [1988] ICR 116; [1988] IRLR 16: EAT, the words 'Sex Discrimination Act or the Race Discrimination Act' were held to be sufficient to comply with the requirement to set out the grounds, with particulars thereof, on which relief was sought. But this is almost certainly not a claim which can sensibly be responded to, both because of the widely differing legal bases of potential claims under such headings (direct and indirect discrimination, victimization, and harassment) and because of the almost infinite variety of factual scenarios which can give rise to them. The respondent is entitled to know, at least in bare outline, the nature of the case it has to meet before it can sensibly respond. In discrimination cases as a minimum, it is suggested, this would appear to require the claimant to identify the event about which complaint is made. However, as in *Grimmer*, a claim form which said merely 'flexible working' might well be capable of sensibly being responded to given the very limited bases on which such claims can be brought before the Tribunal and that the employer will have full knowledge of the process which it followed and its reasons for rejecting the claimant's application for flexible working. Again, if the claimant has never in fact made an application for flexible working, that is a response which can sensibly be made.

4.33 As for monetary claims, where the sum claimed is (or is very likely to be) for an amount which is fixed (directly or indirectly) by statute as in the amount of notice pay (Employment Rights Act 1996, s. 86) or entitlement to holiday pay (Working Time Regulations 1998, reg. 13), merely ticking the appropriate box on the claim form without any further explanation may suffice. But where the amount claimed is at large, such as for unpaid wages, a failure to indicate how much is claimed or at least the time period to which the claim relates, may mean that the claim cannot sensibly be responded to.

(b) *Other claims which cannot sensibly be responded to*

In *May v. Greenwich Council* (UKEAT/0102/10) the EAT held that an **4.34** Employment Judge had no power to reject a claim form merely because the handwritten particulars of the claim were said to be illegible as the parts of the claim which the claimant was required by the Rules to complete—the relevant required information—were all legible. It would seem that under r. 12(1)(b) such a claim form could and probably should be rejected provided it was truly illegible. If the claim form is only partially legible, it was suggested in *May* at para. 19 (albeit *obiter*) that it would not be correct to refuse to accept the claim in its entirety where the refusal would have the effect of precluding the claimant from presenting a more readable copy within the applicable time-limit. The correct course would be to accept the claim and require the claimant to provide a more readable copy within a defined time. Provided enough of the original claim was legible to allow the claim to sensibly be responded to, that would still appear to be the appropriate course of action.

Claim forms which are incomprehensible for other reasons, for example they **4.35** are so badly written that it is impossible to determine the nature of the complaint, or are in a language other than English or Welsh, could also be rejected under this Rule provided that it is proportionate to do so. It must be doubtful that it would ever be proportionate not to reject a claim form which was truly incomprehensible, simply because it has been submitted so close to the end of the limitation period that a replacement could not be presented in time.

(c) *Want of jurisdiction*

A claim or part of one may be rejected if it is one which the Tribunal has no **4.36** jurisdiction to consider (r. 12(1)(a)). Rule 3(2)(b) of the 2004 Rules required the Secretary to reject a claim if it was one which the Tribunal did 'not have *power* to consider' [emphasis added]. It could be said that the 2013 Rules narrow the scope for rejection created by the 2004 Rules as there are several examples of claims which whilst the Tribunal has *jurisdiction* to hear them it has no *power* to do so. The most obvious are complaints of unfair dismissal where the claimant lacks the requisite qualifying service and any claim which is presented after the time-limit has expired. However, it seems likely that the change of wording is not intended to alter the basis on which claims have hitherto been rejected but rather to correct inappropriate use of language in the 2004 Rules.

Thus a claim may only be rejected under this provision if it is one which does **4.37** not fall within the scope of either the Employment Tribunals Act 1996 or any other Act which confers jurisdiction on the Tribunal (ETA, s. 2). For example, a claim for damages for personal injury which is not linked to a discrimination claim; a complaint of defamation; or a complaint against a disciplinary sanction short of dismissal which is not said to be discriminatory. Whether the

Tribunal has jurisdiction must be determined by taking the claimant's claim at face value.

4.38 An English or Welsh Tribunal has no jurisdiction to accept a claim which, by virtue of r. 8(3) should have been presented in Scotland and vice versa. The power under r. 99 to transfer claims between the jurisdictions applies only to claims which could have been started in either.

4.39 It would be wrong in principal to reject a claim under this rule simply because the time-limit for bringing it had expired, even if there does not appear to be a power to extend the time-limit under the appropriate legislation. The Tribunal has jurisdiction to entertain such a claim until it is held to be out of time.

(d) *No qualifying service*

4.40 The position with claims for which a qualifying threshold of service is required when that threshold has not been crossed is less clear. For example the right to bring a complaint of unfair dismissal is created by s. 94(1) of the Employment Rights Act 1996 (ERA). But s. 108 provides that s. 94 'does not apply' if the claimant lacks the requisite qualifying service. If the section does not apply then it would seem that the claimant lacks the right to bring the claim and in consequence it appears to be one that the Tribunal has no jurisdiction to consider. But that is not the current view of the majority of the Tribunal's senior judges. Current practice is to accept such claims and send them to the respondent but require the claimant to show cause why the claim should not be struck out, the respondent being told that there is no requirement to enter a response in the interim. The strike out is dealt with as a purely paper process allowing the claim to be struck out without a hearing even if the claimant makes representations, provided it is clear that the claimant is not alleging that the reason for the dismissal is one of those set out in s. 108(3)(a)–(r) ERA for which no qualifying service is required or that she does in fact have the requisite service.

(e) *Abuse of process*

4.41 A claim form may now be rejected under r. 12(1)(b) if it is an abuse 'of the process'—presumably the Tribunal's process. The Tribunal has always had power to strike out claims which are an abuse of its process and, even though no express power to do so has previously appeared in the Rules, it has probably been the case that it has had power to reject (or previously not to accept) such claims but only where it is apparent on the face of the claim form that it is an abuse. Examples of abuse of process which might be apparent on the face of the claim form include attempts to relitigate points which have already been the subject of a judicial decision (*Ashmore v. British Coal Corporation* [1990] ICR 485; [1990] IRLR 283 CA); attempts to re-open claims which have previously been dismissed after being withdrawn; attempts to re-open claims which have been settled as a result of an Acas conciliation officer's intervention (Employment Tribunals Act 1996, s. 18) or a binding compromise agreement (Employment Rights Act 1996, s. 203; Equality Act 2010, s. 147).

The rule would also cover such claims as an allegation of discriminatory bias **4.42** against an Employment Judge in determining a previous claim, or a claim which whilst apparently disclosing a cause of action appeared to be vexatious because, for example, the particulars of claim amounted to a libel against the employer or a named individual.

A failure to reject a claim on this ground cannot prevent a respondent from **4.43** applying for it to be struck out on the grounds that it is an abuse of process at a later stage in the proceedings, even where the abuse is apparent from the face of the claim. A decision not to reject a claim on this ground, and in particular acceptance by the Tribunal staff of such a claim without referring it to a Judge, does not create an issue estoppel against a respondent who has had no previous notice of the claim.

5. Reconsideration of rejection

(a) *General principles*
'Reconsideration' is the term used in the 2013 Rules in place of 'review' in previ- **4.44** ous Rules. Rule 13 provides a discrete reconsideration regime for rejected claims and in consequence the formal reconsideration regime for judgments at rr. 70–73 does not apply.

The claimant may apply for a reconsideration on the basis either that the **4.45** original decision to reject the claim was wrong or that the defect can be rectified. Rule 13(2) provides that the application must be in writing and presented to, i.e. be received at, the Tribunal office, within fourteen days of the date the notification of rejection was sent, although this time-limit can be extended under r. 5 (see para. 3.12) even if it has already expired. The application must either explain why the original decision was wrong or rectify the defect. Although the rule also provides that if the claimant wishes to request a hearing 'this shall be requested in the application' (words not in the original Underhill draft) a refusal to entertain an application for a hearing made subsequently but before the decision on the reconsideration application had been made, simply because it had not been made in the original application, would be pedantry of the worst kind and almost certainly in breach of the overriding objective. If the claimant requests a hearing the reconsideration application cannot be rejected without a hearing because of access to justice considerations and this still applies whenever the request is made.

It is unclear whether the application for a reconsideration is to be copied to the **4.46** respondent. Rule 13 itself is silent on the point. Rule 92 (see para. 12.13) deals with correspondence with the Tribunal and copying to other parties and is of general application. However, it provides for correspondence from 'any party' to be copied to 'all other parties' but until the claim form has been accepted there are no proceedings and therefore no parties and so r. 92 does not apply. The intention appears to be that the reconsideration application is entirely *ex parte* and in consequence there is no requirement for either the claimant or the Tribunal to copy the application to the respondent.

4.47   If a hearing is held, r. 13(3) provides that it is to be attended only by the claimant and again the intention appears to be that the respondent would not be notified of it. The rule does not say whether the hearing is in public or private and because there are as yet no proceedings to which anything other than r. 13 can apply, it is not obvious that r. 56 ('When preliminary hearings shall be in public') is applicable. Indeed, it is probable that this is not a preliminary hearing for any purpose. It is suggested that Art. 6.1 ECHR would require the hearing to be in public as a refusal of the application would be determinative of the claimant's right to bring the proceedings.

4.48   Even though the reconsideration application finally determines an issue which is capable of finally disposing of the claim, the Judge's decision on the application is expressly excluded from the definition of 'judgment' in r. 1(3)(b). If the application succeeds, the decision presumably becomes a case management order because of r. 1(3)(a), although it seems that the Judge is not required to give reasons for granting the application as r. 62(1) only requires reasons to be given on disputed issues. Being *ex parte* in nature the application for reconsideration is not disputed if that term means, as seems likely, opposed. The Rules therefore appear to require nothing more than an order recording that the decision to reject the claim form is revoked and, because of r. 13(4), to state the date on which the claim form is, in consequence, deemed to have been presented. Rules 60 and 61(2) require that a copy of the order is sent to the respondent. A respondent seeking to challenge the order should apply for it to be varied or set aside under r. 29. For a discussion on the standing of a respondent who has not entered a response to make such an application see para. 7.04. If the claimant's application fails and so there are no proceedings in existence, a case management order would appear to be inappropriate and so the decision would have to be communicated to the claimant by letter.

(b) *Failure to use a prescribed form or provide minimum information*

4.49   For the first time, the administrative decision to reject a claim or response for not being on the prescribed form is made susceptible to judicial reconsideration (r. 13(1)). The question whether the minimum information has been supplied or the prescribed form used seems at first sight to be a purely factual one (a glance at the form will show whether or not it is prescribed and includes the minimum information) and therefore to leave little scope for judicial reconsideration. But even though the initial decision is administrative and appears to admit of only a 'yes'/'no' answer, a decision to reject the claim should not be mechanical, although it must be doubted whether in practice it will be anything other than mechanical. However, on an application to reconsider the rejection of a claim or response for not being on the prescribed form or for failing to provide the minimum information, there can be little doubt from the authorities that the Employment Judge is required to approach the question judicially.

In *R v. Secretary of State for the Home Department, Ex p Jeyeanthan* [2001] 1 **4.50**
WLR 354 CA at 359 Lord Wolf MR said:

Because of what can be the very undesirable consequences of a procedural requirement
which is made so fundamental that any departure from the requirement makes everything
that happens thereafter irreversibly a nullity, it is to be hoped that provisions intended to
have this effect will be few and far between. In the majority of cases, whether the requirement is categorised as directory or mandatory, the tribunal before whom the defect is
properly raised has the task of determining what are to be the consequences of failing to
comply with the requirement in the context of all the facts and circumstances of the case
in which the issue arises. In such a situation that tribunal's task will be to seek to do what
is just in all the circumstances.

Among the consequences to be considered will be whether a fee will be forfeited
or a second fee will have to be paid if the decision to reject is not reconsidered.

It is clear from numerous authorities under the 2004 Rules that the task of the **4.51**
Employment Judge considering whether to reject a claim or response for failing
to supply what was then described as relevant required information (and therefore when reconsidering a decision to reject for an administrative defect under
the 2013 Rules), is anything other than mechanical. In *Richardson v. U Mole Ltd*
[2005] ICR 1664; [2005] IRLR 668 EAT the then President of EAT, Burton J,
speaking of the 2004 Rules in general said [at paras. 4 and 5]:

On the face of it the new Rules are extremely welcome, whereby there is a gateway to
ensure that applications or responses kick off on a sensible and complete basis from the
beginning...If however the result of the imposition of the gateway is not simply to point
out gaps which ought to be corrected, but to drive away a claimant so that...it means
that by the time the completely immaterial defect is corrected the claimant is out of time,
then injustice is inevitably going to be done. I have no doubt that that is not, and if it were
it should not be, the purpose of the Rules, and...there ought to be, and is, an overriding
objective of encouraging dealing with cases justly and fairly...rather than driving meri-
torious claimants, or indeed respondents, from the judgment seat.

I have seen other examples...where respondents have, by error, omitted, for example, in
one case an address, resulting in their response being rejected and their being thus barred
from defending a claim. That is not an appropriate use of the Rules and in my judgment
the better course is to construe the Rules in order to avoid such injustice.

In *Hamling v. Coxlease School Ltd* [2007] ICR 108; [2007] IRLR 8, EAT allow- **4.52**
ing an appeal from a decision to reject a claim for failing to include the relevant
required information of the claimants address when the claim form included full
contact details of her solicitor who had presented the claim on her behalf, Mr
Recorder Luba QC said, at para. 38:

The field of landlord and tenant is notoriously littered with judicial pronouncements on
the adequacy or otherwise of the completion of particular forms and the compliance with
requirements relating to those forms. From that jurisprudence it is plain that the proper
course is for [an Employment Judge] to ask himself whether, even in the face of the mandatory requirement as to the completion of a form, the failure is material or immaterial
in the particular circumstances of a case.

4.53   A claim or response therefore cannot be rejected simply because some of the minimum information is missing. The question for the Judge, having regard to the interest of justice, is whether the omission is material. This inevitably prompts the question, does this now apply to the prescribed form as well? The answer would appear to be 'yes'. Therefore, given that a decision to reject a claim or response because it is not on a prescribed form is now open to judicial reconsideration, the way seems to be open for the acceptance of claims and responses not on prescribed forms provided the failure to use a prescribed form is not material, which may well be the case if all of the information required by the Rules and the prescribed form is provided, and the interests of justice and the overriding objective would not be served if the claim or response were rejected. This point might well arise not expressly in an application for reconsideration but at a subsequent preliminary hearing if a replacement claim form was received after the time-limit had expired.

(c) *Time-limits*

4.54   The reconsideration regime for rejected claims in r. 13 and in particular a new provision, r. 13(4) which concerns time-limits, may lead Judges to err on the side of caution when considering whether a claim which is bereft of detail can sensibly be responded to and whether it should be rejected. The reconsideration regime permits the claimant either to explain why the decision to reject the claim was wrong or to rectify the defect (r. 13(2)) in this case by providing sufficient information to enable the claim to be responded to. Rule 13(4) provides that where on a reconsideration the Judge decides that the original decision to reject the claim was correct but the defect in the claim form has now been rectified, the claim will be treated as having been presented on the date of rectification. Because of the inevitable delay between the initial rejection and the provision of the further information, this may mean that by the time the claim comes to be accepted it is out of time.

4.55   Rules 3(7) and (8) of the 2004 Rules operated so that on a successful review the claim was to be treated as having been received when first presented and this seems also to be the case under the 2013 Rules if the reason for reconsidering the rejection was that the original decision was wrong. Although there was no express provision concerning the rectification of defects in the claim form, it was common practice under the 2004 Rules to overturn on review decisions not to accept claims if the failure to provide any of the relevant required information had been rectified by the claimant. This made sense when the failure related to supplying information required by the Employment Act 2002 (Dispute Resolution) Regulations 2004 as such a failure affected entitlement to bring the proceedings, but less so when it related to failure to provide details of the claim. A similar tendency may emerge under the new Rules in cases where the rejected claim was originally presented in time but rectified after the primary time-limit for the claim has expired, there being an obvious temptation for a Judge to say that the original decision to reject was wrong and to set it aside (thus rendering the claim in time) and to treat the new information provided as voluntary further particulars.

(d) *Reconsideration and issue estoppel*

It is perhaps regrettable, if only for the avoidance of doubt, that r. 3(9) of the **4.56** 2004 Rules (a decision to accept a claim shall not bind any future Tribunal where the original reason for rejection falls to be determined later in the proceedings) has not been replicated in the 2013 Rules, but its omission can scarcely be accidental. It is suggested that such a provision is unnecessary given the *ex parte* nature of the reconsideration proceedings and, in consequence, it would be open to the respondent to raise limitation issues or issues over jurisdiction, either in the response or subsequently, if a decision on reconsideration that the original rejection was wrong, seems flawed. There appears however to be a gap in the rules in that there is no requirement for the Tribunal to send to the respondent with the claim form any of the correspondence between the claimant and the Tribunal over the rejected claim form although the respondent would appear to be entitled to a copy of the order granting the reconsideration application. It is not clear therefore how, until discovery of documents, a respondent would become aware of the possibility that a claim which he has been informed is in time, could in fact be out of time.

6. Public interest disclosure claims

Rule 14 reproduces the effect of rr. 2(3) and (4) of the 2004 Rules and empowers **4.57** (but does not require) the Tribunal to send a copy of any clam form in which it is alleged that a protected disclosure has been made (even where it does not form part of a cause of action) to a Regulator listed in Schedule 1 to the Public Interest Disclosure (Prescribed Persons) Order 1999, provided the claimant has signified her consent to this course of action in the claim form.

5

RESPONDING TO THE CLAIM—RULES 15–25

A. THE RESPONSE TO THE CLAIM—RULES 15–22

1. Overview

Changes are made to the regime governing the presentation of the response **5.01** which attempt to make it mirror, at least to some extent, the regime for presenting the claim. This attempt at symmetry appears to create difficulties with the reconsideration provisions which in some circumstances seem likely to operate in a way which is not human rights compliant. These difficulties arise from the fact that when a claim is rejected there are only putative proceedings with putative parties and in consequence only r. 13 is engaged; whereas with a response there are actual proceedings with actual parties, the Rules as a whole are engaged and the claimant may have acquired a quasi-property right in the form of a judgment or the expectation of obtaining one. The term 'default judgment' disappears as, apparently, does the concept.

2. The response

5.02 Rule 15 provides that the claim form, once accepted, is to be sent to each respondent together with a prescribed response form and a notice informing them whether any part of the claim has been rejected, how to respond to the claim, including the time-limit for doing so, and what happens if no response is submitted. By virtue of r. 4(5) the last date for complying with a time-limit should, wherever practicable, be expressed as a calendar date and the Tribunal's standard service documents are designed so that this is always the case. A claim form sent to a respondent with the last date for returning the response expressed only by reference to a period of twenty-eight days beginning with a specified date or event is arguably not served in compliance with the Rules.

5.03 Subject to the possibilities discussed at paras. 4.49–4.53, the response to the claim must be on the prescribed form, although not necessarily on the form sent with the claim form. Responses may also be submitted online via the Tribunal's website at http://www.justice.gov.uk/tribunals/employment/claims/responding. The response must be presented to the Tribunal office 'within 28 days' of the date the copy of the claim form was sent to the respondent. 'Within 28 days' includes on the twenty-eighth day. There is a very important change from the 2004 Rules with regard to extending this time-limit. New r. 5, which allows the Tribunal to extend any time-limit after it has expired, is, unlike its predecessor, of universal application and therefore applies to the time-limit for presenting a response. However, although in most cases r. 5 permits the Tribunal to grant an extension of time after it has expired on its own initiative, by virtue of r. 18(1) in the case of a response an extension can only be granted if the response 'includes or is accompanied by' an application to extend time. To 'present' means to deliver to the Tribunal office by any means permitted by r. 85 (r. 1(1)). For commentary on what amounts to presentation see paras. 4.03–4.08 which apply equally to responses with one notable exception: there are no restrictions placed on how a response can be presented, even if it includes an employer's contract claim.

5.04 The current practice of permitting more than one respondent to respond to a claim on the same claim form provided they all resist the claim on the same grounds or they do not resist the claim, is retained (r. 16(2)). The Rule is silent as to what amounts to 'the same grounds' and it is suggested that the grounds need not be identical provided that all the respondents accept or deny the same facts. There is no power to reject the response if two or more respondents respond on the same form when it is inappropriate to do so although it may amount to an irregularity under r. 6. It therefore becomes an issue to be addressed at initial consideration under rr. 26–28 (see Chapter 6).

3. Rejection of response

(a) *Prescribed forms and minimum information*

Rule 17(1) provides that a response will be rejected if certain conditions are not **5.05** met, namely that the response is not made on a prescribed form and the specified minimum information has not been provided. When a response is rejected, it is to be returned to the respondent with a notice explaining why it was rejected and how to apply for a reconsideration and (if appropriate) an extension of time. The opening words of r. 17(1) –'The Tribunal shall reject a response if'—suggest, for the reasons given in the commentary to r. 10 (para. 4.15) that the decision is an administrative one.

The minimum information which must be supplied is only the respondent's **5.06** full name and address and whether the respondent wishes to resist any part of the claim. It is noteworthy that the former requirement in r. 4(3)(d) of the 2004 Rules that the response must also include the grounds on which the claim is to be resisted, has gone. Whilst this mirrors the minimum information which the claimant is required to give for a claim not to be rejected, there is no equivalent to r. 12(1)(b), so the concept of rejection for substantive defects does not, at least expressly, apply to responses (although it must presumably be the case that the Tribunal would be able to reject a response which was an abuse of its process e.g. because it did not even indicate whether or not the claim was resisted). A response which gives no clue as to the basis for the defence must therefore be accepted and the defect remedied at initial consideration (rr. 26–28: see paras. 6.01–6.06) if necessary by means of an unless order.

(b) *Response out of time*

Rule 18(1) provides that a response will be rejected if it is received outside the **5.07** twenty-eight day period for presenting a response or any previously granted extension of time, unless an application for an extension or further extension is awaiting consideration. The response will be returned together with a note explaining the reason for rejection and how to apply for a reconsideration. As with r. 17, the Rule does not say whether this is an administrative or judicial decision. Under the 2004 Rules it was a judicial decision and it is suggested that in the absence of express words to the contrary it remains so as whether the response contains an application for an extension of time may be a matter of interpretation. Even if the initial decision is administrative, the Employment Judge must act judicially on any reconsideration application (see paras. 4.44–4.53).

(c) *Extending time*

Rule 20 requires that an application for an extension of time must be in writing **5.08** and copied to the claimant. Rule 92 (see para. 12.13) provides that the Tribunal may order a departure from the requirement for the respondent to copy the application to the claimant 'if it considers it in the interests of justice to do so'. The application must explain why the extension is sought and, if the time-limit has already expired, be accompanied by a draft of the proposed response or an explanation of why that is not possible. If the respondent wishes to request a hearing 'this shall be requested in the application'. For a discussion of why this requirement may not be mandatory see para. 4.45. Unlike r. 13 there is no requirement to hold a hearing, even if one is requested, before rejecting an application under r. 20.

5.09   The claimant has seven days from the date of receipt of the application to object. The Rule does not say that the application may not be determined during that period but that appears to be the intention, subject to the power to shorten time under r. 5 of the Tribunal's own initiative. Given that the seven-day period runs not from the date the application was sent to the claimant but from the date she received it, unless time is shortened under r. 5 the prudent course would be for an Employment Judge not to deal with the application until the 8th day after an application sent to the claimant by email, the 10th day after an application sent by first class post, and the 12th day after an application sent by second class post, unless of course the Judge intends to reject the application in any event. By virtue of r. 18(1) the response cannot be rejected until the application to extend time has been dealt with.

5.10   Rule 20(3) provides that an Employment Judge may determine the application without a hearing. This is so even if the respondent asks for a hearing and the Employment Judge proposes to dismiss the application: note the difference in language between this rule and r. 19(3) (see para. 5.11 below). The hearing would appear to be in the nature of a preliminary hearing to vary a case management order under r. 29, and so would be in private (rr. 53(1)(a) and 56). As the rule does not say otherwise, the claimant would have the right to be notified of and to attend such a hearing and make representations. If the application succeeds, any judgment issued under r. 21 (see paras. 5.17–5.22 below) will be set aside. If the application fails the original decision to reject the response stands (r. 20(4)).

4. Reconsideration

5.11   Rule 19 is the reconsideration regime for rejected responses and it follows the pattern established by r. 13 for claims. Thus the application must be in writing and made within fourteen days of the date that the notice of rejection was sent (r. 19(2)) although this time-limit can be extended under r. 5 even if it has already expired. It must explain why the decision to reject the response is said to be wrong or rectify the defect and say whether the respondent requests a hearing. (This last phrase was how r. 13(2) (reconsideration of rejected claims) was originally worded but the late rewording of that rule is reflected in r. 20 rather than its equivalent, r. 19, which appears to be a drafting error). This latter requirement appears to be directory rather than mandatory as it is suggested that it would be disproportionate to reject an application simply because it fails to say whether a hearing is requested. As the Rule does not permit the application to be dismissed without a hearing if one has been requested (r. 19(3)) no doubt for access to justice reasons, the same considerations would apply whenever the application for a hearing was made.

Rule 19(3) provides that unless the Employment Judge is prepared to accept **5.12** the response in full or no hearing has been requested, there is to be a hearing, but any such hearing shall be 'attended only by the respondent' which mirrors the language in r. 13 with regard to claimant applications for reconsideration. But the consequences are very different in the case of responses. It is not clear from the wording of r. 19 whether the respondent is required to notify the claimant of the reconsideration application, but by virtue of r. 92 it would appear that he is unless the Tribunal orders otherwise. Unlike the position under r.13 the claimant would be entitled to notice of the hearing although seemingly not to attend. Under r. 19(3) the claimant has no right to attend the hearing in his capacity as claimant nor, if the hearing is in private, as a member of the public.

Unlike r. 20 which deals with applications for extensions of time, r. 19 does **5.13** not expressly provide that if the reconsideration application is successful any judgment issued under r. 21 will be set aside. It does provide that if the Judge hearing the application decides that the original decision to reject the response was correct but that the defect has been rectified, the response will be treated as presented on the date the defect was rectified '(but [the Judge] may extend time under r. 5)'. The effect of a successful reconsideration application therefore is either that the response is to be treated as having been received on the original date of presentation or on the later date when the original defect was rectified. In the former case if the original presentation was within the twenty-eight day period or in any case if the Judge extends time under r. 5 to include the date of presentation, any judgment already issued under r. 21 would automatically become a nullity as the fundamental premise for issuing such a judgment—that no response has been presented—is no longer fulfilled. This gives rise to real difficulties.

That r. 19 allows a judgment under r. 21 to be set aside in this way with- **5.14** out permitting the claimant to be heard is clearly anomalous and appears to be a breach of the claimant's human rights. Assume a response rejected because the respondent did not include its address on the response form. A judgment is issued under r. 21. There are three courses open to the respondent: (i) to apply for a reconsideration of the decision to reject under r. 19; (ii) to apply under r. 20 for an extension of time in which to present a fresh response form; (iii) to apply under r. 70 for a reconsideration of the judgment. All three courses of action can result in the judgment being set aside but only (ii) and (iii) give the right to the claimant to make representations on the application and, by necessary implication, the right to attend any hearing of the application.

There appear to be two separate breaches of the claimant's Convention **5.15** rights. The exclusion of the claimant from the reconsideration process breaches his Art. 6 right to a fair hearing in the determination of his civil rights (the problem does not arise under r. 13 because no finding adverse to the respondent can be made—see the discussion at para. 4.56). It also appears to be a breach of Art. 1 of the First Protocol—Protection of Property—which provides that 'Every natural or legal person is entitled to the peaceful enjoyment of his possessions'. 'Property' has been held to include an award of a court or arbitration which is final and enforceable with no right of appeal on the merits: (1) *Stran Greek Refineries* (2) *Stratis Andreadis v. Greece* (1994) 19 EHRR 293; *Pressos Campania Naviera SA & ors v. Belgium* (1997) 21 EHRR 301. Any judgment under r. 21 which includes the remedy would fall within this definition. But following *Matthews v. MoD* [2002] 1 WLR 2621 CA in which it was held that a right of action in tort was a possession for the purposes of the First Protocol, even the entitlement to, or the real possibility of having, a judgment issued under r. 21 would appear to be a possession for this purpose. Rule 19 however permits the Tribunal to strip the claimant of his judgment or the right or expectation to have a judgment issued, without a hearing.

5.16 Section 3 of the Human Rights Act 1998 requires primary and subordinate legislation to be read and given effect to in a way which is compatible with Convention rights only 'so far as it is possible to do so'. It would be difficult if not impossible to interpret r. 19 in a way which allows the claimant to participate fully in the reconsideration process, which is what appears to be required to make it Convention compatible, given the express words of r. 19(3). By virtue of s. 6(2)(b) HRA it would not be unlawful for a Tribunal to act in a way which is incompatible with a Convention right if the Tribunal was acting so as to give effect to a legislative requirement which cannot be read or given effect to in a way which is compatible with the right.

5. 'Default judgments'

5.17 Rule 21 deals with the effect of non-presentation or rejection of a response or an indication in a response that the case is not contested. The familiar phrase from r. 8 of the 2004 Rules, 'default judgment', has disappeared. Where a response has been received and accepted, somewhat surprisingly r. 21(1) only permits a judgment to be issued where the respondent has stated that no part of the claim is contested. Under r. 1(1) 'claim' means any proceedings before an Employment Tribunal making a complaint or complaints. It therefore seems that if a claimant complains of unfair dismissal, failure to pay notice pay and holiday pay, a r. 21 judgment cannot be issued where the monetary complaints are expressly admitted in the response if the unfair dismissal claim is contested. This could have serious consequences for a claimant if there is a delay in bringing the unfair dismissal claim to a hearing and the respondent encounters financial difficulties in the interim. Although old r. 8(2)(c) gave as one of the circumstances in which a default judgment could be issued that the respondent had stated in the response that it 'does not intend to resist the claim', no distinction was made in the 2004 Rules between the claim and the complaints which constituted it. It was the practice in at least some Tribunal regions to issue default judgments when some but not all claims were admitted.

On the expiry of the twenty-eight day period for entering a response (pro- **5.18** vided no application for an extension of time or for reconsideration of a decision to reject a response is outstanding) or if the response indicates that no part of the claim is contested, paras. (2) and (3) of r. 21 apply. Paragraph (2), by the use of the word 'shall' on two occasions, seems to require that a judgment must be issued to the extent that it is possible to do so on the material available to the Judge either on the face of the claim form or provided by way of further information. This would have preserved the effect of the default judgment regime under old r. 8 but it does not seem to have been achieved. Note that the rule contemplates that the Judge may require either party to provide whatever further information is deemed necessary to enable a judgment to be issued. The word 'required' suggests that the process is initiated by the making of a formal order rather than a request, and in the case of a respondent, this would almost certainly be essential. By virtue of s. 7(4)(c) (read with s. 7(3A) and 7(3B)) of the Employment Tribunals Act 1996 a person who without reasonable excuse fails to comply with any requirement imposed by virtue of the Rules 'to give written answers' for the purposes of facilitating the determination of proceedings without a hearing where the claim is not resisted, is guilty of an offence which attracts a fine not exceeding level 3 on the standard scale. It must be presumed that the requirement in r. 21 to provide further information is intended to be such a requirement despite the absence of an express reference to 'written answers'. For the avoidance of doubt any such order should require the party to whom it is addressed to provide written answers rather than further information and the order should be endorsed with a penal notice drawing attention to the provisions of s. 7(4)(c).

The first step for the Judge is to decide whether 'a determination can prop- **5.19** erly be made of the claim, or part of it'. To the extent that a determination can be made a judgment will be issued. To the extent that it cannot, a hearing will be held before a Judge alone. It is not clear what is meant by 'determination can properly be made of the claim'. Old r. 8(1) expressly provided that in the absence of a response a Judge shall issue a default judgement to determine the claim without a hearing but r. 21(2) appears to introduce an element of decision making about whether to issue a judgment, with potentially far reaching consequences. Most obviously it appears to give rise to the question— can a determination 'properly be made of the claim' without a hearing if the claim appears to have little prospect of success or is apparently misconceived e.g. because the wrong respondent may have been cited where there has been a TUPE transfer,[1] or simply because the claimant has failed to give the start and

---

[1] i.e. a transfer to which the Transfer of Undertakings (Protection of Employment) Regulations 2006 applies (SI 2006/246).

finish dates of their employment and the complaint is one for which a minimum qualifying service is required?

5.20　If that is the intention of the Rule then it would denote a radical departure from established (albeit recently established) practice, but would explain why the words 'default judgment' have disappeared. If the intention was merely to simplify old r. 8 and retain the concept of the default judgment with the 'determination' (subject to the point discussed in the next paragraph) being confined to the issue of whether a remedy hearing was required, it is by no means certain that it has been achieved. But there is nothing in the Underhill Review itself to suggest that any change from the regime under the 2004 Rules was intended as the only reference to default judgments is to the simplification of the procedure for setting them aside. This area is likely to be the subject of Presidential guidance under r. 7.

5.21　It is suggested that it is not possible to make a determination on a claim without a hearing where the claim appears to be out of time as limitation provisions have to be taken by the Tribunal since they have the effect of preventing the Tribunal from considering out of time claims, subject to the ability to extend time where appropriate (*Rogers v. Bodfari (Transport) Ltd* [1973] ICR 325 NIRC). It would therefore be wrong in principal for a judgment to be issued in favour of the claimant on an out of time claim without a hearing, and perfectly permissible to dismiss the claim at such a hearing, even though the respondent had neglected to raise the issue. Under old r. 8 the same was not true of 'threshold' conditions such as being a disabled person or being an employee as these were matters which the Tribunal was entitled to assume in the absence of grounds of resistance to the contrary. This may no longer be the case.

5.22　Rule 21(3) provides that where a hearing is required, the respondent is entitled to receive notice of it but is only entitled to participate in it to the extent permitted by the Employment Judge. This is a useful new provision designed to overcome the uncertainty created by old r. 9 and its predecessors—which provided (in effect) that a respondent who had not entered a response could not take any part in such a hearing—as interpreted in such cases as *Tull v. Severin* (1998) ICR 1037 EAT. The Judge's discretion must presumably be exercised in accordance with the overriding objective although it would still appear to be the case that the Judge would have no power to entertain an application to set aside a r. 21 judgment made orally at the hearing (*B.S.M. v. Fowler* UK/EAT/0059/06). For the possibility of such a respondent being able to apply for case management orders see para. 7.04.

6. Notification of acceptance

5.23　Rule 22 requires the Tribunal to send a copy of a response which has been accepted to all other parties to the proceedings. It does not expressly require that the respondent be notified that their response has been accepted but this will continue to be done in practice.

B. EMPLOYER'S CONTRACT CLAIMS—RULES 23–25

1. Overview

Important changes are made to the way in which employer's contract claims, that **5.24**
is, claims under art. 4 of the Employment Tribunals Extension of Jurisdiction
Orders 1994[2]—described under the 2004 Rules as counterclaims—are dealt
with. A new time-limit is introduced and a fee is now payable. The Rules now
treat employer's contract claims as claims and require the claimant to respond
to them, engrafting onto the process the rules relating to responses with one
immaterial exception. A failure to respond to an employer's contract claim may
therefore lead to a judgment being issued under r. 21.

2. Transitional provisions

By virtue of reg. 14(2), the 2004 Rules continue to apply to counterclaims where **5.25**
the respondent receives the claim form from the Tribunal before 29 July 2013.
While it would have eliminated any uncertainty as to which Rules applied to
specify that the relevant date was the date on which the claim form was sent
rather than the date on which it was received, r. 90 applies to create presump-
tions about the date of receipt (see para. 12.10). 'In the ordinary course of post'
normally means two working (or per CPR 6.2(b) 'business') days if sent by first
class post and four if sent by second class post. The presumption is rebuttable
by the respondent.

3. Fees

Where the claim form is received on or after 29 July 2013 a fee of £160 is payable **5.26**
if the respondent wishes to bring an employer's contract claim (art. 4 of and
Schedule 1 to the Fees Order). However, in contrast to the fate of claims presented
without a fee, the employer's contract claim will not be immediately rejected if
not accompanied by a fee. Instead, a notice requiring payment by a specified
date will be sent to the respondent, failure to pay leading only to the employer's
contract claim being dismissed (r. 40(2)(b)).[3] Neither the Rules of Procedure nor
the Fees Order lay down the period of time to be specified in the notice but as a
matter of administrative practice it will be fixed at twenty-one days. As this is not
a time-limit 'specified in these Rules' there is no power to extend it under r. 5 and
none exists in the Fees Order.

---

[2] SI 1994/1623 for England and Wales and SI 1994/1624 for Scotland.
[3] For a discussion of the interpretative problems surrounding r. 40 see para. 7.91.

4. The right to claim

5.27 By virtue of art. 8 of the 1994 Orders, an employer's contract claim may only be brought where there is in existence a contract claim against the respondent by a former employee, although the subsequent withdrawal of the employee's contract claim would not invalidate an employer's contract claim which has already been presented (for an anomaly in the Fees Order over the hearing of such a claim see para. 14.14). The Tribunal's jurisdiction to hear employee's contract claims is created by art. 3 which provides (so far as material):

Proceedings may be brought before an employment tribunal in respect of a claim of an employee for the recovery of damages **or any other sum** ... if —

(a) the claim is one to which section 131(2) of the [Employment Protection (Consolidation) Act 1978] applies and which a court ... would under the law for the time being in force have jurisdiction to hear and determine. [emphasis added]

5.28 Section 131(2) of the now repealed Employment Protection (Consolidation) Act 1978 has been re-enacted as s. 3(2) ETA. Section 3(2)(a) provides that the section applies to a claim for damages for breach of a contract of employment or other contract connected with employment and s. 3(2)(b) applies it to 'a claim for a sum due under such a contract'. By virtue of art. 4 of the 1994 Orders such a claim must arise out of or be outstanding on the termination of the employee's employment. An employee's contract claim therefore cannot be brought if the employee is still employed by the respondent, unless, possibly, they are now employed under a different contract of employment, the former contract having been terminated (see *Hogg v. Dover College* [1990] ICR 39 EAT). While there is no limit on the size of a contract claim which can be pursued in the Employment Tribunal, art. 10 limits the size of any award (including where several claims are made relating to the same contract) to £25,000. The rule in *Henderson v. Henderson* (1843) 3 Hare 100 would appear to preclude the possibility of pursuing the balance of any claim in the civil courts.

5.29 The wording of s. 3(2)(b) in particular suggests that the traditional view that an employer's contract claim can only be brought if the claimant is claiming notice pay or is otherwise expressly alleging a breach of contract, is wrong. The better view is that an employer's contract claim can be brought in any case where the claimant is claiming any sum due under the contract such as wages or holiday pay, provided there is a contractual right to the latter, and provided such claims could have been brought before a civil court. There is no doubt that a claim in respect of unpaid wages can be brought in the civil courts (*Rigby v. Ferodo Ltd* [1988] ICR 29; [1987] IRLR 516 HL(E)), a jurisdiction which was not ousted by the Wages Act 1986, now Part II of the Employment Rights Act 1996. There is no reason to doubt that the same is true of claims in respect of holiday pay as the Tribunal has exclusive jurisdiction only where the claimant relies for entitlement on the Working Time Regulations 1998 which would take the claim outside the ambit of the 1994 Orders in any event.

An equally erroneous view is held by some practitioners that an employer's **5.30** contract claim can be brought where the claimant complains of constructive unfair dismissal as such a claim necessarily involves a complaint that the employer is in breach of the employment contract. But such a claim is neither one to which s. 3(2)(a) or (b) of the 1996 Act applies nor one which a civil court would have jurisdiction to hear as the Employment Tribunal's jurisdiction to hear such claims is, and always has been, exclusive.

5. Making the claim

The 2004 Rules required only that the 'counterclaim' be presented to the Tribunal **5.31** in writing and should (post the 2009 amendments) include the same required information as for claims. The time-limit for doing so was six weeks from the date on which the claim form was received by the respondent (1994 Orders, art. 8(c)(i)) subject to an extension for a further reasonable period if it was not reasonably practicable to comply with that time-limit (art. 8(c)(ii)).

Rule 23 now requires that the employer's contract claim be made as part **5.32** of the response 'presented in accordance with r. 16' i.e. on a prescribed form within twenty-eight days of the date on which the claim form was sent to the respondent. It is understood that the 1994 Extension of Jurisdiction Orders will be amended to make them compatible with this provision although that may not technically be necessary. What is not clear is whether an extension of time can be granted under r. 5 for presenting the employer's contract claim alone. The requirement that it should be included in the response form would suggest not (as the response form would have already been presented to the Tribunal without the employer's contract claim) whereas the overriding objective, particularly the requirement to avoid unnecessary formality and seek flexibility in the proceedings, would suggest that it could (and see also the discussion at paras. 4.49–4.54). However by treating the application as one to amend the response to add the contract claim the problem appears to be overcome, as the contract claim becomes part of the response if the application is granted.

The requirement that the employer's contract claim be made as part of the **5.33** response clearly cannot be an absolute one nor can the time-limit as there may well be circumstances where knowledge of the employee's breach of contract first comes to the employer's attention after the response has been presented. The overriding objective (r. 2) would require that r. 23 be interpreted so as to permit the late addition of such an employer's contract claim. An application to amend after the response has been accepted could, like a corresponding application to amend the claim form, be made by letter given the absence of any requirement for formal pleadings in Employment Tribunals beyond the claim and response form.

6. Rejecting the claim

5.34 Rule 23 provides that an employer's contract claim may be rejected on the same basis as a claimant's claim may be rejected under r. 12 'in which case rule 13 shall apply'. The fact that r. 10 is not expressly engaged does not mean that there is no power to reject an employer's contract claim included in a response which is not on the prescribed form. Rule 23 provides that the contract claim must be included in a response 'presented in accordance with r. 16' which provides that the response must be on a prescribed form. If the response is rejected for this reason, so will the employer's contract claim. For a discussion of r. 12 see paras. 4.27–4.43.

5.35 The unamended use of the reconsideration regime for rejected claims in r. 13, which would have the effect of excluding the claimant from any deliberations over the rejected employer's contract claim, is justified by the fact that although there are by this time proceedings in train to which the claimant is a party, the employer's contract claim, if accepted, will, in essence, be fresh proceedings with its own case number. For a discussion of r. 13 see paras. 4.44–4.56.

7. Responding to the claim

5.36 Rule 24 provides that if a response includes an employer's contract claim the Tribunal will notify the claimant of this when sending the response form in accordance with r. 22. The notice will also include information on how to respond to the claim, the time-limit for doing so and what may happen if the response is not received within time. Thus in contrast to the 2004 Rules (r. 7) a response is now required to all employer's contract claims without the need for an order by an Employment Judge. Note that there is no prescribed form for responding to an employer's contract claim.

5.37 Rule 25 provides that the claimant's response to the employer's contract claim must be presented to the Tribunal within twenty-eight days of the date that the response was sent to the claimant. Presentation may be by any means permitted by r. 85. The time-limit can be extended under r. 5 (see para. 3.12) if the application is made before the twenty-eight day period expires but the more detailed regime of r. 20 (see para. 5.08) will apply after it has expired. Although at first sight this places the claimant seeking an extension of time in which to respond in a more advantageous position than a respondent seeking an extension of time to respond to a claim, as r. 20 sets out a detailed procedure to be followed and r. 5 does not, r. 20 in effect does little more than describe the procedure which would have to be followed by virtue of r. 92 and the normal principles of case management.

5.38 The consequences of failing to present a response are that rr. 20 and 21 apply. This means that failure to present a response to the employer's contract claim may result in a judgment being issued under r. 21. There was no power to issue a default judgment under the 2004 Rules even where an Employment Judge ordered the claimant to enter a response. Rule 20 permits an application for an extension of time to be made after the time-limit has expired and even after a judgment under r. 21 has been issued.

8. Rejection of the response and reconsideration

It should be noted that r. 25 does not engage r. 18—rejection of response **5.39** presented outside the twenty-eight day time-limit. However it seems that in practical terms unless a late submitted response to an employer's contract claim is accompanied by an application for an extension of time under r. 20 it will have to be rejected. Although there is no express power to do so, it cannot be ruled out that other circumstances may arise which would require rejection such as illegibility, incomprehensibility, or abuse of process. In the former case there is no provision in the Rules for the rejection to be reconsidered. In the latter cases, a case management order under r. 29 would be required if, as appears to be the case, only a Judge can order that the response be rejected for such a reason. If so it may subsequently be set aside, suspended, or varied on the application of a party.

6

INITIAL CONSIDERATION
OF CLAIM FORM AND
RESPONSE—RULES 26–28

A. OVERVIEW

It is now universally recognized by the Tribunal's judiciary that just **6.01** decision making is dependent on effective case management, particularly the early and correct identification of the issues, and the more complex the case, the greater this dependency becomes. The requirement in the overriding objective that the parties and their representatives shall co-operate generally with each other and the Tribunal is particularly important in this area. In recent years case management has become increasingly proactive with all case files routinely being scrutinized by a Judge on receipt of the response. This practice now becomes a formal requirement under rr. 26–28 and is described as initial consideration. The Underhill Review (at para. 32) described the purpose of these rules as being to ensure that weak cases which should not proceed are identified and dealt with more effectively and to ensure that Employment Judges are considering the file earlier in the process and dismissing any claim or response where there is 'no arguable complaint or response'. To that end a sifting process is introduced (rr. 27 and 28) requiring Judges to give notice to claimants and respondents whose contentions appear to have no reasonable prospect of success, to give reasons why they should not be dismissed.

6.02 Although r. 26 does little more than formalize as a requirement of the Rules that which is already standard practice, it should have the effect of bringing forward to the initial consideration stage as a matter of routine, the start of the process of identifying the issues where they are not obvious from the claim and response forms. Many Tribunal regions have standardized orders for use in discrimination cases whose intention is to require claimants to present the essentials of their complaint in a way which reflects the structure of the Equality Act, thus demonstrating that they have an arguable claim. It should become the practice for such orders to be sent at the initial consideration stage rather than following a case management discussion.

B. CONSIDERATION OF THE FILE

1. Case management orders

6.03 Rule 26(1) requires that as soon as possible after acceptance of the response the Employment Judge shall consider the file ('all of the documents held by the Tribunal in relation to the claim') with a view to confirming that there are arguable complaints and defences within the jurisdiction of the Tribunal. A Judge may require a party to provide further information for this purpose.

6.04 Unless the Judge decides that the claim or response or part thereof has no reasonable prospect of success and in consequence requires notice under either r. 27 or r. 28 to be sent ordering that the claim or response be dismissed unless reasons to the contrary are given, r. 26(2) requires the Judge to make a case management order 'unless made already' as would be the case with those one-day unfair dismissal claims which are listed for hearing before being sent to the respondent with national standard case management orders included in the notice of hearing. Until the final version of the draft Rules in both r. 26(1) and (2) the requirement was to make case management orders rather than 'a case management order'. The reason for the change is possibly to reflect the language of r. 1(3)(a) which defines a case management order as: 'an order or decision of any kind in relation to the conduct of proceedings, not including the determination of any issue which would be the subject of a judgment'. But given the established canons of statutory interpretation in which the singular includes the plural[1] the power to make more than one case management order survives the amendment. Those orders may include listing the case for a preliminary hearing (which expression now includes what were formerly known as case management discussions (r. 53(1)(a)) or for a final hearing and/or propose judicial mediation

---

[1] Interpretation Act 1978, ss. 6(c) and 23(1).

or other forms of dispute resolution. (For a discussion of the orders which may be made see Chapter 7.)

The reference to mediation is slightly puzzling as under the current proto- **6.05** cols only a Regional Employment Judge may offer judicial mediation and no other form of ADR is available through the Tribunal. Judicial mediation is entirely voluntary and so the intention is presumably that the Judge will do no more than ask the parties whether they are interested in exploring it as a possibility. Mediation is currently only available in cases which are likely to take three days or more to hear and is not available if an equal pay claim is involved.

The requirement to make a written case management order, which appears to **6.06** be mandatory in all cases, is not appropriate for those claims which were designated as 'short track' in the original version of the 2004 Rules and which are still often referred to as such, namely purely monetary claims which are listed for hearing before being sent to the respondent and normally given a time allocation of one hour. The hearing date is usually around eight to ten weeks after the date the claim form is sent to the respondent. No case management orders are made and the intention is that the process is quick, cheap, and relatively informal. It is only on rare occasions that it becomes necessary to make case management orders once the response is received, normally only if it becomes apparent that the case has unexpected complexities or ramifications. It would be surprising if the intention was to change the practice in such cases so that a case management order had to be routinely issued as this would almost inevitably lead to a postponement of the hearing and rob the concept of the 'short track' case of much of its *raison d'être*. An order that no case management order is required would presumably satisfy the requirements of the Rule.

C. DISMISSAL OF CLAIM OR RESPONSE—THE SIFT RULES 27 AND 28

1. When the rules apply

Rule 18(6) of the 2004 Rules allowed an Employment Judge acting on his or her **6.07** own initiative to give notice to a party informing them that it was proposed to strike out their claim or response on one of the grounds listed in r. 18(7) and for a paper determination of the issue should neither party request a hearing. Except where the proposed order was to strike out the claim on the grounds that it was not being actively pursued, this was not commonly done. Although some Judges were prepared to list a case for a pre-hearing review under old r. 18(7)(b)—strike out on the grounds of no reasonable prospect of success—of their own initiative, others were reluctant to do so even on the application of the respondent. This led to much criticism from certain quarters that the Tribunal was 'awash' with weak cases.

6.08   The purpose of new rr. 27 and 28 is to address this criticism by creating what is in effect a sifting process designed to eliminate the weakest claims and responses at the earliest stage. If they are interpreted too restrictively by Judges this purpose will not be achieved. The language of both paragraphs (1)—the Employment Judge considers that the claim/response has no reasonable prospect of success—is capable of narrow interpretation. 'Has no reasonable prospect of success' might be said to pose a higher threshold than '*may have* no reasonable prospect of success' suggesting that the Judge must have virtually decided that the claim is hopeless before the notice can be sent. Such an interpretation, it is suggested, is not justified and would frustrate the intention of the rule.

6.09   The key words are 'considers' and 'reasonable'. To consider something to be the case is not the same as to have concluded that it is the case. The rule seems to require only that the Judge is of the view that it is likely (in the sense of 'it may well be') that the case has no reasonable prospect of success. 'No reasonable prospect' of success is of course not the same as no prospect of success. It contemplates the possibility of the claim succeeding but the possibility being a remote one. It would therefore be wrong to refuse to send the r. 27 notice in any case where it was possible to envisage the claim succeeding if that possibility was not a realistic one. It would be prudent for respondents to expressly plead that a claim has no reasonable prospect of success where they believe that to be the case and to ask for action to be taken under r. 27. It might well be advantageous to both parties, and in accordance with the overriding objective, for Judge's to utilize rr. 27 and 28 as a vehicle for the early clarification of weak claims and responses by using the hearing which must be held before a claim or response can be dismissed if a reply to the notice is received, to make case management orders.

2. The process

6.10 Both rules operate in the same way. The claimant or respondent is to be sent a notice that the Judge is considering striking out the claim or response or part of it on the grounds that it has no reasonable prospect of success or, in the case of the claim, that the Tribunal has no jurisdiction to consider it. The notice informs the party of the Judge's reasons for being of that view and that the claim or response 'will stand dismissed' on a date specified unless before that date the party presents written representations explaining why the claim or response should not be struck out. Should no representations be received the claim or response stands dismissed 'from' the specified date without further order (rr. 27(2) and 28(2)). Note that the requirement to prevent strike out at this stage is merely to respond to the notice with reasons, not for those reasons to show cause. Should the claimant (or respondent as the case may be) make representations then the issue of whether the claim (or response) is to be dismissed must be listed for a hearing unless the Judge is prepared to allow the claim or response to proceed in the light of the representations (rr. 27(3) and 28(3)).

By virtue of r. 4(1) an act required to be done by the Rules or by an order of **6.11**
the Tribunal on or by a particular day may be done at any time before midnight
on that day. The claim or response would therefore not stand dismissed until the
day after the date specified in the notice. No further action on the Tribunal's part
is required to implement the dismissal: it is automatic. In particular no further
judgment or order should be issued (*Neary v. Governing Body of St Alban's Girls
School & anor* [2010] ICR 473 CA). The rule requires only that the Tribunal will
confirm to the parties in writing that the claim or response stands dismissed.

3. The hearing

(a) *The Judge*
Rules 27 and 28 do not say whether the hearing should, or should not be, before **6.12**
the Judge who caused the notice to be sent. As the notice is required to set out
the Judge's reasons for believing that the claim or response has no reasonable
prospect of success, objection might legitimately be taken to the same Judge
conducting the hearing, particularly if the Judge's reasons in the original notice
were strongly expressed and if he or she had also declined to allow the claim or
response to proceed on the basis of the written representations. There would
seem to be real prospects of an appeal against a decision to strike out the claim
or response succeeding on the grounds of apparent (even actual) bias if the same
Judge was to be involved in the process throughout (see *Oni v. Leicester City
NHS Trust* [2012] ICR 91 EAT).

(b) *The nature of the hearing*
The rules are also silent as to the nature of the hearing and whether it should be **6.13**
in public or private. Instinctively they are preliminary hearings, not least because
under r. 53(1)(c) one of the purposes of a preliminary hearing is to consider
whether a claim or response or part should be struck out under r. 37. However,
there are important differences between r. 37 and rr. 27 and 28. Rule 37(1)(a) provides (*inter alia*) that at any stage of the proceedings the Tribunal may of its own
initiative strike out all or any part of a claim or response on the grounds that
it has no reasonable prospect of success but, unlike r. 27 or r. 28, a claim may
be struck out under r. 37 without a hearing unless a hearing is requested by the
affected party. In addition to the procedural differences, r. 26(2) provides that on
initial consideration the Employment Judge may make case management orders
including orders for a preliminary hearing 'Except in a case where notice is given
under r. 27 or [r.] 28' from which it seems to follow that rr. 27 and 28 hearings
are not preliminary hearings for the purposes of the Rules even though clearly
preliminary in nature.

It also seems that there is no express power to make case management **6.14**
orders in respect of them, for example for exchange of witness statements or
disclosure of documents. This interpretation is likely to give rise to several
difficulties as discussed in the following paragraphs. How the difficulties might

be overcome is discussed below at para. 6.18. Given that it involves, at least potentially, the determination of the civil rights of the party to whom notice has been sent, Art. 6 of the Convention would require that a r. 27(3) or r. 28(3) hearing be in public.

6.15   Even though the hearing is not expressly a preliminary hearing rr. 41–50 (other than r. 48) would appear to apply as they are headed 'Rules common to all kinds of hearings'. It seems to be the intention that the hearings will be of the same nature as strike out hearings under the 2004 Rules which were normally listed with a time estimate of one hour or slightly longer and without orders for exchange of witness statements or agreement of a bundle. The thinking behind listing them in this way seems (rightly) to have been that if it isn't obvious within an hour that the claim or response is hopeless by listening to the parties' submissions then it must be allowed to proceed, particularly where there are disputes of fact to be resolved. However, it would not be an error of law at a r. 37(1)(a) preliminary hearing for the Judge to hear evidence, consider documents, and determine disputes of fact (*Eastman v. Tesco Stores Ltd* UKEAT/0143/12). While it seems doubtful that the intention was to permit such formality at rr. 27 and 28 hearings, it is difficult to see how a respondent (claimant) could be precluded from adducing evidence reasonably necessary to support the contention that the claim (response) had no reasonable prospect of success and which they would have been able to adduce if the hearing had been under r. 37, given the consequences (discussed below) of a finding that the claim (response) be allowed to proceed.

(c) *Participation of the respondent*

6.16   It is also unclear what form the hearing will take. Rules 27(3) and 28(3) could have required that the issue be listed for a preliminary hearing under r. 53(1)(c). The fact that they do not suggests that a hearing of a different type is envisaged as do the final sentences of both paragraphs: 'The respondent [claimant] may, but need not attend and participate in the hearing'. This implies an informal, even summary, process and one with which the opposing party need not trouble themselves. But there are hidden dangers in treating it as such. If a respondent does not attend the hearing, or having done so does not pursue the strike out with the vigour which they would have done had it been listed in the normal way under r. 37, it would almost certainly be the case that they would not be able to apply to strike out the claim under r. 37(1)(a) on the grounds that it has no reasonable prospect of success at a later stage of the proceedings—at least not on the same grounds as those set out in the r. 27(1) notice—as the Tribunal's decision will create an issue estoppel. Even if a subsequent application was based on different reasons from those in the r. 27(1) notice, there may be questions of abuse of process if the alternative basis now being advanced could have been put forward at the earlier hearing. It would therefore be most unwise for a respondent (or claimant as the case may be) not to attend the hearing and participate fully.

(d) *Can other issues be considered?*

This raises a further difficulty. It is not in fact clear whether at a hearing under **6.17** rr. 27(3) or 28(3) the Judge would be able to consider any issue other than the one contained in the notice sent under para. (1). The normal practice under the 2004 Rules where a claim was listed for strike out consideration under r. 18(7) (b) (no reasonable prospect of success) was to consider at the same time as an alternative to striking out whether a deposit order should be made under r. 20 (now r. 39). Rule 26(2) would seem to prevent the Judge from taking the initiative and adding a deposit order preliminary hearing under r. 53(1)(d) as the power to list for preliminary hearings and make other case management orders on initial consideration is expressly excluded where a notice has been given under rr. 27 or 28. As a deposit order can only be made at a preliminary hearing (r. 39(1) and r. 53(1)(d)) and it appears that the r. 27(3) hearing is not a preliminary hearing, unless the matter is expressly before the Judge via another route she would seem to have no power to make a deposit order rather than strike the claim out. It would presumably be open to either party to ask for a deposit preliminary hearing to be run in parallel with the rr. 27(3) or 28(3) hearing and there would be some tactical advantage in so doing as the party to whom the notice was addressed may see the opportunity to make a deposit order as offering an attractive, less draconian, alternative to the Judge which she otherwise would not have.

It is suggested that any difficulty caused by a literal interpretation of the restric- **6.18** tions imposed by r. 26(2) in particular and by the failure to designate the hearing as a r. 53 preliminary hearing in general, can be resolved by interpreting r. 26(2) (and other rules which would be applicable but for r. 26(2)) so as to accord with the overriding objective, something which the objective itself requires. Rule 2 provides that cases are to be dealt with fairly and justly which includes dealing with them in ways which save expense and seeking flexibility in the proceedings and it would not seem to be in accordance with either the spirit or the letter of the objective to require the parties to return for a preliminary hearing at a later date when that hearing could have been listed together with the r. 27 or r. 28 hearing. The simplest approach would be to interpret the restriction on making case management orders in r. 26(2) as applying only to preliminary or main merits hearings and not to the r. 27(3) or r.28(3) hearing, or in the case of such hearings as leaving the making of case management orders to the Judge's discretion rather than requiring them to be made. Alternatively, r. 54 provides that a preliminary hearing may be directed by the Tribunal of its own initiative following its initial consideration and the Rule is not said to be subject to r. 26(2). It would therefore seem to be in accordance with the overriding objective for the Judge undertaking the initial consideration to resolve the apparent conflict by utilizing r. 54 to enable her to list the case for a r. 39 deposit hearing to be heard at the same time as the r. 27(3) (or r. 28(3)) hearing, and to make any necessary case management orders under the aegis of that rule. In other words, where a literal reading of rr. 26, 27, and 28 appears to frustrate the overriding objective, it can be (arguably the objective itself requires it to be) trumped by other rules which facilitate it.

4. Reconsideration

6.19 There is no express provision within rr. 27 or 28 for a reconsideration of the dismissal of the claim or response at initial consideration. However, it seems clear that, whether in consequence of a failure to reply to the initial notice or following a hearing, the Judge must issue a judgment in order to finally dispose of the claim or response. Such a judgment could be reconsidered under rr. 70–73. Where it is the claim that is the subject of the hearing, because the hearing is one which is capable of finally disposing of the claim even if it does not in fact do so, by virtue of r. 1(3)(b)(ii) the outcome of the hearing, however it is described by the Judge, qualifies as a judgment and so a decision not to strike out the claim could be reconsidered in the same way. The same is not apparently true of a decision not to strike out a response because striking out the response would not finally dispose of the claim as a Judge would still have to make a determination under r. 21 whether to issue a judgment. There appears to be a lacuna in the Rules (albeit a relatively unimportant one) as it seems there is no power for a claimant to apply for the reconsideration of a decision not to strike out a response following a hearing under r. 28(3).

5. Other matters

6.20 Rules 27(4) and 28(4) require the Employment Judge to make a case management order if the claim or response is allowed to proceed.

6.21 Rule 28(5) provides that where a response is struck out the consequence will be as though no response had been presented and r. 21 applies. This is an important addition to the Rules as there was no express equivalent provision in the 2004 Rules and the position was uncertain although in *North Care Primary Care Trust v. Aynsley* [2009] ICR 1333 EAT it was held that the respondent was to be treated as though a response had not been entered.

7

CASE MANAGEMENT ORDERS AND OTHER POWERS—RULES 29–40

A. OVERVIEW

7.01 The Rules relating to case management (rr. 29–36) are considerably simplified and the process of applying for orders becomes less bureaucratic and prescriptive. A new power is created to designate lead cases for multiple claims and to make the decisions in lead cases binding on the cases stayed behind them. Striking out (r. 37) and the ordering of a deposit (r. 39) are now treated as elements of case management and there are important changes in the latter. The power to make an 'unless order' is retained (r. 38). Rule 40 deals with the non-payment of fees: its wording is ambiguous and its operation uncertain. For the definition of a case management order see r. 1(3)(a).

B. CASE MANAGEMENT ORDERS GENERALLY

1. Orders which can be made

7.02 A notable omission from the 2013 Rules is the extensive catalogue of orders which may be made at case management discussions set out in r. 10(2)(a)–(t) of the 2004 Rules. It would be wrong to assume that its omission implies that orders of the kind listed in old r. 10(2) can no longer be made. The list was only of examples of orders which could be made under the general power to make orders contained in r. 10(1) which provided that an Employment Judge may 'make an order in relation to any matter which appears to him to be appropriate. Such orders may be any of those listed in paragraph (2) *or such other order as he thinks fit*' [emphasis added]. Paragraph (2) itself was headed 'Examples of orders which may be made'. The danger of such an extensive list of examples is that it is regarded not as illustrative but exhaustive and practitioners tended to scrutinize the list to see if there was something in it which met their needs. New rule 29 which is entitled the 'General rule' make the position quite clear: 'The tribunal may at any stage of the proceedings … make a case management order. The particular powers identified in the following rules do not restrict that general power.' The last minute change from the plural to the singular does not confine the power to make orders to a single order on each occasion as the singular is taken to include the plural.[1] The power to make case management orders is therefore not subject to any express limitations in the Rules and it would be wrong to interpret the small number of potential case management orders which now have their own rule as implying a limitation.

7.03   Nor, it is suggested, is it the case that there is no power to make a case management order which is not expressly contemplated by s. 7 ETA. Section 7(1) provides that the Secretary of State may by regulations 'make such provisions as appears to him to be necessary or expedient with respect to proceedings before employment tribunals'. The lengthy list in s. 7(3) is only of those matters for which such regulations 'may, in particular, provide'. It is not an enabling list, that is, a list of those things, and only those things, for which provision can be made. However, in the past, whenever the Rules have been amended to include a new provision, it has always been felt expedient to first amend s. 7(3) to create an express power to do so. If the Secretary of State's powers to make such provisions as appears to him to be necessary or expedient has been translated into a

---

[1] Interpretation Act 1978, ss. 6(c) and 23(1).

similar power of the Tribunal to make case management orders by the broad but express language of r. 29, this suggests something akin to an inherent jurisdiction in the Tribunal to make such orders as appear to it to be necessary in the interests of good case management or in order to protect a person's Convention rights, or secure their EU law rights, subject only to the overriding objective. For a discussion of the recent creative use of this power see the commentary to r. 50 'privacy and restrictions on disclosure' at paras. 8.24–8.39.

2. Who may apply

(a) *Respondents who have not entered a response*

Under both the 1993 and 2001 Rules a respondent who had not entered a response could apply for only two case management orders—an extension of time in which to submit a response and for further particulars of the claim. Under the 2004 Rules they could only apply for an extension of time and only if the time-limit had not already expired (r. 4(4)). Rule 9 of the 2004 Rules provided that, subject to that one exception, a respondent who had not presented a response could take no part in the proceedings other than to apply for a review of a default judgment or, on limited grounds, any other judgment or decision, and in the Rules the words 'party' and 'respondent' included a respondent only to the extent to which they were entitled to take part in the proceedings. The rule applied whether the time for presenting the response had expired or not and so prevented a respondent from applying even for case management orders that appeared to be necessary to enable it to present a full response to the claim. **7.04**

There is no equivalent provision to old r. 9 in the 2013 Rules and the word 'respondent' is defined in r. 3(1) simply as 'the person or persons against whom the claim is made'. That very broad definition is not cut down anywhere in the Rules by reference to whether a response has been presented. As discussed below, there is no apparent requirement for an applicant for an order to be a party to the proceedings so an objection that a respondent who has not entered a response is not a party would not be relevant. Even r. 21, which applies only after the time for entering a response has expired, would seem to allow the respondent to apply for case management orders as the only restriction expressly imposed (and not an absolute one at that) is in respect of participation at hearings. It therefore seems clear that under the 2013 Rules a respondent who has not presented a response to the claim may apply for any case management order, certainly before the twenty-eight-day period for presenting the response has expired and, apparently, even after it has expired, and cannot be required to enter a response as a precondition for making the application. This is an extremely sensible change to the Rules as the rigid application of old r. 9 could work against both the spirit and the letter of the overriding objective and lead to wasted costs through the need to submit 'holding' responses simply in order to acquire the standing to make applications for obviously necessary case management orders. **7.05**

(b) *Non-parties*

7.06   Rule 29, the 'General rule', is, in effect, the preamble to this part of the Rules. Its opening sentence reads: 'The Tribunal may at any stage of the proceedings, on its own initiative, or on application, make a case management order.' In the 2004 Rules, r. 10 which had the heading 'General power to manage proceedings' and performed a similar function to r. 29, provided, by contrast, that: '...the Employment Judge may at any time either on the application **of a party** or on his own initiative make an order...' [emphasis added].

7.07   The omission of the words 'of a party' from the first sentence of r. 29 is striking, not only in comparison with its immediate predecessor but in contrast to the rest of that rule and to other rules in this part of the Rules in which the word 'party' appears. That strongly suggests that the omission is intentional and is designed to allow non-parties to make applications for case management orders where appropriate; indeed, the power in r. 35 to permit any person to participate in the proceedings would seem to require it.

7.08   The impression is strengthened by r. 50(1) 'Privacy and restrictions on disclosure' which also omits the words 'of a party' after the words 'on application'. As that rule makes clear (applying *F v. G* [2012] ICR 246 EAT), the Tribunal may make orders with a view to preventing or restricting the public disclosure of any aspect of the proceedings 'in order to protect the Convention rights of any person...' where Convention rights has the meaning given to it by the Human Rights Act 1998, s. 1. The effectiveness of the rule would be seriously curtailed, and the UK potentially placed in breach of its Convention obligations, if a person whose Convention rights were in need of protection but who was not a party to the proceedings could not make the application. For a fuller discussion of the issues involved see paras. 8.24–8.29.

7.09   However, the wording of r. 31 'Disclosure of documents and information' provides only that the Tribunal may order any person to disclose documents or information to a party. It says nothing about disclosure by a party to any person. This may be thought to imply that such an order cannot be made. It is suggested that the wording of the rule is not fatal to the possibility that non-parties may apply for case management orders of this nature, for two reasons. First, because r. 29 provides that 'The particular powers identified in the following rules do not restrict' the general power to make case management orders created by the first sentence of the rule. Second, r. 31 is almost certainly worded as it is because of the need for the rule to coincide with the wording of s. 7(3)(e) ETA which together with s. 7(4)(b) creates a criminal penalty for non-compliance with orders relating to disclosure to and inspection by a party.

7.10   More problematic, at least at first sight, is r. 30 'Applications for case management orders' which refers only to applications by parties and describes what parties must do when applying (see paras. 7.18 and 7.19 below). Again, this might be read as intending to restrict applications for case management orders to the parties. But the rule can be interpreted perfectly sensibly not as operating so as to prevent applications by non-parties but as creating a regime which does not apply to them. On this interpretation, applications can be validly made by non-parties which do not comply with r. 30, although it would normally be sensible for them to comply.

There is, in short, nothing in the subsequent rules to suggest that the impression, created by the first sentence of r. 29 particularly when contrasted with its immediate predecessor, that a non-party can apply for any case management order, is false. But what orders might be applied for by a non-party and why? The most obvious circumstance—that a non-party wishes to be joined as a party—has its own rule, r. 34 (see paras. 7.37–7.42 below). But, before making such an application a non-party may wish to establish whether it is appropriate to do so: for example by requiring a party to give further particulars of their claim or response, to test whether an assertion or allegation is in fact being made, and if so, with what intent. Similarly an application for disclosure of a specific document or even for full discovery by list. The overriding objective would undoubtedly apply to such applications—only r. 2(a) refers to 'the parties' and the remaining provisions of the overriding objective could require even that provision to be interpreted as including 'potential party' where appropriate. **7.11**

(c) *Case management and legal capacity*
For observations on case management where a party may lack legal capacity (the claimant was said by the respondent to be delusional) see *Johnson v. Edwardian International Hotels Ltd* (UKEAT/0588/07). **7.12**

3. Reasons for orders

Rule 62(1) requires that reasons are given for 'decisions on any disputed issues'. Under the 2004 Rules it was not clear whether reasons had to be given where an application for an order was refused as the requirement was only to give reasons for an order (old r. 30(1)(b)) which was defined as something which required a person to do or not to do something (old r. 28(1)(b) although in *Hart*—see below—it was suggested that 'order' must be interpreted as meaning any decision of the Tribunal). It is now clear from r. 62(1) that a decision to refuse an application for an order is one which requires reasons—presumably even if the application is made by consent but is nonetheless refused by the Judge. **7.13**

4. Varying, suspending, and setting aside

Case management orders include decisions of any kind in relation to the conduct of proceedings (r. 1(3)). The word 'order' therefore includes a decision to refuse an order. A party who has unsuccessfully applied for a case management order cannot normally apply to have the decision rejecting the application set aside; in effect, to apply again for the same order. There are two circumstances where such an application is permissible: where there has been a material change in circumstances since the original application was refused (*Onwuka v. Spherion* **7.14**

Technology UK Ltd [2005] ICR 567 EAT, para. 35) and where the party wishes to argue a significant point which ought reasonably to have been, but was not, advanced at the original hearing (*Hart v. English Heritage (Historic Buildings and Monuments Commission for England)* [2006] ICR 655; [2006] IRLR 915 EAT). In this latter situation the rule in *Henderson v. Henderson* (1843) 3 Hare 100 applies and the question which arises is whether it would be an abuse of process for the point to be taken afresh. In *Hart* it was held that a claimant should have been permitted to revisit an application to amend a claim to include a complaint of unfair dismissal by reason of trade union activities where on the first application the hearing proceeded on the assumption on all sides that the claim form did not include such a complaint and on the application for a review of that decision the claimant wished to argue for the first time that it did.

5. Orders on the Tribunal's own initiative

7.15 Rule 12 of the 2004 Rules prescribed how a Judge might exercise powers on his or her own initiative and how a party affected by such an order might apply for it to be varied or revoked. There is no corresponding rule in the 2013 Rules although the substance of old r. 12 is preserved in other rules—e.g. old r. 12(3) is reflected in the second sentence of r. 29.

7.16 There is no requirement in the Rules for an Employment Judge to give notice to the parties that she intends to make a case management order and invite representations before so doing. Rule 26(1) clearly contemplates that the Judge will make such orders without prior reference to the parties at the initial consideration stage and r. 29 does so impliedly with regard to case management in general by providing that any case management order may be varied, suspended or set aside where that is necessary in the interests of justice 'and in particular where a party affected by the earlier order did not have reasonable opportunity to make representations'. This reflects the position under old r. 12 and long-established practice. There does not appear to be a requirement for a Judge to give reasons for an order made of their own initiative as r. 62(1) only requires reasons to be given 'on any disputed issue' which is taken to mean where an application is opposed. It would however be good practice for brief reasons to be given if a failure to do so would be likely to provoke an application for the order to be set aside.

6. Combining proceedings

7.17 Under the 2004 Rules there was one exception (r. 10(7)) to the general principal that case management orders could be made on the Tribunal's own initiative without prior notice to the parties. That was where the Judge proposed to order 'that different claims be considered together', i.e. that proceedings be combined or consolidated. This requirement is not reproduced in the 2013 Rules which means that new claims can now be added to existing multiples without notice to the parties which will save both time and expense. It is suggested that it would still be prudent to consult parties about any proposed new consolidation order where there is any doubt whether the cases can safely be heard together.

7. Applications for case management orders

New r. 31 replaces the complex and bureaucratic r. 11 of the 2004 Rules with **7.18** a simpler, more flexible procedure for applying for case management orders although in one important respect, r. 31 appears to be more restrictive than its predecessor. The main differences are:

- There is now a single procedure which applies equally to both legally represented parties and other parties.

- No time-scales for making or objecting to the application are prescribed—the other parties must be told by the party applying only that any objections must be sent to the Tribunal office 'as soon as possible'. The requirement to notify the other parties that an order has been applied for can be dispensed with by the Tribunal in the interests of justice (r. 92) but, if the other parties have been notified of an application, the requirement to notify them of the need to send any objection to the Tribunal office as soon as possible cannot be dispensed with, words which would have permitted this having been deleted from r. 31(2) at a late stage in the drafting process, possibly in the mistaken belief that they were unnecessary because of r. 92 (for r. 92 see para. 12.13).

- There is no longer an express power to entertain an application made other than in writing unless it is made at a hearing. Old r. 11(2) provided that an application 'must (*unless an Employment Judge orders otherwise*) be in writing…' [emphasis added]. Rule 31 provides only that an application may be made 'either at a hearing or in writing'. A strict, literal, interpretation of r. 31(1) would therefore suggest that, for example, urgent telephone applications for a hearing to be postponed are no longer permissible. Given that 'writing' includes 'writing delivered by means of electronic communication'[2] (r. 1(1)) urgent applications can be made by email to the Tribunal office even where the other party has not disclosed an email address. However, there are likely to be circumstances in which only a telephone application is practicable. As such an application is not expressly forbidden by the rule, and as r. 31(1) says that applications 'may be made' either at a hearing or in writing, rather than 'must be made', if the situation is truly urgent and no other means of application practicable, the overriding objective to deal with cases fairly and justly would seem to permit (arguably, require) the Tribunal to interpret the rule so as to enable it to entertain a telephone application. In the event of the

---

[2] Defined in the Electronic Communications Act 2000, s. 15(1): and see Communications Act 2003 s. 32 for the definition of 'electronic communications network' which forms part of the former definition.

other party objecting to the Tribunal dealing with the application because it had not been made in writing, it would undoubtedly be open to the Judge, having regard to the overriding objective, to make any appropriate order, including the postponement of the hearing, of his or her own initiative, based on the information contained in the (possibly) technically invalid application.

• There is no longer a requirement to include in the application either the reasons for requesting the order or an explanation of how the order would assist the Tribunal in dealing with the proceedings efficiently and fairly. Nonetheless it is clearly essential for the application to be supported by some explanation of why it is being made and why an order rather than a request to the other party is necessary.

7.19 Although r. 31(2), which requires that applications for case management orders made in writing must notify the other parties of their right to object, appears to be of general application, it must be read as being subject to r. 92 which exempts applications for witness orders from the general rule that all correspondence with the Tribunal be copied to the other parties. An application for a case management order may be dealt with by the Judge in writing or the Judge may direct that it be dealt with at a preliminary hearing (which term now includes case management discussions: r. 53(1)(a)) or at a final hearing (r. 31(3)). Applications for case management orders are not infrequently refused without troubling the other side where, for example, they are manifestly inappropriate or misconceived. Such an application should be treated as a disputed issue for the purposes of r. 62(1) requiring the Judge to give reasons for its peremptory refusal.

C. SPECIFIC ORDERS

1. Disclosure of documents and information

(a) *The scope of the orders*

7.20 The apparently straightforward r. 31 raises some difficult issues of *vires* as it repeats a (previously inidentified) solecism which first appeared in the 2004 Rules. The starting point is s. 7(3) ETA which lists among the provisions which procedure regulations may in particular include at para. (e) on the application of a party 'such discovery or inspection of documents, or the furnishing of such further particulars, as might be ordered by a county court' (or in Scotland by a sheriff, the power in the case of a sheriff being limited to recovery or inspection of documents). Where the Act intends that an order-making power should extend beyond requiring a party to do something, such as in s. 7(3)(d) and 7(3)(h), the formula used is 'for requiring persons'. It therefore seems clear that the intention behind s. 7(3)(e) was that orders for discovery and further particulars be directed only at a party—indeed the phrase 'further particulars' can only apply to a party in respect of their pleaded case. The 1993 and 2001 Rules both expressly provided that such orders could be made against a party.

The current formulation of the rule (apart from the words '(by providing cop- **7.21** ies or otherwise)') which first appeared in the 2004 Rules (r. 10(2)(d)) purports to enable the Tribunal to order 'any person in Great Britain' to disclose documents or 'information' to a party. But there was also a provision in the 2004 Rules (at r. 10(2)(b)) that an order could be made 'that a party provide additional information' presumably the plain English equivalent of 'further particulars'. Thus the 2004 Rules and the 2013 Rules go beyond s. 7(3)(e) in two respects: by extending the ambit of the order to 'any person in Great Britain' and by bringing in an unexplained concept of 'information' which appears to be something other than further particulars of a party's claim or response. If the suggestion in para. 7.03 above is correct, the mere fact that s. 7(3) does not expressly provide for the making of a rule to a certain effect does not mean that such a rule cannot be made, but a problem arises here because while s. 7(3) expressly creates the power to make a rule of a certain type which (if only by necessary implication) is limited in its scope, the resulting rule exceeds that scope. Thus a question mark must hang over the legality of the entirety of this rule to the extent that it purports to give the Tribunal power to make an order against a non-party. There is a further difficulty in respect of non-parties and the provision of information (see para. 7.25).

The Tribunal may order 'any person in Great Britain' to disclose documents or **7.22** information 'as might be ordered by a county court or, in Scotland, by a sheriff'. In consequence, in England and Wales, the order-making provisions of CPR 18 (further information) and CPR 31 (discovery and inspection of documents) are, by necessary implication, incorporated into the Tribunal's Rules of Procedure together, presumably, with similar parts of practice directions made under them, although this was said not necessarily to automatically follow in *South Tyneside District Council v. Anderson* (UKEAT/0002/05).

In the absence of the express incorporation of the whole of CPR 31 it must **7.23** be presumed that in addition to the specific order-making powers, the parts of the rule which are necessary to support those powers, such as the duty of search (CPR 31.7) and the duty of continuing disclosure (CPR 31.11) are also incorporated. However, there does not appear to be any necessity for the incorporation of CPR 31.10, which lays down the procedure for standard disclosure but which is not an order-making power, thus requiring Employment Judges to make such orders for the mechanics of disclosure as appear appropriate to the circumstances of the case. It is not clear whether CPR 31.16 (disclosure before proceedings start) is applied to Employment Tribunals by virtue of r. 31. It seems not, as both s. 7(3)(e) ETA and r. 31 expressly refer to an application by a party, implying that an application under r. 31 can be made only after proceedings have commenced.

CPR 31.17 deals with orders for disclosure against non-parties. It requires **7.24** that applications for orders of disclosure and inspection against non-parties be supported by evidence. An order may only be made where the documents in question are likely to (in the sense of 'might well': *Three Rivers District Council v. Bank of England (No. 4)* [2002] 4 All ER 881 CA) support the case of the party applying for the order or adversely affect the case of the other parties and disclosure is necessary in order to dispose fairly of the claim or to save costs. Assuming that such an application is permissible (see para. 7.21) there is little doubt that CPR 31.17(2) should be followed by a party making an application in the Tribunal for an order for disclosure against a non-party. When considering such an application the Tribunal would also be required to have regard to the overriding objective.

7.25   The qualification in r. 31 of the Tribunal's power to make orders, equating it to that of the county court, is apparently also intended to apply to orders for the provision of further information. However CPR 18, which deals with the provision of further information, is restricted to the making of orders against a party (CPR 18.1(1)) and there does not appear to be a similar power in respect of non-parties. Given the way r. 31 is framed, in the absence of a power under the CPR to order a non-party to provide information there is no power for the Tribunal to do so. That part of r. 31 therefore appears to be redundant. A party wishing to obtain information from a non-party may have to resort to the threat of applying for a witness order unless they supply the information voluntarily.

7.26   Although there is no express power to do so in the rule, where issues of confidentiality arise, the Tribunal may in the first instance order disclosure of the documents to itself for the purpose of determining whether full disclosure should be ordered or only after the redaction of confidential material such as the name of a witness (*Science Research Council v. Nasse* [1979] ICR 921; [1979] IRLR 465 HL). In a case where the documents in question were the witness statements obtained during the employer's investigation into disciplinary offences, it was held that the correct approach for the Tribunal was to receive the unredacted originals together with the employer's suggestions for redaction and, having considered them, if necessary to make alternative proposals for redaction which should first be put to the employer for comments (*Asda Stores Ltd v. Thompson (No. 2)* [2004] IRLR 598 EAT).

(b) *Penal notices*

7.27   The 2004 Rules (r. 10(6)) provided that any order containing a requirement to attend as a witness to give evidence or to disclose documents or information should state that under s. 7(4) ETA any person who without reasonable excuse fails to comply with the order shall be liable on summary conviction to a fine. There is no similar provision in the 2013 Rules. That is hardly surprising as there is no requirement in s. 7 ETA either for the Rules to contain such a provision or for the applicable orders to be so endorsed. The penal notice provisions in the 2004 Rules were, in any event, incorrect. Section 7(4) ETA creates the penal sanction in respect of various provisions in the section, s. 7(4)(b) doing so for s. 7(3) (e) 'with respect to the discovery, recovery or inspection of documents'. Section

7(4) creates no sanction in respect of failure to supply information pursuant to an order whether by a party or otherwise. Therefore even if a penal notice is endorsed on an order to provide information, whether addressed to a party or non-party, it would be invalid and of no effect.

(c) *Disclosure—what may be ordered*

An order may be made for either general or specific disclosure. So far as general **7.28** disclosure is concerned, CPR 31.5 and 31.6 provide for the disclosure only of documents on which a party relies, the documents which adversely affect his own or another party's case or support another party's case and any documents which he is required to disclose by a relevant practice direction (known as standard disclosure). This can be waved or varied to meet the requirements of the over-riding objective. CPR 31.7 imposes the duty on a party of making a reasonable search for documents. What is reasonable depends on the number of documents involved, the nature and complexity of the proceedings, the ease and expense of retrieval of any particular document and the significance of any document which is likely to be located during the search. The duty to disclose is limited (CPR 31.8) to documents which are or have been in the control of the party. That means documents which are or were in his physical possession, over which he has or has had a right to possession or a right to inspect and take copies.

Specific disclosure is dealt with by CPR 31.12. An order for specific disclosure **7.29** is an order that a party do one or more of the following: disclose documents or classes of documents specified in the order; carry out a search to the extent specified in the order; disclose any documents located as a result of that search.

There is no provision in either the Employment Tribunal's Rules or the CPR **7.30** for the giving of disclosure without an order but once a duty of disclosure arises, either upon the making of an order or because the parties have agreed to mutually disclose documents, the obligation to disclose is a continuing one until the proceedings are concluded by the delivery of judgment. The duty calls for the immediate disclosure of any previously undisclosed document as soon as it comes to a party's notice (CPR 31.11).

(d) *Restrictions on disclosure*

A full discussion of the grounds on which the disclosure or inspection of a docu- **7.31** ment can be withheld is outside the scope of this volume. For national security proceedings see r. 94 and the commentary in Chapter 13. For withholding of disclosure or inspection in the public interest generally see CPR 31.19. For legal professional privilege generally see CPR 31.15 [3]–[13]. For legal advice privilege see *R (on the application of Prudential Plc and anor)* v. *Special Commissioners of Income Tax and anor* 2013 UKSC 1. For medical reports see CPR 31.15 [15]. For the restrictions on disclosure of material relating to the assessments of compara-tors in a large-scale redundancy exercise see *British Aerospace v. Green* [1995] ICR 1006; [1995] IRLR 433 CA, although it may be that *Green* is confined to those cases where there is no particularized allegation of unfairness in the way the assessments were made or applied and the request for disclosure is in consequence a disguised fishing expedition in the hope that some unfairness will be revealed by the documents.

2. Witness orders

7.32 The 'requirement to attend to give evidence' in r. 32 replaces r. 10(2)(c) of the 2004 Rules but with the additional words 'or produce information'. As with the 2004 Rules, applications for witness orders and the Tribunal's response to them are not required to be copied to the other parties (r. 92). The Tribunal may order any person in Great Britain to attend to give oral evidence only or to attend to give evidence and to produce documents or provide information. Given the penal sanction for non-compliance created by s. 7(4)(a) ETA, the documents or the information would have to be identified in the order with sufficient certainty to enable any non-compliance to be demonstrated to the criminal level of proof. It is not clear in what circumstances it would be appropriate to apply for an order that a person attend a hearing to produce information rather than give evidence, or how such an order would be complied with. It may be intended to apply, for example, to cases where a specific process needs to be described, or the content of a document which cannot readily be produced at the hearing, explained. Unlike the 2004 Rules there is no requirement for witness orders to be endorsed with a notice warning of the consequences of non-compliance (on summary conviction a fine not exceeding level 3 on the standard scale—currently £1,000) but in practice they will continue to be so endorsed. The penal provision does not extend to orders to attend to produce information in the absence of an amendment to s. 7(4) ETA.

7.33 A witness order will only be granted if the Judge is satisfied that the witness can give relevant evidence and they will not attend unless compelled to do so. An application for an order may be refused if it is made so late in the day that it would be unreasonable to expect the witness to attend at such short notice, unless they have hitherto been willing to attend voluntarily. Given the test in *British Home Stores Ltd v. Burchell* [1978] IRLR 379 EAT a witness who will speak to the question whether the claimant did or did not as a matter of objective fact commit the disciplinary offence in question, is not a relevant witness on liability in an unfair dismissal claim, but may be on remedy. A party may only apply for an order to compel the attendance of a witness who will support that party's case: it is never permissible for a party to seek to call a witness solely for the purpose of cross-examining them. However, it would be open to the Tribunal to issue a witness order of its own initiative so that the witness is not called on behalf of either party and may therefore be cross-examined by all parties.

7.34 A person against whom a witness order is issued may apply under r. 29 for it to be set aside entirely, e.g. because they have no relevant evidence to give; or to be varied, e.g. so as to require their attendance on a specified date only rather than throughout a lengthy hearing. Rule 92 would not apply to such an application as the witness is not a party and it would appear to be a matter for the discretion of the Judge whether to grant the application without first seeking the views of the party in whose favour the witness order was issued.

The Rules are silent as to the mode of service of a witness order and as to **7.35** whose responsibility it is to serve the order. The Tribunal's current practice is to require the party applying for the order to provide an address for service and for the Tribunal to serve the order itself by recorded delivery at that address. There appears to be no warrant for adopting this procedure, which is a purely administrative instruction to staff, other than practical efficacy, in particular the ability to prove service. It would, however, be wrong in principal to refuse to issue an order merely because the party applying does not have an address for service or wishes to serve the order personally for some other reason, for example because of the imminence of the hearing.

3. Evidence from other EU Member States

The purpose of rule 33 is informative rather than regulatory, drawing attention **7.36** to the possibility of obtaining evidence for use in Employment Tribunal proceedings from witnesses based in Member States by means of the procedure contained in Council Regulation (EC) No. 1026/2001. The Tribunal has no power to issue a witness order against such a person. A discussion of the procedure involved is outside the scope of this volume but practitioners may find CPR 34.22 and 34.23 of assistance.

4. Addition, substitution, and removal of parties

Rule 34 combines old r. 10(2)(k) (joining as a respondent any person who the **7.37** Tribunal considers may be liable for the remedy claimed); r. 10(2)(l) (dismissing from the proceedings a respondent who is no longer directly interested in the claim); and r. 10(2)(r) (joining as a party any person who the Tribunal considers has an interest in the outcome of the proceedings). The wording of the new rule however is in some respects broader and in others apparently narrower than its predecessors, although given that the various sub-paragraphs of r. 10(2) were only illustrative of the general power to make case management orders contained in r. 10(1), a situation which is replicated in r. 29, it would not generally be helpful to compare the old and the new provisions with a view to drawing conclusions about apparent changes in the Tribunal's powers. The Tribunal's overall power to make orders in this general area has neither been increased nor diminished although it may be necessary to proceed with care when determining whether an order can be made under r. 34 or only under r. 29. Although the wording of the new rule to some extent reflects CPR 19.2–19.5 (addition and substitution of parties) there is no warrant for importing into the Rule, or interpreting it to accord with, the limitations in CPR 19 on what is intended to be a broad general power.

7.38   However, there is one respect in which the Tribunal's express powers may have been consciously changed. Under the 2004 Rules a respondent could be added if they may be liable for the remedy claimed and any person who had an interest in the outcome could be joined as a party. Rule 34 provides for joinder or substitution 'if it appears that there are issues between that person and any of the existing parties falling within the jurisdiction of the Tribunal which it is in the interests of justice to have determined in the proceedings'. The language is that of CPR 19.2(2)(b) although none of the other grounds for changing parties in CPR 19.2 are mentioned in the Rule, in particular the power of substitution in CPR 19.2(4). It is not immediately obvious what, if anything, might be caught by the new wording which would not have been caught by the old.

7.39   However, it is not clear whether everything that was caught by the old wording is caught by the new. Old r. 10(2)(r) was introduced to resolve the problem encountered in *Rutherford v. Secretary of State for Trade and Industry (No. 1)* [2003] IRLR 388 EAT where the claimant, who was over 65, alleged that the rules preventing him bringing a complaint of unfair dismissal and from receiving a redundancy payment were indirectly discriminatory against men. In order to resolve the matter the Tribunal needed to have statistics relating to the impact of the cut-off at age 65 and to hear argument on objective justification. The problem was resolved by the Secretary of State consenting to be a party. Whilst the Secretary of State would, as the author of the rules in question, clearly have had an interest in the outcome of the Tribunal proceedings, any issues between the Secretary of State and the parties in respect of the Rules could only be resolved in the High Court, not the Tribunal. The Secretary of State could therefore not be joined under new r. 34 in similar circumstances. However he or she could still be joined by consent and the Tribunal would apparently still have power to make an order in the same terms as old r. 10(2)(r) under the general order-making power in r. 29. New r. 35 may also be applicable (see para. 7.43 below).

7.40   The most striking difference between the 2004 Rules and r. 34 is that the latter gives the power to add a claimant as well as a respondent to the proceedings as the reference is to adding 'any person as a party'. The jurisprudence on applications to amend a claim form by the addition of a fresh cause of action (*Selkent Bus Co Ltd v. Moore* [1996] ICR 836; [1996] IRLR 661 EAT) will be of some assistance in such cases but a power in the Rules to add a claimant to existing proceedings cannot trump statutory limitation provisions. A claimant who is out of time for bringing fresh proceedings therefore cannot improve their position by seeking to add their claim to an existing one under r. 34. Although r. 34 permits the Tribunal to act of its own initiative, it is difficult to imagine any circumstance in which it would be appropriate to add a person as a claimant other than on their own application. On the other hand, where the original claim was in time and the application is to add a new respondent (or the Tribunal is proposing to do so of its own initiative) the fact that the claim is now out of time against that respondent is only one of the factors to be considered: it is not an absolute bar: see *Cocking v. Sandhurst (Stationers) Ltd* [1974] ICR 650 EAT, at 656 and 657.

There is also an important difference in wording between old r. 10(2)(l) which 7.41
permitted the dismissal of a claim against a respondent who is no longer interested in the claim and r. 34 which refers to the removal of any party 'apparently
wrongly included' although given the general rule-making power under r. 29,
the former order is still permissible. The importance of the new wording is that
it is now explicit that the Tribunal may of its own initiative, and, if necessary,
against the wishes of the claimant, dismiss from any proceedings which can only
be brought against the claimant's employer, persons such as managers or owners
of limited companies erroneously named as respondents.

The power of substitution can be used to substitute one respondent for 7.42
another even after judgment, provided (*per Cocking v. Sandhurst* (above) at 657,
proposition (6)) the mistake sought to be corrected was a genuine one, was not
misleading, and would not cause reasonable doubt as to the identity of the person to be claimed against. If, on that test, substitution was appropriate, there is
no requirement for the original judgment to be set aside (*Watts v. Seven Kings
Motor Co Ltd* (1983) ICR 135 EAT).

5. Participation by other persons

Rule 35 is a new provision and seemingly very broad in scope. It appears to cre- 7.43
ate an unfettered discretion in the Tribunal to permit a non-party to participate
in the proceedings and on what terms, although such a discretion does not mean
that a decision to refuse an application to participate would be un-appealable.
The discretion must be exercised rationally and not capriciously and in accordance with the purpose of the rule, taking all relevant factors into account and
ignoring irrelevant ones. On appeal the question will be whether the Judge's decision was permissible on the evidence (*Neary v. Governing Body of St Alban's
Girls' School and anor* [2010] ICR 473, para 49). A relevant factor is always likely
to be, having regard to the overriding objective, balancing the prejudice caused
to the applicant for the order through not being able to be heard in respect of
their legitimate interests, against any prejudice to the parties in terms of delay
and additional cost caused by allowing them to be heard.

Although the rule does not expressly say so, it does seem to envisage, by the 7.44
use of the word 'permit', the need for an application to be made by the person
wishing to participate in the proceedings. Thus the Tribunal would not appear
to be able to require any person to participate, for example by way of being an
amicus, without their consent. So in a case such as *Rutherford* (see para. 7.39
above) unless the Secretary of State applied to participate in the proceedings,
r. 35 would not solve the problem that existed prior to the introduction of old
r. 19(2)(r) and which may now have re-emerged. Note that the application is
not to become a party (which is permitted by r. 34) but merely to participate
in the proceedings on such terms as may be specified, those terms, ultimately,
being dictated by the Tribunal as a condition of the permission to participate.
The terms would appear to be at large and might, therefore, include the calling

of witnesses by the person applying for the order and the cross-examination by them of the parties' witnesses: indeed anything up to but excluding actually becoming a party. The rule does not expressly say so, but given that the terms which the Tribunal may grant or impose are at large, the terms on which participation might be granted could include that the person concerned be represented, even though the rule is couched in terms of personal participation.

7.45   As the applicant for the order is by definition a non-party, rr. 30 and 92 would not apply to the application itself, although it should be copied to the parties, if necessary by the Tribunal, who must be given the opportunity to comment given the potential impact of intervention on the proceedings. Once made, the application becomes an application for a case management order and the Rules as a whole therefore apply to its disposal. It should be dealt with like any other application for a case management order either on paper or at a preliminary hearing under r. 53(1)(a) by way of case management discussion which would appear to be the better course (unless the application is plainly hopeless) if it is not supported by all the parties to the proceedings or the terms on which it is to be granted require discussion. A party aggrieved by the granting of a r. 35 application to participate in proceedings would be able to appeal the order but only on the basis that the exercise of the Judge's discretion was improper. An appeal would also appear to lie to the EAT from a refusal to make the order as it would be 'a decision . . . arising in . . . proceedings before an employment tribunal' (ETA s. 21(1)).

7.46   Participation in the proceedings can only be permitted in respect of matters in which the person applying has a legitimate interest. In the case of an order under r. 50 (privacy and restrictions on disclosure) the right to be heard in objection to such an order arises by virtue of r. 50(4) not r. 35. There is no provision comparable to r. 35 in the CPR.

6. Lead cases

7.47   The purpose of r. 36 is to overcome the difficulties encountered in the *Preston* litigation (part-time worker pension cases) and subsequent large-scale equal pay claims involving local government and National Health Service employees.[3] Although in those cases so-called test cases were designated and their outcomes treated as binding, this could only be achieved by consent. Strictly, no party not involved in the test cases was bound by the outcome and so every individual claimant whose claim would fail as a consequence of a test case was required to show cause why it should not be struck out on the grounds that it had no reasonable prospect of success. Although the system worked in practice, it could not have done so if a large proportion of the claimants had not been represented by

---

[3] It also brings the Employment Tribunals into line with other Tribunals e.g. r. 18 of the Rules of Procedure of both the Tax Chamber and the General Regulatory Chamber.

a relatively small number of representatives and if the representatives had not actively co-operated in the process. Even so, it was administratively complex, time-consuming and expensive.

Although there are some common elements and both apply to claims which 'give rise to common or related issues of fact or law', the system which has been designed for the Employment Tribunal differs in material respects from, and is less complex than, the CPR equivalent, CPR 19.10–19.15 and CPR PD 19B (group litigation). In particular there is no equivalent of the Group Litigation Order (CPR 19.10 and 19.11) nor to CPR 19 Part II, representative parties, and no requirement for a group register to be established, although for the system to be workable in practice a central record of all of the affected claims would have to be kept at the Tribunal office handling the multiple, something which is already routinely done. Although under CPR PD19B, para. 3.1 a Group Litigation Order can be made before any proceedings are commenced, there is no power under r. 36 for the Tribunal to act in respect of a potential multiple. At least two claims must have been presented before a 'Lead Cases' order can be made. **7.48**

There is also no equivalent in r. 36 to CPR PD 19B paras. 4 and 3.3(3) which prevent a county court judge making a Group Litigation Order of his or her own initiative without first obtaining the consent of the Head of Civil Justice. However, it is long-established practice within the Employment Tribunal that whenever a multiple claim affects more than one region, either the Regional Employment Judges concerned or the parties must refer the matter to the President for directions. One of the reasons for the difference between the two systems seems to be that the Group Litigation Order is aimed at large-scale, potentially national, litigation whereas r. 36 is equally applicable to small-scale, single region multiple claims—the rule expressly applies where two or more claims are involved. **7.49**

Observance of the overriding objective, particularly the requirement for the parties to assist the Tribunal to further the aims of the objective and to co-operate with each other and with the Tribunal, will be of paramount importance in the effective management of cases subject to r. 36. Failure by a party to do so would be an irregularity or non-compliance for the purpose of r. 6, thus inviting a sanction. **7.50**

The principal features of r. 36 are as follows: **7.51**

- The designation by an Employment Judge or the President of lead cases which may be done without consulting the parties, although where the issues are likely to be complex it would be usual to hold a preliminary hearing under r. 53(1)(a) (case management) at an early stage although not necessarily as a first step. Note that the claimants in cases stayed behind the lead case and the claimant in the lead case itself are unlikely to constitute a fee group for the purpose of the Fees Order (see para. 14.04).

- The staying (in Scotland, sisting) of all other claims in the multiple behind the lead cases. The stayed (sisted) cases are referred to as the related cases. The power to stay (sist) related cases extends to future claims as well as those existing at the date the order is made. Note that there is no power in the Rules or otherwise for a respondent to agree not to take time-limit points in the hope of encouraging potential claimants not to issue proceedings but await the outcome of the lead case hearings, thus reducing the respondent's workload in dealing with claims. Any purported agreement to that effect cannot bind the Tribunal which is obliged to take limitation points even if the respondent does not as they go to the Tribunals jurisdiction to hear a claim (*Rogers v. Bodfari (Transport) Ltd* [1973] ICR 325 NIRC).

• There is no express requirement in the rule for a party in a related case to be notified that it is stayed behind a lead case or for the issues in the lead case which are said to be common or related to the issues in the related cases to be described or explained to them. However, r. 60 would require the former to be done and it is clearly advisable for the latter also to be done, possibly in the form of reasons attaching to the order staying the proceedings.

• There is no provision in r. 36 for a party in a related case to apply for the stay to be lifted in respect of that case, whether on the grounds of insufficient commonality with the lead cases or otherwise, but there seems to be no reason why such an application could not be made under r. 29.

• A copy of any decision in respect of the lead cases must be sent to, and the outcome is binding on, all parties in the related cases subject to r. 36(3) (see below).

• If the lead case or cases are withdrawn before a decision is made on all the common or related issues, the Tribunal must make an order as to whether another claim or claims be specified as lead cases and whether any existing order affecting the related cases should be set aside and varied.

7.52   A party in a related case may apply in writing, within twenty-eight days of the date on which a 'decision in respect of the common or related issues' was sent to it, for an order that the decision does not apply to and is not binding on the parties to a particular related case. The time-limit can be extended by virtue of r. 5 even after it has expired. Rule 36(3) does not specify the nature of the application or the procedure to be followed although if the application was made in respect of a case management order in the lead case rather than a judgment, rr. 29 and 53(1)(a) would almost certainly apply. Rule 92 applies in any event and so the applying party must send a copy of the application 'to all other parties'. It is not clear whether in this case that means only the parties in the particular related case or all parties in the multiple. Because of what appears to be the very narrow basis on which the application can be made and the near impossibility of the party applying knowing the identity and contact details of all other parties in a large multiple, it is almost certainly the former.

7.53   It is important to note that this is not an application for a reconsideration of a judgment in the lead case under rr. 70–73, as r. 36(3) does not appear to give scope for any challenge to be made to the decision itself (where the decision is a case management order, r. 29 might give scope for it to be challenged but only to the extent to which it affects the particular related case). There is also no equivalent of CPR 19.12(2) which permits a party in a related case adversely affected by a judgment in a lead case to seek permission to appeal that judgment. The basis on which an application can be made under r. 36(3) in respect of a judgment would therefore appear to be limited to a claim that the issues between the parties in the related case are not sufficiently similar to the issues between the parties in the lead case for the judgment to be binding.

There is no express requirement in r. 36(3) for the application to include an **7.54** explanation of why it is made, although it would clearly be necessary for an explanation to be given in advance of any hearing of the application to enable the other party to know the nature of the case it has to meet. There is also no express power to reject an application on the basis that it has no reasonable prospect of success although one can probably be implied by virtue of the overriding objective. There is no express provision for a hearing of the application, although where the decision is a judgment, by virtue of rr. 53(1)(b) and 56 and Art. 6 ECHR a public hearing of the application would appear to be necessary if it was not otherwise disposed of e.g. by consent. Where the other party to the related case disputes the facts on which the applying party relies for their contention that the case is not sufficiently related to the lead case, it would seem that evidence would have to be called.

7. Striking out

(a) *Generally*

The purpose of rule 37 is to give more prominence to the power to strike out a **7.55** case at any stage: 'which should lead to increased awareness by all parties and potentially, more consistent use by Judges' (Underhill Review, para. 33). Rule 37(1)(a)–(e) reproduces old r. 18(7)(b)–(f) and enables a claim or response or part of one, to be struck out on the now familiar grounds, with one difference in wording which is discussed below. The Tribunal can act in response to an application by a party or of its own initiative. Although there is no requirement in the rule for notice to be sent to the party in question, as a claim or response cannot be struck out unless that party has been given a reasonable opportunity to make representations (r. 37(2)), a notice must be sent. Rule 30 makes this explicit where the possibility of strike out is on application by a party, but it must equally be the case where the Tribunal acts of its own initiative. A reasonable opportunity to make representations would seem to entail that both the ground on which it is proposed to strike out the claim or response and the reason why strike out is deemed appropriate, must be spelled out. A hearing must be held if the party in question requests it (r. 37(2)). Hearings of strike out applications must be held in public (r. 56) unless r. 50 ('Privacy and restrictions on disclosure') or r. 94 ('National security proceedings') apply.

(b) *'Vexatious' or no reasonable prospect of success*

7.56 A vexatious claim (r. 37(1)(a)) is one brought for an improper motive, to harass or oppress the respondent (*E T Marler Ltd v. Robertson* [1974] ICR 72 NIRC). Having no reasonable prospect of success (r. 37(1)(a)) means having no realistic prospect of success. While it is unusual for the hearing of an application to strike out a claim on the grounds that it has no reasonable prospect of success to involve the determination of disputes of fact, it would not be an error of law for the Judge to hear evidence and consider documents in order to do so: see *Eastman v. Tesco Stores Ltd* (UKEAT/0143/12) where the issues determined by the Judge were whether the claimant had signed a career break letter and whether she had been given an undertaking that her job would be available to her at the end of the career break period. Where there are disputes of fact it can only be in the most extreme cases, e.g. that the claimant is now denying something which he clearly admitted previously, that the Tribunal can properly conclude that the factual dispute will be resolved against the claimant without first hearing evidence.

7.57 Lady Smith P in *Balls v. Downham Market High School* [2011] IRLR 217 EAT stated it thus:

> The general rule is that where the facts are disputed and if on the claimant's account the claim could succeed, the strike out application should be refused. Where strike out is sought or contemplated on the ground that the claim has no reasonable prospects of success, the structure of the exercise that the tribunal has to carry out is the same; the tribunal must first consider whether, on a careful consideration of all the available material, it can properly conclude that the claim has no reasonable prospects of success. I stress the word 'no' because it shows that the test is not whether the claimant's claim is likely to fail nor is it a matter of asking whether it is possible that his claim will fail. Nor is it a test which can be satisfied by considering what is put forward by the respondent either in the ET3 or in submissions and deciding whether their written or oral assertions regarding disputed matters are likely to be established as facts. It is, in short, a high test. There must be no reasonable prospects.

(c) *Unreasonable conduct of proceedings*

7.58 Where the basis of the application for a strike out is the unreasonable conduct of proceedings (r. 37(1)(b)) there are two cardinal conditions, at least one of which must be met: that the unreasonable conduct has taken the form of deliberate and persistent disregard of required procedural steps or it has made a fair trial impossible. If one of those conditions is met, the Tribunal must then consider whether striking out is proportionate (*Blockbuster Entertainments Ltd v. James* [2006] IRLR 630 CA). There is an interesting difference between the wording of this provision and the wording of the corresponding provision in the costs rule (r. 76(1)(a)). The words 'abusively' and 'disruptively' appear in the latter but not the former and in r. 76(1)(a) the word 'otherwise' appears before the word 'unreasonably'. This dichotomy was also present in previous iterations of the Rules. For a discussion of the significance of the word 'otherwise' see paras. 11.14–11.17. It is suggested that despite the difference in wording the two rules are addressing if not the same conduct then conduct of the same degree of seriousness and the difference is merely a drafting anomaly which has been perpetuated over the years.

(d) *Non-compliance with the Rules or orders*

Where the basis of the application is non-compliance with the Rules or with an **7.59** order of the Tribunal (r. 37(1)(c)) 'It is well established that a party guilty of persistent and deliberate failure to comply with a court order should expect no mercy' (*Neary v. Governing Body of St Albans Girls' School and anor* [2010] ICR 473 CA, para. 60) otherwise the determining issues are likely to be: (i) whether a fair trial remains possible despite the non-compliance; and (ii) proportionality. If an award of costs against the offending party would remedy the mischief, striking out is likely to be disproportionate.

(e) *Not being actively pursued*

A claim or response should only be struck out on the grounds that it is not being **7.60** actively pursued (r. 37(1)(d)) where any default on the part of the party in question, by for example failing to reply to correspondence from the Tribunal or to comply with orders, has been intentional or contumelious (contemptuous) or there has been inordinate and inexcusable delay either by the party or his representative such that there is no longer any prospect of a fair trial or there is substantial prejudice to the other party (*Birkett v. James* [1978] A.C. 297 HL(E)); (r. 38(1)d).

Employment Tribunals routinely strike out claims on the grounds that they **7.61** are not being actively pursued once contact with the claimant appears to have been lost or there is a simple failure to reply to correspondence particularly where a hearing is imminent and the claimant appears to have lost interest in the proceedings. This may be more difficult under the 2013 Rules as r. 37(2) provides that a claim or response may not be struck out unless the party in question has been given a reasonable opportunity to make representations. Where there is reason to believe that the party may no longer be at the address they have given for receiving documents, sending the notice to that address may not be giving them the requisite opportunity to make representations and so the prudent course may be for an order for substituted service of the notice to be made under r. 89.

(f) *Fair hearing no longer possible*

The 2004 Rules provided for the striking out of the claim where a fair hearing **7.62** of the proceedings was no longer possible. The 2013 Rules (in r. 37(1)(e)) provide that a claim or response may be struck out where it is no longer possible to have a fair hearing of the claim or response. The change may have been made in the name of equalizing the treatment afforded to claimants and respondents as far as possible but could have some unexpected consequences. The requirement that a fair hearing be no longer possible was always a necessary condition for striking out where there was non-compliance with the Rules or an order of the Tribunal or where the conduct of the proceedings, including whether they were being actively pursued, was in issue, but since the 2004 Rules it has become a condition which is both necessary and sufficient. It is presumably meant to apply when none of the other grounds for strike out are available, for example in claims which could not be said to be not being actively pursued because the claimant vigorously appealed every order made but in doing so caused so much delay that a fair trial had become impossible.

7.63　The wording of the 2004 Rules was certainly capable, at least in theory, of causing an injustice as the test was not why a fair trial was no longer possible but simply whether it was no longer possible, and there was no power to strike out the response (assuming that none of the grounds for striking out which were blameworthy was available). The wording of r. 37(1)(e) also does not expressly provide that the culpability of the parties is a factor for the Tribunal to take into consideration. Either the claim or response may be struck out and there is a very obvious paradox here in that the fact that a fair hearing of the response is no longer possible may lead to the claim being struck out (and vice versa), even if no-one is to blame, for example if the respondent's only witness suddenly dies before a proof of evidence is taken. However, the intention must be presumed to be that if the reason why a fair hearing is no longer possible is because of something done or not done by the claimant where the act or omission falls short of being a ground for striking out in its own right, it will be the claim which is truck out and vice versa.

7.64　Where a response is struck out, r. 21 applies, a judgment may be issued and the respondent would be entitled to take part in any future hearing (e.g. as to remedy) only to the extent permitted by the Employment Judge who chairs the hearing. The decision striking out either the claim or response is itself a judgment and therefore may be reconsidered under r. 70.

8. Unless orders

(a) *Nature of the order*

7.65　Rule 38(1) replaces r. 13(2) of the 2004 Rules but with an important change of wording. Under old r. 13(2) if the order was not complied with 'the claim or...response shall be struck out on the date of non-compliance...'. There was no power to strike out only part of the claim or response and so non-compliance with an order which related to only one of a number of complaints resulted in the whole claim being struck out (*Royal Bank of Scotland v. Abraham* UKEAT/0305/09). The new Rule provides that an order may be made 'in terms that specify that if it is not complied with the claim or response, or part of it, will be dismissed...'. This wording seems to leave open the possibility that the order may provide that the whole of a claim or response shall stand dismissed if the order is not complied with even if the order relates only to one of a number of complaints, but in the absence of an express provision to that effect then only that part of the claim (or response) to which the order applies will be dismissed.

The words 'will be dismissed without further order' make it clear that the **7.66** operation of an unless order is automatic and that no further action is required on the part of the Tribunal to bring it to an end. This was also the position under the 2004 Rules although the wording was less clear (*Scottish Ambulance Service v. Laing* UKEAT/0038/12). The Tribunal is only required to give written notice to the parties confirming what has occurred (r. 38(1)). The Tribunal should resolve any disputes over the question of compliance. Whether an order has been substantially complied with so as to avoid the sanction is to be interpreted qualitatively not quantitatively (*Johnson v. Oldham Metropolitan Borough Council* UKEAT/0095/13).

(b) *Relief from sanction*

The fact that no further order of the Tribunal is required to bring the claim (or **7.67** response) to an end makes the wording of r. 38(2) problematic, at least at first sight. It provides that a party whose claim or response has been dismissed as a result of non-compliance with an unless order may, within fourteen days of the date written notice of the effect of non-compliance was sent, 'apply to have *the order* set aside on the grounds that it is in the interests of justice to do so' [emphasis added]. There is of course no 'order' dismissing the claim or response and the original unless order, being a case management order, could be set aside under r. 29 in any event. The right to apply to have 'the order' set aside is therefore either otiose or is aimed at the dismissal of the claim or response rather than the original unless order itself. The presumption must be that the right is not otiose and there will certainly be cases where no challenge could be made in the interests of justice to the original order but where the consequent dismissal would be unjust if no challenge could be made to it, e.g. where the information required by the order was provided timeously but lost or delayed in the post.

By providing that the 'order' can be set aside, the rule is following the effect of **7.68** *Uyanwu-Odu & anor v. Schools Offices Services & anor* (UKEAT/0294/05) which held that the unless order itself was a provisional judgment in the case of a claim and *North Care Primary Care Trust v. Aynsley* [2009] ICR 1333 EAT which provided that it was a provisional case management order in the case of a response, which in both cases became final on non-compliance and therefore susceptible to review under old r. 34 or old r.10(2)(n) respectively. The subject of the application referred to in r. 38(2) is therefore the dismissal into which the original unless order has crystallized. The rule simplifies and removes any uncertainty from the position under the 2004 Rules by treating both the dismissal of claims and responses alike and expressly providing a power to set aside.

The time-limit for applying for the order to be set aside can be extended under **7.69** r. 5. Although the application must be dealt with at a hearing if one is requested by the party in default, it would clearly be in breach of the overriding objective to require both parties to attend a hearing if the application was not opposed unless a hearing was required in any event, for example to make case management orders. The rule is silent both as to the process to be followed and the nature of the hearing. From the fact that r. 38 appears in the section of the Rules dealing with case management and other powers and that the language of r. 38(2) is that of order rather than judgment, it seems that the hearing will be a preliminary hearing for the purposes of case management under r. 53(1)(a) and therefore in private. That being so r. 36 applies and the party applying must notify the other parties of the application. It is suggested that it could never be in the interests of justice for this requirement to be dispensed with by the Tribunal under r. 92 in the case of an application to set aside a dismissal for non-compliance with an unless order. The other party would have the right to request a hearing but would not be entitled to one.

(c) *Applicability of CPR 3.9(1)*

7.70   Under the 2004 Rules, which did not expressly provide for relief from the consequences of non-compliance with an unless order, a line of appellate authority developed which recognized the existence of such a right by equating the consequence with a judgment in the case of a claim and an order in the case of a response. These authorities held that CPR 3.9(1) applied directly to an application for relief from the sanction of dismissal and therefore it was an error of law for an Employment Judge considering such an application not to expressly apply each of the nine factors listed under that rule. In *Neary v. Governing Body of St Alban's Girls School and anor* [2010] ICR 473 CA it was held that as CPR 3.9(1) was not expressly incorporated into the 2004 Rules it was not an error of law for a Judge not to follow it. It was at best a helpful checklist of factors to be considered but in the context of relevancy.

7.71   The correct approach to be adopted by a Judge when considering whether to grant relief from sanction in such a case was discussed by Smith LJ in *Neary*. Having identified (at para. 49) that it was a matter of judgment not discretion, she said:

> But this may be a distinction without a difference in that, in both cases, there is a duty on the judge to decide the case rationally and not capriciously and to make his decision in accordance with the purpose of the relevant legislation, taking all relevant factors or circumstances into account. He must also avoid taking irrelevant factors into account... with an exercise of judgment the question [on appeal] will be whether the decision was fair.
>
> 50. What factors or circumstances are relevant to a decision will be case sensitive. However, there are certain types of decision in which it is predictable that particular factors are likely (although not certain) to be relevant. The factors listed in...CPR 3.9(1) are good examples of this situation. However, in each case, it must be recognised that not all the factors will have any relevance in a particular case. Also, there may well be other factors not mentioned in the list which may be highly material in the individual case.

7.72   Thus, CPR 3.9(1) had the status under the 2004 Rules as nothing more than an *aide memoire* of likely relevant issues. Is this status affected by the fact that the 2013 Rules expressly provide a relief from the sanction of dismissal? In *Neary* it was accepted that the correct approach (at least where it was the claim which had been struck out) was for the Judge to apply old r. 34(3) which listed a number of bases on which a decision could be reviewed, only one of which (that the interests of justice require it) 'is of possible application in the present circumstances' (*Neary*, para. 48). Rule 39(2) provides (in effect) that the only ground on which the dismissal can be set aside is that it is in the interests of justice to do so. Thus *Neary* would appear to apply equally to the 2013 Rules and the status of CPR 3.9(1) remains as it was, merely a helpful checklist. Whether it should enjoy even this diminished status is discussed at paras. 1.10–1.12.

(d) *Where the response is dismissed*

Rule 38(3) provides that where it is the response which is dismissed r. 21 applies, 7.73 permitting a Judge to issue a judgment in favour of the claimant. For a discussion of r. 21 see paras. 5.17–5.22.

9. Deposit orders

(a) *Generally*

Rule 39 combines and simplifies old rr. 20 and 47 and some important changes 7.74 are made, in particular to the question of forfeiture of the deposit. There is one very important omission from r. 39. Old r. 18(9) provided that if the payment of a deposit had been 'considered' at a pre-hearing review, the Judge who conducted it should not be a member of the Tribunal at the final hearing: in other words the disqualification applied even if no deposit was ordered. This provision is not repeated in the 2013 Rules although it is understood that the Presidents of both England and Wales and Scotland wish it to continue to be the case in practice.

Considerations of apparent (indeed actual) bias would make it at least pru- 7.75 dent, and in some cases obviously necessary, for any Judge who has ordered the payment of a deposit to disqualify themselves from any further participation in the proceedings, including possibly a later preliminary hearing to consider making case management orders under r. 53(1)(a) which would not have been prevented by old r. 18(9), but, absent a Presidential practice direction under reg. 11, it would appear to be a matter for the Judge. It is suggested that it would be good practice for a Judge who does not disqualify himself from further participation in the proceedings having made a deposit order, to explain why he has not done so as part of the reasons required by r. 39(3). There may indeed be perfectly good reasons for a Judge not to disqualify herself from a future hearing, for example where the application for a deposit was refused without controversy or the Judge spent time discussing the pros and cons of various contentions and in so doing gained the confidence of the parties who would in consequence welcome her continued involvement in the proceedings.

There are two discretions to be exercised by the Judge. The first is whether 7.76 to make a deposit order at all. The words of both the 2004 and 2013 Rules are 'may make an order'. Thus it is perfectly permissible for a Judge to conclude that although a complaint or response has little reasonable prospect of success no deposit will be ordered. However, if that is against the wishes of the other party, reasons would have to be given (r. 62(1)) and if the reasons show that the Judge has exercised their discretion wrongly an appeal would lie. The second discretion is as to the amount of the deposit—see below paras. 7.81 and 7.82.

(b) *The hearing*

7.77 A deposit order can only be made at a preliminary hearing. However it appears that the preliminary hearing need not have been listed expressly for that purpose. Rule 39(1) provides that 'If at a preliminary hearing the tribunal considers that any complaint or response has little reasonable prospect of success...', it may make a deposit order. There is a requirement to specify in advance the subject matter of a preliminary hearing only where it is to be held to determine a 'preliminary issue' as defined in r. 53(1)(b), the power to make a deposit order not being a preliminary issue for this purpose. It therefore seems that 'a preliminary hearing' in the opening words of r. 39(1) means 'any preliminary hearing'. The Tribunal is only required to give reasonable notice of a deposit order hearing and no minimum period is specified. It may therefore be possible for a deposit order to be made on no prior notice other than an oral indication to the parties during a preliminary hearing into another matter (even one for the purposes of case management under r. 53(1)(a)), that the Judge has it in mind to make such an order, and a short adjournment to enable submissions to be prepared. Whether this is appropriate in any particular case is likely to be determined largely by reference to the overriding objective.

7.78 A preliminary hearing called expressly for the purpose of making a deposit order is to be held in private (r. 56) unless (as will usually be the case) it is coupled with an application to strike out the claim on the grounds that it has no reasonable prospect of success, as any part of the hearing relating to the strike out application must be in public and the Tribunal 'may direct' that the entirety of the hearing be in public. As the making of a deposit order is usually considered to be a lesser alternative to strike out with no separate submissions being made, the whole hearing would normally be in public.

(c) *Applicability of the order*

7.79 The 2004 Rules did not distinguish between claims and complaints as the 2013 Rules do and according to the Underhill Review (at para. 63) deposit orders under the 2004 Rules could not be attached to anything other than a whole claim or response 'under current legislation', a reference to ETA s. 9(2). However old r. 20 provided for a deposit to be paid in respect of a 'contention' by a party 'in relation to a matter required to be determined by a tribunal' and provided for a deposit order to be made as a condition of being permitted to take part in the proceedings 'in relation to that matter'. That was generally understood to mean, and was widely interpreted in practice as meaning, that it was possible to order a deposit in respect of something which was not only less than the full claim but less than a complaint as defined in the 2013 rules. A late amendment to the draft 2013 Rules prompted by s. 21(2) of the Enterprise and Regulatory Reform Act 2013, which amends s. 9(2) of the ETA to correct the difficulty referred to in the Underhill Review, ensures that under the 2013 Rules that is indeed the case. A deposit may now be ordered in respect of 'any specific allegation or argument' in either a claim or response which the Tribunal considers has little reasonable prospect of success, as a condition of continuing to advance that allegation or argument.

There is no litmus test for determining when something has 'little reasonable **7.80** prospect of success'. On a spectrum, one extreme of which is 'no prospect of success' and the next band 'no reasonable prospect', it appears to be the next available band of degree of unlikelihood of success. But how many such bands there are between the extreme and the mid-point of having a 50–50 chance of success is a matter of speculation. Attempting to define those bands in such terms as 'not much' 'some' etc looks suspiciously like splitting hairs. The rule means what it says: having 'little reasonable prospect' entails having some small prospect of success. If the prospect of success appears to be better than small, no deposit can be ordered. As with striking out for having no reasonable prospect of success 'little reasonable prospect of success' is likely to mean 'little realistic prospect of success'.

(d) *The party's means*

Rule 39(2) reproduces the effect of old r. 20(2). The Tribunal must make reason- **7.81** able enquiries into the paying party's ability to pay the deposit and 'have regard to any such information' when deciding the amount of the deposit, which may be up to £1,000. It is important to note that this is not a requirement to temper the wind to the shorn lamb: in other words to reduce the deposit which would otherwise have been ordered on the sole ground of lack of means to pay. The amount of the deposit is a matter for the discretion of the Judge, that discretion to be exercised on the usual principles with regards to relevance and fairness and having regard to the overriding objective. The rule merely stipulates that the party's means to pay is always a relevant, but not determinative, consideration.

It is suggested that, having regard to the overriding objective, it would not be **7.82** appropriate for the Judge to adjourn the hearing having decided that a deposit order should be made, simply because the paying party has failed to bring the necessary financial information to the hearing with them, certainly where to do so would be to put the other party to irrecoverable expense and probably any-way. The requirement is only to make reasonable, not exhaustive, enquires into the party's ability to pay the deposit, rather than their means as a whole, and the onus must be on the party against whom the deposit order is sought to provide the necessary evidence at the original hearing.

(e) *Reasons*

Rule 39(3) provides that the Judge's reasons for making the deposit order must **7.83** be provided with the order and the paying party must be notified of the potential consequences of the order, which must include not only failure to pay the deposit but what will happen should the deposit be paid and the claim be ultimately unsuccessful. Rule 62(4) provides that the reasons given for any decision should be proportionate to the significance of the issues and for decisions other than judgments (thus including deposit orders) may be very short. They must however be detailed enough to enable the Tribunal which eventually hears the case to both understand the allegation or argument to which the order relates and the reasons for making the order, as a deposit can only be forfeited if the reason for finding against the party at the final hearing was 'substantially the reason given in the deposit order' (r. 39(5)).

7.84   Although not expressly provided for in the Rules, the practice used to be that the reasons for the making of a deposit order (and in consequence the fact that an order had been made) be placed in a sealed brown envelope in the file, not to be opened until the conclusion of the hearing. This is no longer the case which means that both the fact of, and the reasons for, making a deposit order can be included in an order dealing with other matters, such as the rejection of an application to strike out the claim or response, and also in the final hearing bundle and so be known to the Tribunal before the final hearing begins.

(f) *Effect of non-payment*

7.85   Previous Rules have always provided that a deposit must be paid within twenty-one days of the written notice being sent to the parties as did all drafts of the 2013 Rules until the last. The length of time which a party has to pay the deposit now seems to be a matter for the Judge when making the order although r. 39 is silent on the point. By virtue of r. 4(5) the last date for compliance should be given as a calendar date. By virtue of r. 4(3) if a period of time, say twenty-one days, is specified for payment, the day the notice is sent is to be ignored in calculating the twenty-one days so that where the notice is sent on the 5th of a month, the last date for compliance is the 26th.

7.86   The notice requiring payment includes details of how and where to make the payment. The time may be extended under r. 5 even after the original period has expired, provided the allegation or argument to which the deposit relates has not already been struck out. This is because r. 39(4) only provides that the allegation or argument 'will be struck out' which appears to require further action by a Judge in signing the appropriate judgment: strike out is not automatic as in the case of non-compliance with an unless order. It is essential that in both the notice sent to the claimant and in the deposit order itself the allegation or argument in question is clearly identified and the strike out judgment faithfully reflects the order. It is important to avoid any confusion over what has been struck out as there is obviously scope for something much less than a full complaint or even a full cause of action to be the subject of a deposit order. Although the rule is mandatory in its effect with regard to strike out and there is no further discretion to be exercised by the Judge, it is still a judicial decision (*Sodexho v. Gibbons* [2005] ICR 1647; [2005] IR.L.R. 836 EAT) and the strike out judgment would therefore be susceptible to reconsideration under r. 70. Where the response is struck out, r. 21 applies so that a judgment may be issued and the respondent limited to taking part in any hearings to the extent permitted by the Employment Judge chairing the hearing (r. 39(4)).

(g) *Forfeiture*

Rule 39(5) makes significant changes to the consequences for the paying party **7.87** where they have paid the deposit, continued with the claim but lost 'for substantially the reasons given in the deposit order'. It now seems to be the case that a party may be largely successful at the final hearing but still forfeit their deposit because they were unsuccessful in respect of the allegation or argument which caused the order to be made. However, depending on the nature of the allegation or argument, it may well be difficult for the other party to show that identifiable costs have been incurred in defending it, thus preventing a costs order being made in addition to the forfeiture.

Old r. 47(1) only required the Tribunal to consider whether to make a costs **7.88** or preparation time order against the unsuccessful party on the grounds that, by persevering in the face of the deposit order, the proceedings had been conducted unreasonably. Rule 39(5) considerably strengthens the effect of the deposit order in such circumstances, first by creating a rebuttable presumption that the proceedings have been conducted unreasonably for the purposes of the costs regime in respect of the specific allegation or argument; and, second, by providing for the deposit to be forfeited in favour of the winning party or parties (the rule appears to allow for the whole of the deposit to be forfeited in favour of one of a number of parties or paid to all parties in proportions to be determined by the Tribunal) even if no costs order is then made in the exercise of the Tribunal's discretion. Where a costs or preparation time order is made, the deposit counts 'towards the settlement of that order' (r. 39(6)).

Rule 39(5) creates the presumption mentioned above 'unless the contrary is **7.89** shown'. It must be assumed that this does not anticipate a further hearing after the Tribunal's decision has been announced to give the paying party the opportunity to rebut the presumption as it will almost always be the case that any evidence that the paying party wished to call on the issue which was the subject of the deposit order will have been called during the main merits hearing. Showing the contrary therefore seems likely to be a matter for submissions on evidence which the Tribunal has already heard.

There is a further significant change from old r. 47(2), this time a liberalization. **7.90** Under r. 39(5) the deposit is to be repaid to a losing paying party if the reason why they were unsuccessful at final hearing was not substantially the reason given in the deposit order, even if a costs or preparation time order is made against that party for a different reason. Under old r. 47(2) a deposit would be forfeited whenever an order for costs or preparation time was made, whether the award of costs arose out of the same proceedings as had given rise to the deposit order 'or out of proceedings relating to any other matter considered with that matter...'.

10. Non-payment of fees

7.91 The purpose of new r. 40 is to provide the Tribunal with a sanction where a party has not paid a relevant Tribunal fee. The rule is subject to r. 11 and therefore does not apply where a claim is rejected under that rule. The possibility of the claim being reinstated by way of an application under r. 40(5) is therefore not available to a claimant whose claim has been rejected under r. 11 leaving such a claimant apparently without remedy short of judicial review. Rule 40 provides for the dismissal of a claim, a response, an employer's contract claim or an 'application' (as defined in the Fees Order) if a relevant Tribunal fee is not paid and a remission application has not been made or has been unsuccessful, if the fee is not then paid after a notice requiring payment has been sent to the party. In the case of a fee for judicial mediation, the sanction is that the mediation will not take place.

7.92 There is a fundamental disjunct between what this rule, when read with the Fees Order, art. 4(1)(b), (2) and (3) and Schedule 3, para. 9(2) appear to say and what the administration believes it to say. Because the effect of the rule in bringing proceedings to an end is automatic upon the happening of a given event, it is a matter of concern that there is room for doubt as to what that event is. The administration believes that r. 40(1) envisages a two-stage process and that it should be read as follows (added words in **bold**):

> Subject to rule 11, where a party has not paid a relevant fee **pursuant to a notice issued under art 4(1)(b), (2) or (3) of or paragraph 9(2) of Schedule 3 to the Fees Order** or presented a remission application in respect of that fee the Tribunal will send the party **an unless** notice specifying a date for payment of the Tribunal fee or presentation of a remission application.

It is understood that the unless notice will give the paying party a further seven days in which to pay the fee and it is upon the expiration of the unless notice that the automatic dismissal provisions of r. 40(2) will operate.

7.93 The argument appears to be that the non-payment of a fee envisaged in r. 40(1) can only occur after a party has been told what the fee is. But that is not how the system works. A party does not pay a relevant fee or present a remission application on any occasion when a fee is payable other than when the claim form is presented and r. 40(1) does not apply to r. 11. Instead, they are sent a notice telling them how much to pay. The natural meaning of the rule therefore is that the notice referred to is the art. 4 or para. 9(2) notice and it is upon the expiration of that notice that the automatic dismissal provisions operate, making it a one-stage process. If a two-stage process was envisaged, as the wording above demonstrates, it would have been simple enough to make that clear. As it is, there are likely to be challenges by respondents where claimants pay the fee after the first notice expires but before the unless notice has expired, on the grounds that the two-stage process is outwith the Rules and the claim is at an end by virtue of r. 40(2).

Neither the rule nor the Fees Order specifies the length of the notice to be **7.94** given under art. 4 but it is understood that it will be set at twenty-one days. As the time-limit is not one specified in the Rules it cannot be extended under r. 5 nor can the time-limit for compliance with the unless notice. Both are purely administrative. It is not known whether applications for extensions of time will be entertained and if so who will deal with them. It does not appear to be a judicial matter. Once the deadline for payment has passed, the claim, employer's contract claim or application 'shall be dismissed without further order', a sanction equivalent to non-compliance with an unless order and therefore automatic, not requiring the making of a further order or judgment (*Scottish Ambulance Service v. Laing* UKEAT/0038/12).

Relief from the sanction of dismissal is provided in r. 40(5). It provides that **7.95** upon application 'the Tribunal may order a reinstatement'. No time-limit is prescribed for the making of the application and there is no requirement for the grounds on which the application is made to be spelled out. This process would seem to allow a party to challenge the rejection of a remission application or the amount of the fee they have been required to pay following a partial remission. A reinstatement shall be effective only if the fee is paid or a remission application 'is presented and accepted, by the date specified in the order'. This last provision must presumably mean the remission application has to be made by the date specified in the order and subsequently accepted as it would be wholly unjust if delay by Tribunal staff in processing the remission application caused the reinstatement to fail. What r. 40(5) does not say is by whom a reinstatement application is to be considered but as this is an application for relief from sanction of what is in effect an unless order resulting in the dismissal of proceedings, it seems that this now becomes a judicial rather than an administrative matter.

It is understood that the administration may take the view that r. 40(5) is avail- **7.96** able only to correct administrative errors such as where a fee has in fact been paid within the period specified in the notice to pay but this has been overlooked and the party is told that their claim or application has been dismissed. But in such a case there has been no dismissal under r. 40(2) because there has been no triggering event. All that has happened is that the party has been given erroneous information. In consequence the question of reinstatement simply doesn't arise. Rule 40(5) is clearly of much wider effect.

8

HEARINGS—RULES 41–50 AND 53–59

A. RULES COMMON TO ALL KINDS OF HEARINGS—RULES 41–50

1. Overview

As has been noted in earlier chapters, there are several requirements in the Rules **8.01** to hold hearings to determine a variety of issues—e.g. under r. 13(3) reconsideration of the rejection of a claim; r. 19(3) reconsideration of the rejection of a response; rr. 27(3) and 28(3) requirement to show cause why a claim or response should not be struck out at initial consideration—none of which are characterized as preliminary or final hearings. This section of the Rules applies to those hearings as well as preliminary and final hearings.

8.02   The insertion of the phrase 'The Tribunal may regulate its own procedure...' at the beginning of r. 41, the general rule, raises some interesting questions. The three previous Rules all had this as a miscellaneous or general power to the effect that 'subject to the provisions of these Rules, the Tribunal may regulate its own procedure'. The intention now appears to be that the power to regulate its own procedure is confined to the way in which the Tribunal conducts a hearing. If the consequence is that such power as the Tribunal may have previously had to regulate its procedure generally (subject to the exercise of that power not being incompatible with the Rules) has gone, the gap is not filled by the overriding objective to which the Tribunal must give effect 'in interpreting or exercising any power given to it by the Rules'. Whether this change is material will only become apparent should a party seek to challenge on appeal something done by the Tribunal for which there is no express warrant in the Rules. Given the very broad concept of the case management order (r. 29) such a challenge might be difficult to mount.

8.03   There are changes in the language from the 2004 Rules in a number of the provisions relating to hearings which affect the way they will operate in practice.

2. The general rule

8.04   Rule 41 requires the Tribunal to conduct the hearing in the manner it considers fair having regard to the overriding objective, effectively restating in a phrase the basis of the objective itself, that general power not to be restricted by the specific powers contained in the other rules in this section. The rule reproduces old r. 14(2) and (3) but replaces what appeared to be a requirement for the Tribunal to make such enquiries of witnesses as it deemed appropriate with a power to do so ('may' instead of 'shall') and the requirement to seek to avoid formality (r. 14(2)) becomes a requirement to seek to avoid 'undue' formality. Both may be acknowledgments of how far Employment Tribunal proceedings have migrated from the original Donovan ideals[1] as a direct consequence of the increasing complexity of employment law and in doing so have become more formal and adversarial and less inquisitorial. The discretion which this gives to the Tribunal in the way it conducts a hearing must be exercised judicially and is challengeable on appeal (*Aberdeen Steak Houses Group plc v. Ibrahim* [1988] ICR 550; [1988] IRLR 420 EAT). Whilst Employment Judges are experienced in the need to adjust the level of formality to match the complexities of the case and the abilities of the parties, all cases tend to follow the normal civil court format

---

[1] Royal Commission on Trade Unions and Employers Associations 1965–1968 Cmnd 3623—the Donovan Commission—para. 572.

of the party who must establish the case (which in an unfair dismissal claim is the respondent who must establish the reason for dismissal if dismissal is admitted) leading their evidence first, witnesses being cross-examined and after the other party has lead its evidence and its witnesses have been cross-examined, closing submissions being made. Opening statements whilst permissible are very rare.

The statement in the final sentence of the rule, that the Tribunal 'is not **8.05** bound by any rule of law relating to the admissibility of evidence...' is a departure from previous Rules which stated that the Tribunal was not bound by '*any enactment* or rule of law relating to the admissibility of evidence' [emphasis added] the change of wording perhaps being a recognition of the fact that the Rules cannot trump primary legislation. But appellate authority clearly demonstrates that neither r. 41 nor its predecessors can mean what they say, even absent the reference to enactments in the former. The rule with regard to the non-admissibility of privileged communications, most notably of without prejudice discussions with a view to settlement, undoubtedly applies to Employment Tribunal proceedings (*Gallop v. Newport City Council* UKEAT/0586/10) as do the established exceptions to it. Thus evidence of without prejudice discussions might be admitted under the 'unambiguous impropriety' or other abuse exceptions if it was necessary to do so to found a complaint of victimization (*BNP Paribas v. Mezzotero* [2004] IRLR 508 EAT) or if the privilege had been waived by both parties (*Brunel University and anor v. Vaseghi and anor* [2007] IRLR 209 EAT) but not otherwise. The prohibition on the introduction in evidence of a spent conviction (Rehabilitation of Offenders Act 1974) cannot be overcome other than by applying one of the exceptions in the Act e.g. s. 7(3) (*A v. B* UKEAT/0025/13). The Tribunal should be at least as concerned as civil courts to exclude irrelevant or only marginally relevant evidence (*HSBC Asia Holdings B.V. and anor v. Gillespie* [2011] IRLR 209 EAT).

Despite the apparent imperative and all-embracing language of the sentence, **8.06** it can only sensibly be construed as approximating to a declaration that in the interests of justice and having regard to the overriding objective and the need to avoid undue formality, the Tribunal may disregard certain rules concerning the admissibility of evidence. It is also clear that a Tribunal's decision relating exclusively to the admissibility of evidence may be successfully challenged on appeal; see for example *HSBC Asia Holdings B.V. and anor v. Gillespie* (above). While the extent of the limitations on the Tribunal's freedom to ignore the rules of evidence can only be fully established through future cases, the existence of such a limitation is not in doubt. Notwithstanding the very broad purported reach of the Rule, in practice it is generally invoked to permit the admission of what would otherwise be inadmissible hearsay evidence and the unsworn statements of witnesses who are not present to give evidence on oath, although the latter are always treated with great caution.

3. Written representations

8.07 Rule 42 reproduces the effect of old r. 14(5). The rule provides that the Tribunal 'shall', that is, must, consider any written representations from a party if they are delivered to the Tribunal and all other parties not less than seven days prior to the hearing. The rule however appears to give the Tribunal a discretion to consider representations submitted late, or which have not been copied to the other parties although it would clearly be wrong in principle for the Tribunal to consider such representations without disclosing them to the other parties. By virtue of r. 4(4) the date of the hearing is not included in the computation of the seven-day period.

4. Witnesses

8.08 Rule 43 amalgamates old r. 27(2), (3) and (4) with no changes other than a slight change of language (but not substance) to the provision that was formerly r. 27(3). Although initially much resisted in some regions the norm is now for statements of all witnesses to be taken as read, thus bringing Employment Tribunal practice into line with the civil courts (CPR 32.5(2)) and a party wishing to have his or her statement or that of one of their witnesses read out in open Tribunal would be required, in effect, to show cause why this should be done given the implications for the length of the hearing, and in consequence, the costs. One case where the reading aloud of a statement may be appropriate is if there are doubts about the *bona fides* of a claimant's claims of the extent to which his or her feelings have been injured in a discrimination case. The insertion of the word 'oral' before the word 'evidence' makes it clear that there is no requirement for the written witness statement to be in the form of an affidavit. The witness will however be required to confirm the truthfulness of their written statement at the beginning of their oral evidence.

8.09 Where statements are taken as read it is customary to permit supplementary questions to be asked in chief and for the Tribunal to ask any questions it has of the witness to clarify points of uncertainty or ambiguity before cross-examination. The conditions attaching to the giving of additional oral evidence imposed by CPR 32.5(3) and (4)—i.e. that a witness may with the permission of the court amplify their witness statement and give evidence in relation to new matters which have arisen since the witness statement was served, such permission only being granted if the court is satisfied that there is good reason for not confining the witness to the content of his statement—are not reproduced in the Rules and in consequence there can be no warrant for implying them into the Rules. Given that the first sentence of r. 43 precisely replicates CPR 32.5(2) the omission of CPR 32.5(3) and (4) must be presumed to be deliberate. However, those paragraphs do little more than reflect the way in which the Tribunal's discretion is likely to be exercised, having regard to the overriding objective, should a witness wish to amplify their statement.

There is seemingly no power to allow a witness to give evidence other than on **8.10** oath or affirmation. Any person—which would include a party—may be excluded from the hearing until such time as they give their evidence if the Tribunal considers it in the interests of justice to do so. Thus there would be power to exclude a respondent who has alleged to have sexually harassed the claimant if she found his presence so intimidating that she was unable to give her evidence. Although the exclusion of witnesses is the normal practice in civil proceedings in Scotland it would appear that in the Employment Tribunals they can only be excluded if it is in the interests of justice to do so.

5. Inspection of witness statements

The purpose of r. 44 is to obviate problems which naturally arise relating to the **8.11** interests of open and public justice when witness statements are taken as read. It mirrors in essence the provisions of CPR 32.13. The Rule is subject to r. 50 ('Privacy and restrictions on disclosure') and r. 94 ('National security proceedings'). Witness statements are not routinely copied for members of the public and are only to be made available to the extent that their contents are not ruled inadmissible by the Tribunal. It is unclear whether the intention is that all statements are to be automatically made available to the public or only after an application to the Tribunal to give the parties the opportunity to object. The rule does not require every member of the public attending the hearing to be given a copy of all of the statements, only that any statement 'be available for inspection during the course of the hearing' presumably at the Tribunal's own expense.

There is no requirement in the rule, nor expressly in CPR 32.13, for a copy of **8.12** the hearing bundle to be made available alongside the witness statement even if the statements rely heavily on the contents of documents, only paraphrasing or hinting at their content.

6. Timetabling

Rule 45 is a new provision whose purpose is to give formal regulatory author- **8.13** ity to an existing and growing practice among Employment Judges, particularly those familiar with modern civil court practice, and to encourage greater consistency in the use of that practice[2] in order to avoid the detrimental effect of hearings which overrun on both the Tribunals themselves and parties in other cases. Although there can be no doubt that the power exists under the overriding objective (*per* Lewison LJ in *Davies v. Sandwell Metropolitan Borough Council* [2013] IRLR 375 CA: a particularly poignant appellate *cri de cœur*) by giving timetabling a specific rule, the practice is bolstered by the sanctions available under r. 6.

---

[2] Underhill Review, para. 44.

8.14   There are some important differences between r. 45 and the timetabling provisions in the CPR. The first and most striking is that where the court sets a timetable for the trial it will do so in consultation with the parties (CPR 39.4). Rule 45 expressly provides that the Tribunal 'may impose limits on the time that a party may take in presenting evidence, questioning witnesses or making submissions...'. The reason for the different approaches is apparent from the placing of r. 45 in this section of the Rules dealing with hearings rather than in the section on case management: its use is intended to be as much ad hoc as part of a structured approach to organizing in advance how the hearing will proceed. Setting a timetable as an element of case management is frequently done before or at the start of a hearing and always in consultation with the parties. During hearings, the power is more apt to bridle the unruly horse that is the overenthusiastic or obsessive litigant in person or incompetent representative.

8.15   The absence of timetabling from that part of the Rules dealing with case management does not of course mean that there is no power to make a case management order that amounts to a timetable even if the parties are unable to agree the details. Such an order would clearly be permitted under the general rule, r. 29.

8.16   Although r. 45 does not incorporate a sanction for breach of the timetable or explain how in practical terms the Tribunal 'may prevent the party from proceeding beyond any time allotted' the answer is to be found in r. 6, which is headed 'Irregularities and non-compliance'. It provides a list of four sanctions for failing to comply with any provision of the Rules or any order of the Tribunal which includes striking out the claim or response, barring or restricting any party's participation in the proceedings (although not that of a representative), and awarding costs. Where the representative is at fault it would almost certainly first be necessary for the Tribunal to give the party they represent the option of dispensing with their services or facing the consequences of any future breach of the timetabling order.[3] It would appear to be necessary in order for r. 6 to bite for the Tribunal to make it clear that what it is imposing on the party is a formal order. Persistent breaches of a timetabling order are also likely to be regarded as unreasonable conduct of the proceedings for the purposes of r. 37(1)(b) (strike out) or r. 76(1)(a) (costs).

7. Hearings by electronic communication

8.17   Rule 46 succeeds in encapsulating in four lines the essence of the whole of old r. 15 without changing the substance and is largely self-explanatory. The requirement is a simple one: if electronic communications are used (as defined by s. 15(1) of the Electronic Communications Act 2000) the public attending the hearing must be able to hear what the Tribunal hears 'and see any witnesses as seen by the Tribunal'. This suggests that in an appropriate case there would be no objection

---

[3] For a commentary on r. 6 see para. 3.13.

to the taking of evidence over the telephone rather than by video link provided the evidence was being broadcast into the hearing room via a speaker system. The starting point for conducting any part of a hearing by means of electronic communication must be that the Tribunal considers that to do so will not prejudice the fairness of the hearing. While the widespread lack of video conferencing facilities at Tribunal offices is likely to severely restrict the use to which this rule can be put in full hearings and other hearings where evidence is to be given, the use of telephone conferencing facilities in case management discussions is now almost universal and has greatly increased the Tribunal's ability to manage cases effectively.

8. Non-attendance

Rule 47 repeats the substance of old r. 27(5) but adds a very important qualification to the right to dismiss a claim when the claimant fails to attend or to proceed in the respondent's absence. In the past, different guidance has been given by successive Presidents, and on occasion by the EAT, about what if any steps should be taken to establish why a party has failed to attend a hearing. The rule resolves this difficulty by requiring that the Tribunal 'shall consider any information which is available to it after any enquiries that may be practicable, about the reasons for the party's absence'. That obligation necessarily entails a prior obligation to make such enquiries. Note that the obligation is to make any enquiries that may be practicable not that may be reasonable which suggests that issues of proportionality do not arise. In practice what is practicable is likely to be attempting to contact the missing party via any telephone numbers known to the Tribunal and, possibly, by email if the email address is known. Once those enquiries are made the Tribunal is only obliged to 'consider' the information obtained. Any party who has a genuine reason for non-attendance can of course apply for a reconsideration of the Tribunal's judgment. **8.18**

Old r. 27(6) provided that before the Tribunal could dismiss a claim or dispose of the proceedings in a party's absence 'it shall first consider any information in its possession which has been made available to it by the parties'. This was not expressed to be information about the missing party's absence and in practice was taken to mean information provided by the parties about the claim—something akin to written representations. In r. 47 similar wording is expressly linked to the reason for the missing party's absence. However, it would be unwise for a Tribunal proceeding to hear a claim in the absence of the respondent not to take into consideration matters raised in the response form or contained in any documents supplied by the respondent. **8.19**

9. Conversion from preliminary to final hearing

Rule 48 is new, although what it provides for could previously have been achieved with the consent of the parties. It is not clear whether anything of substance is **8.20** added to what could already be achieved by that route other than in extreme cases. While the rule does not require the parties to consent to the conversion of a preliminary hearing to a final hearing and vice versa, it can only be done if the Tribunal is properly constituted and if it is satisfied that neither party will be substantially prejudiced by the change. Consent of the parties therefore still has a part to play, as problems over proper constitution can usually only be resolved by consent unless members can be drafted in at short notice. Section 4(3)(e) ETA provides that proceedings which normally require a full Tribunal can be heard by an Employment Judge sitting alone provided all parties consent in writing. In practice, difficulties are only likely to arise on converting a preliminary hearing (particularly one called under r. 53(1)(a) for case management purposes), into a final hearing. Conversion of a final hearing into a preliminary hearing is seldom likely to be controversial given that preliminary hearings only require an Employment Judge sitting alone and questions of prejudice are unlikely to arise unless the preliminary issue has only been identified at the start of the final hearing and has taken everyone by surprise.

8.21   The use of the word 'conversion' and the present tense seem to contemplate a seamless transition during a single hearing and so when contemplating the conversion of a preliminary hearing to a final hearing the real issue is likely to be that of prejudice. It would be wrong in principle for a Judge to impose such a conversion if either party were genuinely ill-prepared, particular care being needed where unrepresented parties are involved. In practice therefore the rule is unlikely to alter the way the Tribunal currently approaches these issues save in those relatively rare cases where the Judge is satisfied that, despite a party's protestations, they could not improve their position through an adjournment and the overriding objective and the need to save expense requires the conversion to be made.

10. Majority decisions

8.22   Rule 49 reproduces old r. 28(4) with slightly modified wording and no change of substance. While majority decisions are discouraged (*Anglian Home Improvements Ltd v. Kelly* [2005] ICR 242; [2004] IRLR 793 CA) and while it is clearly preferable for a unanimous decision to be reached if possible, it would be not only wrong in principle but an abdication of their judicial responsibility for any member of a Tribunal to abandon a strongly held view merely for the sake of conformity. The losing party is entitled to know that they had persuaded one member of the Tribunal and there is an obligation upon the Employment Judge to ensure that the grounds for any dissenting view are faithfully recorded in the reasons.

8.23   There is a tactical problem to be faced by the parties when confronted with a Tribunal composed of only two persons: do they consent to the hearing proceeding before both or only the Employment Judge who after all has a second or casting vote, so that the reality would appear to be that the Judge's view will always prevail? Faced with such a situation the parties are entitled to know from which panel the remaining lay member is drawn (*Rabahallah v. BTC Group* [2005] ICR 184; [2005] IRLR 184 EAT) although it would be unwise to assume that a member drawn from the employer's panel will always favour the employer just as it would be unwise to assume that a woman member will always favour a woman claimant. Note that there is no obligation on the Tribunal to comply with the parties' wishes in the sense that if the parties agree to a two-person Tribunal or the judge sitting alone, the Tribunal still has the right to require itself to be properly constituted even if that would involve a postponement of the hearing.

B. PRIVACY AND RESTRICTIONS ON DISCLOSURE—RULE 50

1. Overview

Although included in the section of the Rules dealing will all kinds of hearings, **8.24** the changes made to the Rules concerning privacy and restrictions on disclosure of information are so fundamental and wide-ranging that they deserve separate treatment.

The purpose of new r. 50 is to bring together old r. 16 'Hearings which may **8.25** be held in private'; old r. 49 'Sexual offences and the register' which required the anonymization of judgments and other record of proceedings so as to prevent the identification of persons affected by the making of an allegation of a sexual offence; and old r. 50 'Restricted reporting orders'; and also to incorporate recent appellate authority which identified other powers within the Rules which enabled Tribunals to make orders analogous to old rr. 49 and 50 orders in certain circumstances where those rules failed to meet an obligation of the Tribunal to protect a person's rights. However, while the rule has gone beyond the ambit of the current jurisprudence by adding a new circumstance in which orders can be made, namely where it is necessary in the interests of justice to do so, and extending the power to sit in private previously confined to r. 16 cases, to all such cases and creating a new power for witness identity to be concealed, a late amendment deleting the express power to make orders analogous to old rr. 49 and 50 restricted reporting orders has robbed the new provision of some of the clarity of earlier drafts but cannot have changed the power of the Tribunal.

There are two important procedural changes. The first is that under old r. 49 **8.26** the anonymization of documents was an automatic duty of the Secretary in certain circumstances. That has gone, and an anonymization order must either be applied for or made on the Tribunal's own initiative. The second is that the concept of the temporary restricted reporting order has also gone. All orders under the new rule are made in the same way as any other case management order, that is on application or on the Tribunal's own initiative and are effective until varied or revoked under r. 29 or, if time limited, until they lapse.

2. Historical background

8.27 The relevant statutory provisions are ss. 10A, 11 and 12 ETA. Section 10A provides that Employment Tribunal regulations may provide for the Tribunal to sit in private for the purpose of hearing evidence which is likely to consist of information which could not be disclosed without contravening a prohibition imposed by any enactment, or which has been obtained in confidence or which, with exceptions, might cause substantial injury to the undertaking in which the witness worked. Old r. 16 replicated s. 10A(1).

8.28 Section 11 enables procedure regulations to make provision for restricted reporting orders in cases involving sexual misconduct, such an order prohibiting the publication of 'identifying matter' as defined in s. 11(6) in a 'relevant programme' as defined in the Sexual Offences (Amendment) Act 1992. However s. 11(1)(b) restricts the duration of the order to the promulgation of the Tribunal's decision (which old r. 50(8)(b) clarified as the final decision on remedy) or the order's earlier revocation, and restricts the right to apply for such an order to a party to the proceedings, although an order could be made on the Tribunal's own initiative. Section 12 of the ETA is a similar provision in respect of complaints of disability discrimination where evidence is to be given of a personal nature, except that in this case only the claimant may apply for the order.

8.29 Old r. 50 was obviously deficient in two respects: the duration of the order, which could not be longer than the length of time it took the Tribunal to promulgate its final decision, and the limitations placed on the persons who could apply for the order. Sections 11 and 12 are deficient in that they do not permit the making of a restricted reporting order other than in those defined circumstances. In *X v. Commissioner of Police for the Metropolis* [2003] ICR 1031 EAT it was held that the Tribunal had the power, under its general case management power in old r. 10(1), to make an order analogous to an old r. 49 anonymization order where a failure to do so would infringe the EU law principle of effectiveness, as the claimant would have been deterred from bringing the proceedings if the order was not made. The provision of EU law relied on was Art. 6 of the Equal Treatment Directive 76/207/EEC (now Art. 17.1, 2006/54/EC). In *A v. B* [2010] ICR 849 EAT it was held that the Tribunal had power to make orders analogous to old r. 50 restricted reporting orders where the duration of the order permitted under the rule was insufficiently long to afford the necessary protection. In *F v. G* [2012] ICR 246 EAT it was held that an analogous order could be made to protect the rights under Art. 8 ECHR—the right to respect for private and family life—of disabled people and members of the respondent's staff who cared for them who were not themselves party to the proceedings and who therefore could not apply for an order which, moreover, would have to be permanent in nature in order to properly protect those rights. In *F v. G* Underhill P suggested, *obiter* and without quoting examples, that there might be other provisions which could require the making of a restricted reporting order, including non-Convention cases and non-principle of effectiveness cases. That observation is likely to be the genesis of the new 'interests of justice' provision in the new r. 50.

3. Rule 50

(a) *General principles*

Old r. 16 is not reproduced in the 2013 rules but it is clear that r. 50 applies to the circumstances covered by that rule as s. 10A ETA is referred to in paragraph (1). In consequence, not only is the power to hold hearings in private (formerly restricted to r. 16 cases) extended to other types of case, restricted reporting orders and their analogues and the new provisions with regard to witness protection, apply equally to old r. 16 cases as to old r. 50 cases and the cases discussed in para 8.29. Rule 50(1) refers to the making of orders with a view to preventing or restricting the public disclosure of any aspect of the proceedings in certain circumstances. Those circumstances are: that it is necessary in the interests of justice (discussed in the preceding and next following paragraphs); or in order to protect the Convention rights of any person (as defined in s. 1 of the Human Rights Act 1998—r. 50(6)); or in the circumstances identified in s. 10A. Note that the order may be made on the Tribunal's own initiative 'or on application', no mention being made of who may make the application thus allowing for applications by persons who are neither parties nor witnesses. **8.30**

Although no express reference is made to the need to protect a claimant's EU law rights, it cannot be doubted following *X v. Commissioner of Police* (above) that they are also covered by r. 50. What is not clear from the authorities, but is likely to be the case, is whether for the principle of effectiveness to be engaged, the EU law right relied on must be framed in terms similar to Art. 17.1 of 2006/54/EC. While r. 50 may be used to protect the Convention rights of any person, the EU law principle of effectiveness applies only to claimants. **8.31**

An important aspect of r. 50(1) is that, apart from the reference to s. 10A, neither the nature of the claim before the Tribunal nor the nature of the evidence to be given are the basis on which the order making power is predicated. It is the effect of the failure to prevent the disclosure of the evidence or even the nature, and possibly even the existence of, the proceedings ('any aspect of those proceedings') which is the trigger for the rule-making power. **8.32**

Rule 50(2) provides that in considering whether to make any order under r. 50 the Tribunal shall give full weight to the principles of open justice and to the Convention right to freedom of expression. For a discussion of the balancing exercise to be carried out see *In re Guardian News and Media Ltd* [2010] 2 AC 697 and *F v. G* (above) at paras. 34–52. There is a conceptual difficulty here which the Rule leaves unresolved. Where there is a claim that the EU law principle of effectiveness would be infringed if an order were not made, it seems that there may be no balancing exercise to be carried out as the claimant's right to bring the proceedings—the right not to have the EU principle of effectiveness infringed—appears to be absolute and so would trump any competing Convention rights. **8.33**

(b) *The orders*

8.34 Note that the list of orders in r. 50(3) is not exhaustive but merely illustrative; 'Such orders may include...'. The orders which may be made include (r. 50(3)(a)) that the hearing or part may be in private. As there is no express statutory warrant for this provision other than in respect of cases covered by s. 10A ETA (commercial confidentiality cases)[4] this provision seems vulnerable to attack by virtue of Art. 6 ECHR—although permitting a case to be heard in private where that is genuinely in the interests of justice would not be a breach of Art. 6 (*R v. Bow Street County Court ex p Pelling (No. 2)* [2001] UKHRR 165). Whilst it may not be difficult to imagine the need for private hearings where issues of domestic violence or the obtaining of urgent injunctions are concerned, it is very difficult to envisage Employment Tribunal proceedings where s. 10A is not engaged where it would be justified. It is suggested that very exceptional circumstances would have to apply, probably requiring compelling evidence that the other potential orders listed in the paragraph would not afford the requisite protection because, for example, of the malicious intent of a member of the press or public or because of a well-founded concern that the absence of a penal sanction for any order other than an order derived from s. 11 or s. 12 ETA makes the other available orders inadequate.

8.35 Rule 50(3)(b) is the new anonymization provision but goes further than old r. 49 as it permits the identity of specified parties, witnesses or other persons to be suppressed during the course of a hearing as well as in documents which are available to the public (i.e. the judgment and reasons). Rule 50(3)(c) is entirely new and unheralded by recent authority. It permits orders to be made 'preventing witnesses at a public hearing being identifiable by members of the public'. Once again, the warrant for this provision must be open to question as it seems to contemplate—in non-national security proceedings—witnesses giving evidence from behind screens. It is very difficult to imagine any circumstances in which such an order could be justified in Employment Tribunal proceedings, not least because the identity of the witness would presumably be known to all of the parties and their representatives through the exchange of witness statements although it would be a less draconian step than holding the hearing or part of it in private.

8.36 Rule 50(3)(d) permits the making of 'traditional' restricted reporting orders under ss. 11 and 12 ETA. As originally drafted an additional subparagraph, r. 50(3)(e), gave express sanction to the making of analogous orders (see para. 8.29 above) where those sections are too restrictive to provide the necessary protection. It was in these terms:

...an order having similar effect to such a restricted reporting order but made in circumstances other than those identified in those sections and/or extending beyond the date of

---

[4] National security cases have their own provisions for secret hearings (r. 94(1) and (2)) and in consequence r. 50(3)(a) is not aimed at such cases. For national security cases generally, see Chapter 13.

promulgation of the decision of the Tribunal, either indefinitely or to such date as the Tribunal may specify.

It is wholly unclear why it was thought either necessary or desirable to delete the subparagraph as it accurately reflects the powers which the cases discussed above say that the Tribunal has. The rule should be read as though subparagraph (3)(e) was still included in it. It is however important to note that the penal sanctions available for breach of ETA-derived orders (a fine not exceeding level 5 on the standard scale)[5] probably do not apply to breaches of such analogous orders.

(c) *Objecting to an order*

Rule 50(4) provides that not only a party but any 'other person with a legiti- **8.37** mate interest' who has not had a reasonable opportunity to make representations before an order is made may apply in writing for it to be 'revoked or discharged'. The difference between revocation and discharge is not dealt with in the rule but the effect of revocation is likely to be that the order has never been made—meaning there would be no restriction on reporting 'identifying matter' which emerged prior to the date of revocation whereas discharge would preserve the effect of the Rule until the date of discharge. Whilst it is most likely to be the media who would make use of this provision, it would be open to others, such as a campaign group fighting the closure of a local hospital to apply to prevent reporting restrictions in a case concerning the hospital's former Chief Executive, for example. The application for the revocation or discharge of the order may be dealt with on paper although the rule seems to require a hearing to be held if one is requested. The nature of that hearing is not specified. If it takes place before the start of the final hearing it would appear to be a preliminary hearing for the purposes of case management under r. 53(1)(a) and so be in private by virtue of r. 56. If made during or at the start of the final hearing, it would be subject to the order already made, or subject to fresh orders made under r. 50(3) if a failure to make those orders would defeat the object of the order being challenged in the event of that challenge failing.

A potential lacuna in the rule which may make it more difficult to mount a suc- **8.38** cessful challenge to the order is that there is no requirement for any order made with the consent of the parties to include any reasons for the order—although by virtue of r. 62(1) if the application for the order was contested, reasons must be given. Even so, there is no requirement in the rule for copies of the order to be made available to third parties although as a matter of administrative practice this will be done. They are only entitled, it seems, to notice of the fact that an order has been made.

---

[5] Sections 11(2) and 12(3).

(d) *Restricted reporting orders*

8.39 Rule 50(5) applies only to restricted reporting orders made under ss. 11 and 12 ETA and their analogues. These provisions differ in some respects from their predecessors in old r. 50—some, but not all, of the differences being necessitated by the concept of the analogous order (these difference being retained despite the removal from the rule of the express power to make analogous orders!). New r. 50(5)(a) requires that the order must specify the person whose identity is protected and may, but need not, specify particular matters 'of which publication is prohibited'. Paragraph (5)(b) requires that the duration of the order must be specified. This is an essential requirement given the possibility not only of indefinite orders but of orders of finite duration which extend beyond the promulgation of the Tribunal's final decision.

8.40 Paragraph (5)(c) replicates old r. 50(8)(c) and requires that the Tribunal must display a notice of the fact that an order has been made on the notice board which holds the daily cause list and also on the door of the Tribunal. The notice is not required by the rule to contain any details of the order made but— although not a requirement of the rule—will in practice state that a copy of the order may be obtained on application to the office manager. As the details which the media will need in order to avoid committing a criminal offence are only to be found in the order, which is not a public document (orders are not placed on the Register—reg. 14(1), it is perhaps strange that this critical step in the process remains a matter of administrative practice.

8.41 Paragraph (5)(d) reproduces old r. 50(9) and provides that the Tribunal may order that the restricted reporting order applies to any other proceedings being heard as part of the same hearing. This is an important precaution as, for example, a claim may include a complaint of sexual harassment and unlawful deduction of wages; and while a restricted reporting order might not be available for the wages claim in isolation, it would be prudent for the order to be extended to avoid the inadvertent disclosure of identifying matter by the otherwise legitimate reporting of the wages claim.

C. PRELIMINARY HEARINGS—RULES 53–56

1. Overview

8.42 Preliminary hearings under the 2013 Rules encompass the majority of that section of the 2004 Rules headed 'Pre-hearing reviews' (apart from interim relief applications which are now dealt with at r. 95), although the substantive powers to strike out and order the payment of a deposit which were formerly included in this section of the Rules are dealt with elsewhere (striking out r. 37: see paras. 7.55–7.64; deposit orders r. 39: see paras. 7. 74–7.90). Case management discussions which were not pre-hearing reviews under the 2004 Rules now become a form of preliminary hearing. The purpose of this, it was said in the Underhill Review[6] was to avoid the necessity for two hearings in certain cases, thus saving costs. It was envisaged that the two procedures—pre-hearing reviews and case management discussions—would be combined into one 'preliminary hearing' which would consider any case management issues alongside the detail of the case itself. The better judicial practice under the old rules[7] was to list the case for pre-hearing review where it seemed that a preliminary issue might arise, in the knowledge that case management orders could be made if the claim was not struck out, or alternatively to list for both at the same time. Given that where a preliminary issue is to be considered, the notice of hearing must specify the issue in question, there appears to be no changes of substance in the new rule other than in the length of notice to be given of preliminary hearings and the constitution of the Tribunal. There is only a potential change in the nature of case management discussions.

2. Scope of preliminary hearings

(a) *Generally*

Unlike case management orders where the Rules only give illustrative examples **8.43** of a wide-ranging and general power to make such orders as may be appropriate (although these latter words do not actually appear in r. 29), the list of things which a Tribunal may do at a preliminary hearing in r. 53 appears to be exhaustive. However, given that one of those things is to make case management orders and another is to consider 'preliminary issues' which are only loosely defined, the Tribunal nonetheless has scope for the early determination of a wide range of issues.

(b) *'Case management discussions'*

This phrase does not appear in the new Rules but is likely to continue in use to **8.44** differentiate preliminary hearings held under r. 53(1)(a)—which refers to preliminary consideration of the claim with the parties and the making of case management orders, from other preliminary hearings. For case management orders generally see Chapter 7. There is an important change to the nature of case management discussions. In the 2004 Rules, r. 17(2) provided that a person's civil rights or obligations shall not be dealt with at a CMD and that the orders and judgments listed at old r. 18(7)—strike outs and determinations about entitlement to bring the proceedings—may not be made at one. There is no equivalent restriction in the 2013 Rules and as r. 53 describes a preliminary hearing as a hearing at which the Tribunal will do one or more of the following including making case management orders, striking out, ordering a deposit or making a determination as to entitlement to bring proceedings, provided any difficulties

---

[6] At paras. 34 and 35.
[7] Sanctioned by r. 60(2).

with regard to notice (r. 54) and the need for certain preliminary hearings to be in public (r. 56) can be overcome—there would appear to be no objection in principle to a determination of a person's civil rights being made at a r. 53(1)(a) hearing. The prudent course would be to list as an attended hearing any case management discussion at which it seems likely that other preliminary issues may need to be dealt with.

(c) *Preliminary issues*

8.45 The Tribunal may determine any preliminary issue at a preliminary hearing. The phrase 'preliminary issue' is a term of art, being referred to in subsequent rules. However, its definition is incomplete. It is 'any substantive issue which may determine liability' (r. 53(3)). 'Substantive' presumably here means having an existence independent of the claim itself. The definition, supported by the example given (namely 'an issue as to jurisdiction or as to whether an employee was dismissed') suggests that this is the equivalent of old r. 18(7) (a) and deals with issues surrounding entitlement to bring proceedings which are capable of determining liability in the negative sense. 'Preliminary issues' therefore include:

- out of time points;
- whether the claimant is a disabled person for the purposes of the Equality Act 2010;
- whether there has been a transfer of an undertaking for the purposes of the Transfer of Undertakings (Protection of Employment) Regulations 2006 (SI 2006 /246);
- whether the claimant was an employee of the respondent or has the requisite length of service; and
- whether the claimant made a protected disclosure.

(d) *Exploring the possibility of settlement*

8.46 Rule 53(1)(e) provides that one of the things which a Tribunal may do at a preliminary hearing is 'explore the possibility of settlement or alternative dispute resolution (including judicial mediation)'. This provision seems unnecessary (other than as a reminder) given r. 3 which imposes something akin to a duty on the Tribunal, 'wherever practicable and appropriate' to encourage the use of ADR. However, the form of words used is perhaps surprising as no other form of alternative dispute resolution is currently available through the Tribunal. It must be assumed that the inclusion of this provision does not signal any change in the current protocols which surround the offering of judicial mediation which ultimately lies in the gift of each Regional Employment Judge if he or she feels that it is an appropriate case for judicial mediation and meets the President's (unpublished) guidelines.

3. Notice of preliminary hearings

Rule 54 deals with the notice required for preliminary hearings. Having first **8.47** recited that a preliminary hearing may be held on the application of a party or be directed by the Tribunal, two minimum notice periods are laid down. For all preliminary hearings other than those involving the determination of any preliminary issue (that is, a hearing under r. 53(1)(b)) for which fourteen days notice is required, only reasonable notice is required. This is a change from the 2004 Rules as only case management discussions could be called on shorter notice than fourteen days unless the parties consented to shorter notice.

No guidance is given on what amounts to reasonable notice, no doubt because **8.48** what is reasonable is clearly heavily context dependent and the dictates of the overriding objective and issues of proportionality will also be critically important factors. Thus it might well be reasonable to give only a few hours notice of an urgent 'case management discussion' if the parties were in dispute about an issue such as disclosure of documents which, unless resolved, was likely to cause the postponement of an imminent hearing, particularly if substantial costs might be thrown away. It might also be reasonable to give only an hours' notice of a proposal to strike out a claim or part of one if facts had emerged at a preliminary hearing called only under r. 53(1)(a) which pointed to the claim or part having no reasonable prospect of success. The complexity and novelty of the point at issue as well as the claimant's ability to deal with the point at short notice would be important factors. And see also r. 48 (para. 8.20) which enables a Tribunal to convert any preliminary hearing into a final hearing provided the Tribunal is properly constituted and neither party is substantially prejudiced.

There is no provision in the rule for objecting to the length of notice of the **8.49** hearing on the grounds that it is not reasonable. However, it is suggested that if the objection is itself reasonable the Tribunal should make every effort to accommodate the party in difficulties as any judgment or order made as a result of a preliminary hearing called on what is deemed on appeal to have been less than reasonable notice is likely to be a nullity. A party who simply fails to attend a hearing without first having objected to the length of notice or who objects unreasonably, will be bound by any judgment or order made in their absence subject to the right to apply for a reconsideration of a judgment under r. 70 or the variation or revocation of an order under r. 29.

Where the preliminary hearing involves the determination of a preliminary **8.50** issue 'at least 14 days notice' must be given which appears to require that the notice of hearing be received at least fourteen days prior to the hearing (see para. 8.56). This would not appear to be a time-limit for the purposes of r. 5 and so cannot be shortened by the Tribunal. It may of course be shortened if all parties consent. There is also a requirement where the hearing involves the determination of a preliminary issue for the issue which will or may be determined to be specified in the notice of hearing.

4. Constitution of the Tribunal

8.51 Rule 55 provides that all preliminary hearings will take place before an Employment Judge alone with the possible exception of a hearing which involves the determination of a preliminary issue when a party may request a full Tribunal. If such a request is made an Employment Judge shall determine whether a hearing before a full Tribunal would be 'desirable'. Old r. 18(3)(b) also used the word 'desirable' but in conjunction with their being 'one or more substantive issues of fact' likely to require determination. Given the increasing trend for Employment Judges to sit without members it is suggested that it would be a rare case where it would be desirable for a full Tribunal to sit, particularly as many preliminary issues will be as much about the law as fact. No guidance is given in the rule about when a full Tribunal would be desirable and the Judge's discretion is therefore at large. The refusal of an application for a full Tribunal would however require the Judge to give reasons (r. 62(1)) which should demonstrate whether he or she has failed to take into account a relevant matter or has taken into account an irrelevant matter. Experience of the 2004 Rules suggests that parties much prefer preliminary hearings to be before an Employment Judge sitting alone. Although the 2004 Rules did not expressly confine applications for full Tribunals to r. 18(7)(a) cases (the equivalent to preliminary issue cases) as they were the ones most likely to involve the need to determine substantive issues of fact, r. 55 seems to involve a change of form rather than substance.

5. When preliminary hearings will be in public

8.52 In its response to the consultation on the Underhill Review, the government (at para. 31) expressed the hope that Employment Judges would, wherever possible, hold preliminary hearings by telephone and that 'the new rules should help reassure parties that the preliminary hearing will, in most cases, be held in private as case management discussions currently are'. That misunderstands the effect of new rr. 53 and 56. It is likely that in practice r. 56 does not change the current position. The difficulty here is that old r. 20 was silent as to whether deposit hearings should be in public or private although r. 20(1) read with r. 18(1) suggested that they should be heard in public. In practice they were almost invariably held in tandem with applications under r. 18(7)(b) to strike out a claim which had to be held in public, something which is likely to continue. Under r. 56, should an application for a deposit order be heard in isolation from any other preliminary issue, it will be heard in private.

8.53 Only applications for the determination of a preliminary issue and a strike out application under r. 37 now have to be held in public (subject of course to r. 50 ('Privacy and restrictions on disclosure') and to r. 94 ('National security proceedings')). However, where the Tribunal is also considering other preliminary issues at the same time the Tribunal may direct that the entirety of the proceedings be in public. This avoids the obvious practical problems when at the conclusion of a preliminary issues hearing or strike out application the Judge goes on to make case management orders. In consequence the achievement of the stated ambition at para. 34 of the Underhill Review to hold a single hearing rather than two would be likely to decrease the number of preliminary hearings held in private.

Rule 93(2), which in earlier drafts formed the last sentence of r. 56, permits **8.54** a 'representative of Acas' to attend preliminary hearings such as 'case management discussions' which are held in private. This provision is necessitated by the practice in the London regions of inviting an Acas conciliator to sit in on case management discussions of complex discrimination cases, a practice which has been found to materially assist the conciliation process.

D. FINAL HEARINGS—RULES 57–59

These rules largely replicate (minus the use of the upper-case H for Hearing) the **8.55** corresponding provisions of the 2004 Rules, although changes of wording in the interests of simplification introduce a measure of uncertainty in one instance (r. 58). Rule 57 (scope of final hearing) reproduces old r. 26(1). The composition of the Tribunal is not dealt with in the Rules as it is dictated by the provisions of s. 4 ETA.

Rule 58 (notice of final hearing) appears at first sight to be a straightforward **8.56** requirement to give fourteen days notice of the hearing. By virtue of r. 4(4) the date of the hearing is not to be included when computing the fourteen-day period. But a comparison with old r. 14(4) suggests that the requirement is anything other than straightforward. Under old r. 14(4) the requirement was to *send* the notice not less than fourteen days before the date fixed for the hearing. Old reg. 15(5) explained that the requirement was merely to place the notice of hearing in the post not less than fourteen days prior to the hearing and gave as an example that if the hearing was on 15 October the last day for posting the notice was 1 October. Old reg. 15(5) is not reproduced in the 2013 Rules although the other provisions in reg. 15 with regard to time now appear as r. 4 (see paras. 3.07–3.11). Whereas old r. 14(4) spoke of sending notice, r. 58 speaks of the parties being 'given' notice. Although it is far from clear whether this was the intention, it seems that r. 58 requires the notice of a hearing on 15 October to be actually received by the parties not later than 1 October. As this appears to be an entitlement, a party who has not received such notice can insist on the hearing being adjourned. Rule 90 offers a measure of protection from dishonest claims of short notice as it provides that where a document is sent to a party it shall, unless the contrary is proved, be taken to have been delivered, if sent by post, on the day on which it would have been delivered in the ordinary course of post. This is taken to be two working days for first class post or four for second-class.

Rule 59 replaces old r. 26(3) and requires the hearing to be in public subject **8.57** to r. 50 ('Privacy and restrictions on disclosure') and r. 94 ('National security proceedings'). Old r. 26(3) was expressly subject only to r. 16 which permitted hearings to be held in private where the disclosure of confidential information was involved. This provision is not reproduced in the 2013 Rules as such but its effect is subsumed into r. 50. It was also subject to old r. 54 ('National security proceedings'). A hearing held in a room to which the public have no access, such as an Employment Judge's chambers, is void even if no error of law is disclosed by the judgment, no other hearing rooms were available, and the hearing was on the public cause list (*Storer v. British Gas plc* [2000] ICR 603; [2000] IRLR 495 CA).

8.58   Practitioners should note r. 47 which permits, but does not require, separate final hearings for liability and remedy. Unless the notice of hearing specifies to the contrary the working assumption must be that the hearing will deal with both.

9

WITHDRAWALS—RULES 51 AND 52

A. OVERVIEW

9.01 The purpose of rr. 51 and 52 is to preserve the distinction in the Rules of Procedure between the discontinuance of a claim and its withdrawal purportedly introduced in the 2004 Rules as r. 25 following *Ako v. Rothschild Asset Management Ltd* [2002] ICR 348; [2002] IRLR 348 CA. However, there is an important change in procedure, expressly introduced to save expense (Underhill Review, para. 40), which to some extent causes a reversion to the pre-2004 position and may, unless care is taken by Judges, claimants, and their advisors, seriously undermine this distinction. The danger was recognized by some respondents to the government's consultation on the Underhill Review (para. 39) of some claimants being unaware of the significance of withdrawing a claim, but suggestions that steps needed to be taken to ensure that the consequences were drawn to their attention have not found their way into the Rules. Rule 51 replicates the effect of old r. 25(3) and r. 52 replaces the much criticized and ill-drafted r. 25(4).

9.02 Old r. 25A 'Automatic dismissal of proceedings following withdrawal of a claim (or part of a claim) where an ACAS settlement has been reached' introduced into the 2004 Rules by the 2008 Amendment Regulations[1] has entirely gone. It added little or nothing to r. 25 other than bureaucratic complexity and appears to have been designed to boost the significance of ACAS settlements.

---

[1] SI 2008/3240.

B. DISCONTINUANCE AND WITHDRAWAL

9.03 In order to fully understand the mechanics of the rule and the differing available outcomes following the withdrawal of a claim, it is necessary to know something of the history of the rule and its predecessors and the jurisprudence attaching to them.

9.04 The 1993 Rules (r. 13(2)(a)) and the 2001 Rules (r. 15(2)(a)) dealt with withdrawal of proceedings only under miscellaneous powers which listed the things which a Tribunal may do, including: 'If the applicant [claimant] at any time gives notice of the withdrawal of his originating application [claim]…dismiss the proceedings'. Despite the use of the word 'may' in the rule, the near universal practice was to issue a judgment dismissing the claim on withdrawal as a paper exercise without further enquiry. Importantly, there was no requirement for the respondent to apply for the claim to be dismissed. A refusal to issue a judgment where a Judge suspected from the wording of the claimant's letter that the withdrawal was as a result of what the claimant described as improper pressure by the respondent, almost always a threat to apply for costs, had unfortunate repercussions more than once with claimants facing a costs application having pressed on with the claim when invited to do so by the Judge and it becoming apparent that things were not quite as portrayed in the original letter of withdrawal.

9.05 In fact there was never any power to go behind a notice of withdrawal which was effective as soon as received and could not itself be withdrawn by the claimant (*Khan v. Heywood and Middleton Primary Care Trust* [2007] ICR 24; [2006] IRLR 345 CA). Although it was said in *Staffordshire County Council v. Barber* [1996] ICR 379 CA, 397C that the Tribunal had to be satisfied before issuing a judgment that a withdrawal was properly made, this was only in the context of the statutory prohibition on contracting out which renders void any agreement to preclude a person from bringing proceedings before the Tribunal (now s. 203 ERA; s. 144 EQA).

9.06 Although routine to the point of being virtually automatic in its operation, the resulting dismissal of the proceedings was nonetheless a judicial decision not an administrative act despite the absence of a reasoned decision on either the facts or the law and no evidence or argument having been heard (*Barber*, *per* Neill LJ at 397B). As such it operated by way of *res judicata* to prevent the claimant from bringing fresh proceedings based on the same or substantially the same grounds and the claimant could not avoid the consequences of the earlier withdrawal by seeking to place the claim in a different legal framework (*Barber*).The only exception (apart from the possibility of exceptional circumstances which might allow a claim to proceed which could have been brought in the earlier proceedings but which was not[2] and was therefore not strictly caught

---

[2] Subject of course to challenges of abuse of process based on *Henderson v. Henderson* (1843) 3 Hare 100.

by the rule (*Barber*)), was if the original withdrawal had been tainted by fraud or collusion sufficient to justify setting aside the dismissal (*Arnold v. National Westminster Bank plc* [1991] 2 AC 93, 104, *per* Lord Keith of Kinkel). Otherwise the bar was 'absolute'.

In *Lennon v. Birmingham City Council* [2001] IRLR 826 CA it was held that **9.07** the doctrine of *res judicata* 'turns…. on the simple fact that the order was in fact made' and not on the reasons why the court's decision to dismiss the claim was consented to by the party making the claim. However, a claimant's reasons for withdrawing the claim, if communicated to the Tribunal prior to the issuing of a judgment dismissing the claim on withdrawal, were capable of preventing a cause of action estoppel arising. In *Sajid v. Sussex Muslim Society* [2002] IRLR 1136 CA it was held that no cause of action estoppel was created where the reason for withdrawing a breach of contract claim in the Tribunal was to enable the claimant to pursue it in the High Court, the value of the claim exceeding the Tribunal's jurisdiction.

The point was fully argued in *Ako v. Rothschild Asset Management* (above). **9.08** Mrs Ako had commenced Tribunal proceedings only against Rothschild's alleging unfair dismissal and race discrimination. She wished to add a second respondent but rather than apply to the Tribunal for permission to do so, relying on an out-of-date textbook she withdrew the claim without giving reasons and substituted a fresh one naming both respondents. Before doing so the first claim had been formally dismissed. Rothschild's successfully applied to have the second claim struck out as against them on the grounds that a cause of action estoppel had been created by the Judge's decision dismissing the first claim. In the Court of Appeal, Mummery LJ examined the difference between the procedure of the civil courts in which a claimant could discontinue a claim, thereby preserving the cause of action, and the Employment Tribunal where the Rules of Procedure contained no such provision. At para. 30 (Dyson and Jonathan Parker LJJs concurring) he said:

> In my judgment, the reasoning in *Barber* and *Lennon* does not require that cause of action estoppel, as applied in the ordinary courts, should apply to employment tribunal cases where it is clear, on an examination of the surrounding circumstances, that the withdrawal of the application (claim) is in substance a discontinuance of the proceedings. Discontinuance does not release or discharge the cause of action. It preserves the right to establish an untried claim on the merits in other proceedings. If, as I have explained, this is so in ordinary courts, it does not make any sense that the position should be more strict in its application in the less formal setting of the employment tribunals.

The central question is the intention of the claimant in withdrawing the claim. **9.09** At para. 41 Dyson LJ said:

> In my view, what emerges from these authorities is that there is no inflexible rule to the effect that a withdrawal or judgment by consent invariably gives rise to a cause of action or issue estoppel. If it is clear that the party withdrawing is not intending to abandon the claim or issue that is being withdrawn, then he or she will not be barred from raising

the point in subsequent proceedings unless it would be an abuse of process for that to occur....

9.10   As Dyson LJ hinted at para. 41, the discontinuance of a claim does not preserve the right to pursue the cause of action unfettered by restrictions. CPR 38.7 requires that where the defendant has filed a defence to the claim, fresh proceedings arising out of facts which are the same or substantially the same can only be brought with the leave of the court. The commentary at CPR 38.7 [1] suggests that permission will not be easily given since the new claim risks being struck out under CPR 3.4 as an abuse of process, and that conditions with regard to the payment of the costs of the discontinued proceedings or making a payment into court by way of security for costs are likely to be attached.

C. EFFECT OF THE RULES

1. The nature of the act of withdrawal

9.11   Either the whole claim or a part of it may be withdrawn. Withdrawal is a unilateral act on the part of the claimant requiring neither the consent of the respondent nor the Tribunal nor, unlike under the CPR (CPR 38.2(2)(c)) in a multi-claimant case, the consent of the other claimants. It is wrong in principle for the Tribunal to require the claimant to consent to the dismissal of a claim as a condition of being allowed to withdraw it (*Verdin v. Harrods Ltd* [2006] ICR 396; [2006] IRLR 339 EAT).

2. Is discontinuance still available?

9.12   Despite the judgment of the Court of Appeal in *Ako* which clearly contemplated the introduction of a power to discontinue proceedings as the means of remedying the difficulty which Mrs Ako had faced, neither old r. 25 nor new rr. 51 and 52 expressly provide for the discontinuance of a claim. A claimant wishing to discontinue a claim in order to preserve their cause of action must therefore still first withdraw it—although in *British Association for Shooting and Conservation v. Cokayne* [2008] ICR 185 EAT it was said that by virtue of old r. 25, withdrawal was now the equivalent of discontinuance. Old r. 25(4) provided a potentially effective safeguard against the premature dismissal of a withdrawn claim by requiring the respondent to apply for the dismissal of the claim within twenty-eight days of the notice of withdrawal being sent to them. The rule then explained the consequences 'if the respondent's application is granted' indicating that it might be refused. Old r. 11(4) or (5) required that the respondent's application be copied to the claimant, who then had the right to object, although to be effective the objection had to make it clear that there was no intention to abandon the claim and explain why. Thus the claim could not be dismissed and in consequence a cause of action estoppel created, without the claimant's prior knowledge.

Whether the claim for equivalence made in *Cokayne* could now be made in the **9.13** light of the changes which r. 52 has introduced is doubtful. There is no longer a requirement for an application by either party,[3] for the claim to be dismissed, this being the cost saving measure identified in the Underhill Review. Instead, r. 52 requires the Tribunal to issue a judgment dismissing the claim unless the claimant has expressed *at the time of withdrawal* a wish to reserve the right to bring a further claim and the Tribunal is satisfied that there would be a legitimate reason for doing so, or the Tribunal believes that it would not be in the interests of justice to dismiss the claim. Thus the claimant must not only express the wish to reserve the right to bring fresh proceedings but explain why. There is therefore a presumption in favour of withdrawal rather than discontinuance. Under old r. 25 the Tribunal's stance was neutral.

This new provision takes the Tribunal's Rules further away from the position **9.14** in the civil courts and, in practical terms, almost back to the pre *Ako* situation. It therefore appears to be a retrograde step. There are three major issues. The first is that unlike the civil court there is still no right to discontinue—it remains at the Tribunal's discretion. The starting premise is that the claim is withdrawn as opposed to discontinued unless the contrary is shown. The second is that the reason for withdrawal must be given when the application is made: in practice reasons are not always given. The third is that the reason for wishing to bring a further claim must be 'legitimate'. Whether the reason for seeking to discontinue is legitimate, it is suggested, should be a matter for the court or Tribunal before which the claimant seeks to bring the fresh proceedings. It would be wholly wrong for the claimant to be faced with a cause of action estoppel when seeking to bring civil proceedings because an Employment Judge failed to appreciate the legitimacy of their reason or that the reason would not necessarily have amounted to an abuse of process of the civil court.

In *Ako* at para. 30 Mummery LJ said: **9.15**

Unless and until the regulations of the employment tribunals are amended to deal with this point [the absence of a right to discontinue] it would be advisable for employment tribunals on being notified of the withdrawal of [a claim], to ask the [claimant] for a statement of the circumstances of the decision to withdraw before deciding to make an order dismissing the proceedings.

It appears that r. 52(a) expressly prevents that step from being taken unless Employment Judges are prepared to adopt the view that, given the draconian consequences of a judgment dismissing the proceedings, it would not be in the interests of justice to issue a judgment until more is known about the claimant's reasons. However, that would be to use r. 52(b) to defeat r. 52(a) which without

---

[3] The requirement in the Fees Order for the respondent to pay a fee of £60 on making an application to strike out following a withdrawal appears to be very largely if not entirely redundant.

some indication that what the Judge is dealing with isn't a straightforward withdrawal, would be unjustified.

9.16   All would not however be lost as the claimant would have the right to apply for a reconsideration of the judgment dismissing the claim under r. 70. What the claimant could not do would be to commence fresh proceedings and assert in them for the first time that it was always their intention to do so (*British Association for Shooting and Conservation v. Cokayne* (above)). On reconsideration the sole test is whether it is necessary in the interests of justice to revoke the judgment which, it is suggested, might only require the Judge to be satisfied that the claimant did not wish to abandon their cause of action and that their reason for not doing so was not an improper one or was not misconceived. It would however very often be a feature of such reconsideration applications that they would be made long out of time and only on discovering that a challenge is being made to the legitimacy of the new claim.

3. Effect of the notice

9.17   As r. 51 makes clear, the notice of withdrawal is effective to terminate the proceedings as soon as it is received: they 'thereupon' come to an end. The claim however notionally survives for the purpose of allowing the respondent to make an application for costs, preparation time, or wasted costs only. Note however that a claim can only be withdrawn orally at a hearing: to be effective in other circumstances the withdrawal must be in writing. Thus if a claimant who purports to withdraw a claim over the telephone fails to confirm the withdrawal in writing the only course open to the Tribunal is to require the claimant to give reasons why the claim should not be struck out under r. 37(1)(d) on the grounds that it is not being actively pursued.

9.18   It is important to note that even if a claim is discontinued rather than dismissed on withdrawal it is nonetheless at an end: that claim cannot be revived. The claimant has merely preserved the cause of action which, in order to be brought to fruition, must become the subject of fresh proceedings which must survive any challenge of being an abuse of process. So even if a claimant successfully applies for a reconsideration of a judgment dismissing the claim under r. 52, the claim is not resurrected. The effect is merely to prevent a cause of action estoppel arising. As noted above, the notice of withdrawal cannot itself be withdrawn or set aside. For such a power to exist there would have to be express provision in the Rules (*Khan v. Heywood and Middleton Primary Care Trust* (above)).

4. Fresh proceedings

9.19   Rule 52 recites the cause of action estoppel which arises when a withdrawn claim is dismissed, namely that the claimant may not commence a fresh claim against the respondent raising the same, or substantially the same, complaint. No cause of action estoppel would arise in respect of a respondent who was not a party to the first claim (*Ako v. Rothschild Asset Management* (above)).

Where a withdrawn claim is not dismissed and so is effectively only discontinued, unlike CPR 38.7 there is no requirement in the Rules for the claimant to obtain the permission of the Tribunal to commence fresh proceedings against the same respondent based on the same or substantially the same facts. The Tribunal may have a supervisory role to play on receipt of the new application as a claim may be rejected under r. 12(1)(b) if it is an abuse of the Tribunal's process, but it is suggested that the preferable course is for the Tribunal to accept such a claim and leave it to the respondent to take the point if appropriate. The principal reason for this suggestion is that on an application for a reconsideration of the rejection of the claim the respondent has no right to be heard (and will almost certainly be unaware of the reconsideration application) but is very likely to have information which would be of assistance to the Tribunal in determining whether the new proceedings are an abuse. **9.20**

10

DECISIONS, REASONS AND RECONSIDERATION OF JUDGMENTS—RULES 60–73

A. DECISIONS AND REASONS—RULES 60–69

1. Overview

The purpose of new rr. 61 and 62 is to tidy up and simplify, so as to reflect **10.01** current best practice, a number of provisions concerning decisions and reasons which were spread across three rules (old rr. 28–30) which were poorly drafted and had some notable gaps. Some important new requirements concerning the giving of written reasons are introduced. The remaining provisions in this section of the Rules are also simplified but with little change of substance. A new rule (r. 66) concerning time for compliance with judgments and orders to pay money is problematic.

2. Decisions made without a hearing

10.02 The requirement in r. 60 for decisions made without a hearing to be communicated in writing identifying the Judge who made the decision is new but reflects the directions of the current and immediate past Presidents. The rule applies whether the decision is communicated formally or in a letter.

3. Decisions made at or following a hearing

10.03 Rule 61(1) derives from old r. 28(3) although now with a requirement that the reserved decision is to be sent to the parties as soon as practicable rather than merely 'later'. In England and Wales the normal practice is for both decisions and reasons to be given orally at the end of the hearing with only decisions in long or legally complex cases being reserved. The administrative target for sending judgments to parties is 'within 28 days' which in the case of reserved decisions runs from the date of the chambers meeting at which the Tribunal reached its decision. However successive Presidents have imposed a strict three-month time-limit from the last hearing date rather than the in-chambers deliberation which if missed, requires the Judge to write to the President explaining why. Parties should therefore be contacting the Tribunal office enquiring about the delay if a reserved decision has not been received within three months of the last hearing date.

10.04 Delay by itself is not a ground of appeal against a decision even if it is said that the delay has led to material factual errors and omissions as an appeal lies only on a point of law. However, in exceptional cases unreasonable delay by the Tribunal could properly be treated as a procedural error or material irregularity giving rise to a question of law in respect of the proceedings for the purposes of s. 21(1) ETA (*Bangs v. Connex South Eastern Ltd* [2005] ICR 763; [2005] IRLR 389 CA). Delay could also be a factor contributing to a decision not being '*Meek*' compliant (see para. 10.15 below). The Rule also legitimizes the practice of reserving in part as it refers to the Tribunal announcing its decision 'in relation to any issue'.

10.05 Rule 61(2) and r. 65 (see para. 10.22) read together draw for the first time the important distinction between the judgment or order which is pronounced at the hearing and the written record of it which is sent to the parties. The requirement to send a written record of the judgment or order to the parties as soon as practicable after the hearing is new as the 2004 Rules only expressly required a written judgment to be sent where judgment had been reserved (old r. 29(1)).

10.06 The wording of the final bracketed sentence of r. 61(2) '(Decisions concerned only with the conduct of a hearing need not be identified in *the record of that hearing* unless a party requests that a specific decision is so recorded)' [emphasis added] is problematic. Given the heading of r. 61 and the first two lines of r. 61(2), the emphasized words must be taken to refer to the written record of the decision which has been announced at the hearing i.e. the written judgment or order, rather than the reasons for that decision which are dealt with in r. 62. As such they are likely to be of limited practical importance as it is already the case that decisions concerned only with the conduct of a hearing would not normally be identified in the record of the decision unless they required a formal case management order to be made. The bracketed sentence notwithstanding, such an order would still be required in at least some circumstances even if not requested by a party, for example if a restricted reporting order under r. 50(3)(d) was made during the course of the hearing. The sentence may be aimed at such things as whether certain evidence is admissible, or the order in which evidence be heard—which would not normally require a specific case management order. Rule 62(1) would however require the Tribunal to give its reasons for any decision concerning the conduct of the hearing if it was a matter of dispute, as the requirement to give reasons extends to procedural issues.

Old r. 29(3) (which was presumably intended to refer to all written judgments **10.07** but which, by virtue of old r. 29(1) being thus limited, could have been intended to refer only to reserved judgments) provided that where the judgment included an award of compensation or required another sum to be paid, 'the document shall also contain a statement of the amount of compensation awarded, or of the sum required to be paid'. There is no equivalent provision in the 2013 Rules. However, none is required as the written record of the decision would not be such if it did not incorporate a reference to any compensation or other sum to be paid.

4. Reasons

(a) *When reasons must be given*
Rule 62(1) introduces an important change in the requirement to give reasons. **10.08** Reasons must now be given for a decision 'on any disputed issue, whether substantive or procedural...'. The requirement to give reasons where procedural disputes are determined is new, at least so far as the Rules are concerned, although reasons should always have been given as a matter of good judicial practice. Under old r. 30(1)(b) it appeared that there was no requirement to give reasons if an application for a case management order was refused as the requirement was only to give reasons if requested to do so before or at the hearing 'where the order was made': if the application was refused no order was made. That was almost certainly an unintended drafting anomaly which has now been rectified and the obligation to give reasons is automatic if the issue giving rise to the order has been disputed, there being no requirement for a party to apply for reasons. Note that this is only a requirement to give oral reasons, not written reasons which are dealt with in r. 62(3) discussed below.

(b) *Written reasons*
The purpose of r. 62(2) according to the Underhill Review, is clarification **10.09** and to ensure that Employment Judges deal with requests for written reasons

consistently. It begins with a requirement to give reasons in writing 'In the case of a decision given in writing...' which must be intended as a reference to r. 61(1) which requires decisions to be in writing where the decision has been reserved. It is clearly not intended to be a reference to the written record of a decision required by r. 61(2) otherwise all reasons would have to be in writing. An interesting omission from the rule is an express requirement for the reasons where judgment has been reserved to be sent to the parties at the same time as the written decision (the judgment) itself although that is a long-standing Presidential requirement. However in the next sentence there is an express provision that the decision and reasons need not be in the same document where the decision has been announced at the hearing but the reasons have been reserved, implying that in all other cases dealt with by this paragraph they are to be in the same document.

10.10   The requirement in both rr. 61(3) and 62(2) for the written record of the decision and the written reasons to be signed by the Employment Judge is subject to r. 63 (see paras. 10.18 and 10.19 below).

10.11   Rule 62(3) largely reproduces old r. 39(3) and (5) but with an important addition. While the basic restrictions on the provision of written reasons at the request of the parties remains the same—only to be provided if requested at the hearing or in writing within fourteen days of the written record of the decision being sent to the parties (which time period can be extended under r. 5)—there is now a requirement for the Judge to announce at the hearing that that is the case and for the written record of the decision to repeat that information. The wording of the rule suggests that where a request is made within the fourteen-day time-limit written reasons must be provided. Although written in a negative sense—no obligation to provide unless the request is so made—the implication must be that if so made an obligation arises. Such an interpretation eliminates the risk of a Judge refusing a request for written reasons made by the winning party on the grounds that written reasons are only necessary if an appeal is contemplated. Absent a request by a party, the Tribunal shall only provide written reasons if requested to do so by the Employment Appeal Tribunal or (a new provision) a court.

10.12   The EAT may not only order a Tribunal to provide written reasons where none have been provided, it may require reasons which have been given to be clarified or amplified. An order to this effect is generally referred to as a *Burns/Barke* order following the cases of *Burns v. Consignia (No. 2)* [2004] ICR 1103; [2004] IRLR 425 EAT in which the practice was first established and *Barke v. Seetec Business Technology Centre Ltd* [2005] ICR 1373; [2005] IRLR 633 CA in which it was approved by the Court of Appeal. For a full discussion of the rationale behind such orders and the circumstances in which they may be made see the judgment in *Barke.*

(c) *Applications by non-parties*

10.13   There is an interesting gap in the Rules in that there is no provision for a non-party to apply for written reasons even when it might appear they have a pressing need for them, for example a person intending to bring a harassment claim on the heels of a successful harassment claim against the same respondent by another person. If the factual backgrounds of the allegations are sufficiently similar the findings of the first Tribunal might even be of probative value in the subsequent hearing. The wording of r. 62(3) is in fact capable of being interpreted as expressly preventing such an application.

(d) The content of reasons

Rule 62(4), whilst new, only enshrines into the Rules best judicial practice. Reasons should always be proportionate and for orders will seldom need to be of length, although where an appeal is likely, for example on a contested application to stay proceedings or for specific disclosure of sensitive documents, fuller reasons along the lines of those contemplated for judgments by r. 62(5) would appear to be called for. Reasons must however always meet the minimum requirements of appellate authority irrespective of the rule. In short, parties are entitled to know why they have won or lost, even on a narrow case management point, and the reasons must identify the issues which were vital to the conclusion, how they were resolved, and if evidence was rejected, the reason why (*English v. Emery Riembold & Strick Ltd* [2003] IRLR 710 CA). This latter requirement is not, in general, met merely by stating that the evidence of one witness was preferred to that of another without giving reasons (*Anya v. University of Oxford* [2001] ICR 847; [2001] IRLR 377 CA). **10.14**

Rule 62(5) largely replicates old r. 30(6) which was designed to ensure that reasons followed a defined structure which reflected best judicial practice following the judgment of the Court of Appeal in *Meek v. City of Birmingham District Council* [1987] IRLR 250 which held that the reasons should outline the evidence given, indicate the Tribunal's factual findings, contain a statement of the reasons leading to the Tribunal's conclusions and enable an appellate court to determine whether a question of law arose. It is not an error of law on which an appeal can be mounted not to expressly follow the structure of the rule provided it is clear that in practice the structure has been followed (*Balfour Beatty Power Networks Ltd v. Wilcox* [2007] IRLR 63 CA) although Tribunals were advised by the court to recite the terms of old r. 30(6) and to indicate how their decision fulfils its requirements. **10.15**

There is one potentially important difference between r. 62(5) and its predecessor. Whereas r. 62(5) requires the Tribunal only to identify the issues which it has determined, old r. 30(6) required it to include the issues which it has identified as being relevant to the claim and if some issues were not determined, to identify them and explain why. It might well be important for a Tribunal to identify issues which it is not subsequently required to determine, e.g. because the outcome of the case is determined by logically prior issues, as those other issues might take on new significance should the Tribunal be upset on appeal over its finding on the logically prior issues and the point arise as to whether those other issues were before the Tribunal at all. It is suggested that the better judicial practice remains that required by old r. 30(6)(a) and (b). **10.16**

10.17   What is meant by 'the issues' is a matter for debate. It is not just a list of the claims before the Tribunal (*Sinclair Roche & Temperley v. Heard (No. 1)* [2004] IRLR 763 EAT). 'The issues' might be said to be the questions to which the Tribunal is required to provide answers in order to reach its decision, but that could be taken to include every disputed contention of fact which would clearly be disproportionate. In an indirect discrimination claim, the issue would not be whether the claimant had been the victim of indirect discrimination but whether the respondent had applied a named provision, criterion or practice which puts persons who share an identified characteristic at a specified alleged disadvantage: whether the claimant has been put at that disadvantage and, if so, whether the respondent can satisfy the Tribunal that the provision, criterion or practice is a proportionate means of achieving a named legitimate end (EQA s. 19). In other words, the applicable statutory framework with brief factual contentions substituted for concepts.

5. Absence of Employment Judge

10.18   Rule 63 replaces old r. 31 with one change of substance and a simpler structure. The requirement for judgments, orders, and reasons to be signed by the Employment Judge is necessarily subject to the Judge being able to do so. Whereas old r. 31 referred to it being 'not possible' for the Judge to sign, r. 63 applies it if is 'impossible or not practicable' for him or her to sign. However, the applicable circumstances, namely death, incapacity, or absence, are the same. Rule 63 therefore would appear to cover a rather wider range of, though not materially different, circumstances than old r. 31. The change of substance is that there is no longer a requirement for the person signing in the Judge's absence to certify that the Judge is unable to sign. In the case of a Judge alone the usual alternate signatory is likely to be the Judge's Regional Employment Judge or in Scotland the Vice President, although the Presidents may also sign. In the case of a Tribunal which included members it shall be signed by the other member or members. It is not clear from the rule whether such a judgment is validly signed if the hearing was before a three-person Tribunal and only one of the members is available or willing to sign. The rule (and, it is suggested, for obvious reasons best practice) appears to require both to sign, the reference to 'the other member' probably being intended to relate to a two-person Tribunal.

10.19   There is no requirement in the Rules for the Tribunal's reasons to be written by the Employment Judge although that will almost invariably be the case. However, if the Tribunal has reached a decision there is nothing in the Rules to prevent the members or one of them drafting the reasons should the Judge then become incapacitated and unable to do so. It therefore behoves both members and Judges when deliberating their decisions to ensure that full notes of the reasons why they reach their decision are made. In practice, this problem should arise only extremely rarely (if at all) as the President expects Employment Judges to dictate the reasons for reserved decisions in the presence of the members (that is as part of the in chambers deliberation) to ensure that they are content with them.

6. Consent orders and judgments

Rule 64 replaces old r. 28(2) with one change. The rule provides that if the parties **10.20** agree in writing or orally at a hearing upon the terms of any order or judgment a Tribunal may 'if it thinks fit' make such order or judgment. The rule therefore expressly contemplates the possibility that the consent application will not be granted. While it seems clear from both the overriding objective (r. 2) and the general discretion to make case management orders (r. 29) that a Judge may refuse to grant an agreed application for a case management order (for example refusing an agreed application that the case should be the subject of judicial mediation because, in the Judge's view, it does not fall within the parameters of the current Presidential protocol for offering mediation) it is much less clear on what, if any, basis a Judge may refuse to enter judgement by consent as neither the Rules nor statute require the Tribunal's approval to be given in any circumstances. Even though persons lacking legal capacity are occasionally party to Employment Tribunal proceedings no provision is made for them in the Rules. Even where the terms of the settlement fall outside the Tribunal's statutory jurisdiction, for example they include an assignment of intellectual property rights, or the sum to be paid on a breach of contract claim exceeds £25,000, there would be nothing to prevent ACAS conciliating a settlement including such terms. However, a Judge might be on stronger ground for refusing to issue a judgment in such a case if troubled by questions of enforceability coupled with the creation of a cause of action estoppel which might be seriously detrimental to an unrepresented or lay represented claimant. It would seem that by virtue of r. 62(1) a Judge refusing to issue a consent judgment would have to give reasons for doing so as this would be a disputed procedural issue at least.

The only change from the 2004 Rules is that there is now a requirement **10.21** (normally observed in practice in any event) for a consent judgment or order to be identified as such. This is an important provision because of the severe limitations placed on a party's ability to appeal a judgment or order made by consent.

7. When a judgment or order takes effect

Rule 65 appears to be a new provision, although it does not change the legal sta- **10.22** tus of Employment Tribunal decisions delivered orally as it reflects long-standing common law practice that a judgment or order takes effect when pronounced. It is presumably included for the avoidance of doubt.

8. Time for compliance

Rule 66 is also a new provision, inserted into the draft Rules at a late stage **10.23** and reflects government policy. Its purpose seems to be to implement the idea canvassed as part of the consultation process into the review of the Rules of the need to ensure that the law supports prompt satisfaction of judgments.[1] However, both its intention and its standing are uncertain. It provides that a party shall comply with a judgment or order for the payment of an amount of money within fourteen days of the date of the judgment or order unless the judgment or order or the Rules specify otherwise, or the proceedings or the judgment are stayed. This implies, but does not expressly say, that prior to the expiration of the fourteen-day period the judgment or order is unenforceable. 'The date of the judgment' is not defined but a reasonable working assumption, given r. 65, is that it is the day on which an oral judgment or order is pronounced (as would be the case under CPR 40). Where there has been no prior oral pronouncement it would presumably be the date on which the written judgment or order was signed by the Judge, albeit that that is not always the date on which the judgment is sent to the parties.

10.24   The principal difficulty is, what is the rule intended to apply to, as it doesn't say to whom the money is to be paid? The problem arises because of the use of the word 'order'. While orders usually require a party to make a payment to another party as in the case of costs, preparation time or wasted costs orders, an order may also require a party to make a payment to the Tribunal, for example, of a deposit under r. 39 (from which, coincidentally, the time-limit for making the payment was deleted in the same draft of the Rules in which r. 66 first appeared). Is the rule intended to apply only to payments by one party to another, which would always be the case with judgments? That was certainly all that was discussed in the consultation. But, if so, its legal validity is highly questionable. While there is no express provision in the ETA about the time for payment of moneys ordered under a judgment, s. 15, which deals with enforcement of Tribunal judgments, provides that any sum payable in pursuance of a decision of the Tribunal '…which has been registered in accordance with employment tribunal procedure regulations shall be recoverable by execution issued from a county court…'. That appears to mean that immediately upon entry in the register (see reg. 14 and r. 67) the judgment becomes enforceable. If that is right, any attempt to change it other than by primary legislation would be *ultra vires*.

10.25   The original recommendation was that the judgment or order should include a statement to the effect that there was a fourteen-day deadline for payment but that has not found its way into the rule. The Employment Tribunals (Interest) Order 1990[2] has been amended by the Employment Tribunals (Interest) Order (Amendment) Order 2013[3] to complement r. 66 by providing for interest on awards to accrue from the date of judgment except where the judgment is paid in full within fourteen days.

---

[1] Underhill Review, para. 72.
[2] SI 1990/479.
[3] SI 2013/1671.

9. The Register

Rule 67 requires copies of any judgments or written reasons to be entered in the **10.26** Register. This requirement is subject to r. 50 ('Privacy and restrictions on disclosure') and r. 94 ('National security proceedings'). In the former case the reasons which will be entered are the redacted reasons if ordered under r. 50(2)(b). In the latter case, para. 6 of Schedule 2 applies which may result in no reasons or only heavily redacted reasons being sent to the Register.

B. RECONSIDERATION OF JUDGMENTS—RULES 70–73

1. Overview

The term 'judgment' is defined in r. 1(3)(b). Rules 70 to 73 replace the provisions **10.27** in the 2004 Rules which permitted both judgments and some other decisions to be reviewed. Along with the change of name from review to reconsideration come some important changes of substance. These can be summarized as follows:

- The reconsideration regime in rr. 70–73 applies only to judgments. Other decisions have their own regimes e.g. case management orders (r. 29); rejection of claim form (r. 13); rejection of response (r. 19). Where no reconsideration regime is provided e.g. rejection of response to employer's contract claim, rr. 70–73 cannot fill the gap unless a judgment has been issued.

- Old r. 33 has gone completely meaning that default judgments, or more accurately judgments issued under r. 21, now have the same reconsideration regime as all other judgments.

- The grounds on which a judgment can be reconsidered are reduced from five to one single ground: that reconsideration is necessary in the interests of justice.

- A gap may have been created in respect of applications to suspend Health and Safety Act prohibition notices (see para. 10.33 below).

The process whereby judgments are reviewed/reconsidered has been clari- **10.28** fied and some sensible changes introduced. But there are also some areas of uncertainty.

2. Principles

(a) *Taking hearings again*
Rule 70 replaces in four lines the five-paragraph r. 34 whilst adding the refer- **10.29** ence to the Tribunal's initiative possibly reflecting a request by the EAT. The last two sentences of the rule leave open a question which was specifically dealt with in the 2004 Rules. Old r. 36(3) provided that on reconsideration the original

decision may be confirmed, varied, or revoked—as does r. 70. However, whereas the old rule very prescriptively provided that if the original decision was revoked it 'must' be taken again and if it was taken by an Employment Judge without a hearing the new decision may be taken without 'hearing the parties', but if taken at a hearing a new hearing must be held; by contrast new r. 70 provides simply that if the decision is revoked 'it may be taken again'. It must be presumed that this is a conscious change of wording designed to remove an unnecessary fetter on the overriding objective which might well enable the original decision to be revisited without a hearing, particularly if all parties consent. Although it was almost certainly the case that no other change of substance was intended, two appear to have occurred. The first is in the grounds on which an application for a reconsideration can be made. The second is with regard to applications to suspend Health and Safety Act prohibition notices.

(b) *The grounds*

10.30   The only ground on which a judgment can be reconsidered is that it is necessary in the interests of justice to do so. That was the fifth of the five grounds for reviewing a decision in old r. 34(3) the others being that the decision was wrongly made as a result of administrative error; a party did not receive notice of the proceedings leading to the decision; the decision was made in the absence of a party; and, new evidence has become available since the conclusion of the hearing whose existence could not reasonably have been known of or foreseen. The question which naturally arises is whether the omission of the other four grounds signifies either a liberalization or a hardening of the review/reconsideration regime. The answer, it is suggested, is to be found in the history of the Rules themselves.

10.31   The wording of the interests of justice ground for review has remained (in substance) constant since the earliest Rules. Prior to the introduction into the Rules of the overriding objective in 2001 it had been narrowly construed so as to be limited to situations where some specific event such as a procedural mishap (*Trimble v. Supertravel Ltd* [1982] ICR 440; [1982] IRLR 451 EAT) or post-decision change of circumstance, had occurred; or, perhaps more rarely, where the Tribunal could be persuaded that its reasoning was faulty. Following the introduction of the overriding objective it was held in *Sodexho Ltd v. Gibbons* [2005] ICR 1647; [2005] IRLR 836 EAT that the correct approach was now to deal with the matter justly by balancing the interests of both parties. In *Sodexho* an Employment Judge's decision to set aside a strike out for failing to pay a deposit where the notice requiring the claimant to do so had not reached his solicitor because the claimant had misstated his postcode on the claim form was upheld on appeal, the Judge basing her decision on both the administrative error and interests of justice grounds. The introduction into r. 70 of the phrase '(which may reflect a request from the Employment Appeal Tribunal)' is itself a reflection of both an existing practice of the EAT and the practice of some Employment Judges to call cases in for review on realizing, upon reading grounds of appeal lodged with the EAT, that a rectifiable error may have been made and that the cheapest way to rectify it is by means of review/reconsideration rather than appeal.

Given these recent developments in the interpretation of the interests of **10.32** justice ground which have considerably broadened its scope, it seems that the requirement to identify other specific grounds for reviewing/reconsidering a judgment falls away as they become no more than non-exhaustive illustrations of circumstances in which the interests of justice ground might apply. That being so, the 2013 Rules represent neither a widening nor a narrowing of the review/reconsideration grounds since the 2001 Rules. However, an important question remains which is whether previously recognized limitations in two specific areas survive the advent of the overriding objective. It is suggested that the fundamental principle must continue to be that there is no 'second bite of the cherry' without cause. Thus a simple failure on the part of a party's representative to take a point or to take it satisfactorily, will still not be grounds to vary or revoke a judgment (*Lindsay v. Ironsides Ray and Vials* [1994] ICR 384; [1994] IRLR 318 EAT) although if that failure had in some way been induced by another party or the Tribunal it might be. It is also suggested that cases concerning the admissibility of newly discovered evidence such as *Bagga v. Heavy Electricals (India) Ltd* [1972] ICR 118 NIRC remain good law. Thus the fresh evidence must be credible, might have had a decisive impact on the Tribunal's decision and there is a reasonable explanation for the failure to make it available at the hearing.

(c) *Health and Safety appeals*

While the first of the apparent changes of substance proves largely illusory, **10.33** an unintended gap in the review/reconsideration regime does appear to have been created in respect of decisions on applications to suspend the operation of prohibition notices. Old r. 34(1)(c) included among the judgments and decisions which may be reviewed, 'decisions' under r. 6(3) of Schedule 4, that is a decision by an Employment Judge on an application to suspend the operation of a prohibition notice issued under s. 22 of the Health and Safety at Work etc Act 1974 pending the determination of the appeal. By virtue of s. 24(3)(b) the operation of such an order is only suspended if an application to that effect is granted. Rule 6(3) of Schedule 4 gave the Judge four possible outcomes, one of which was to dismiss the application, the others being described as orders. Schedule 4 is not reproduced in the 2013 Rules. Instead r. 105 applies Schedule 1 (the main Rules of Procedure) to such appeals subject only to the modification of the terminology applied to the parties. Section 24(3)(b) itself provides that the operation of the notice shall only be suspended if the Tribunal so 'directs'.

In an early draft of the Rules the reconsideration provisions were available for **10.34** judgments and other decisions and would therefore have covered a decision on an application to suspend a prohibition order.[4] They do not now appear to do so as the Judge's decision on such an application does not obviously satisfy the definition of a judgment in r. 1(3) and r. 29 would also appear to be unavailable as the Judge's determination would not be a decision 'in relation to the conduct of the proceedings' and therefore not a case management order.

3. Applications

10.35 Rule 71 replaces old r. 35(1) and (2). Old r. 35(2) provided that the review application 'must identify the grounds of the application in accordance with r. 34(3)' which, if interpreted literally, required the ground relied on to be identified rather than a narrative explanation of why the application should be granted. Rule 71 makes it clear that what is required is a statement of why reconsideration of the original decision is necessary. The rule also introduces a second period of fourteen days within which an application for reconsideration is to be made in cases where the written record of the judgment is sent to the parties before the written reasons, time running from the latter event. The time can of course be extended under r. 5.

4. Process

10.36 Rule 72 sets out a two-stage process which in an earlier draft of the Rules were referred to as stage 1 and stage 2 and it is convenient to think of it in those terms. Stage 1 (r. 72(1)) requires the Judge to reject an application if he or she considers there is no reasonable prospect of the original decision being varied or revoked and, importantly, includes within that concept where substantially the same application has already been made and refused, unless there are special reasons. If the application is not rejected a notice shall be sent to the parties setting a time-limit for any response to the application and seeking the parties' views on whether a hearing is necessary.

10.37   In another important addition to the procedure, the notice may 'set out the Judge's provisional views on the application'. This is slightly dangerous territory for the Judge as, given the provisions of r. 72(3), discussed below, it will in most cases be the same Judge who eventually determines the application. He or she should therefore avoid using language which suggests a predetermination of the application which might lead to a subsequent allegation of bias and an application for recusal at stage 2 (*Oni v. NHS Leicester City* [2013] ICR 91 EAT). Used sensibly this is a useful provision as it gives the Judge the opportunity to say to the other party that, subject to any point they wish to raise, the Judge is minded to grant the application and to explain why, thus hopefully obviating the need

---

[4] Although the word 'decision' is used throughout rr. 71–73 rather than 'judgment', r. 70 makes it clear that reconsideration applies only to judgments.

for a hearing. It is suggested that, in the context of a later bias challenge, it might not be helpful to give the provisional view that the application is likely to fail.

At stage 2 (r. 72(2)), which is the reconsideration itself, there is no obligation **10.38** to hold a hearing just because one has been requested, merely a presumption that there will be a hearing unless the Judge considers that a hearing is not necessary in the interests of justice 'having regard to any response to the notice'. The wording of this provision certainly gives the Judge licence to deal with the application on paper even if the other party or parties object to the judgment being varied or revoked. However, the rule does require that if the Judge decides not to hold a hearing the parties must be given a further opportunity to make written representations before the application is finally disposed of. Where a hearing is held, the parties will be informed in the notice of hearing whether the decision will be taken again on the same day as the reconsideration application if it is successful, or at a later date.

Rule 72(3) replicates the substance of old rr. 35(1) and 36(1). The initial con- **10.39** sideration of the application at stage 1 will be undertaken by the Judge who made the decision complained of or who chaired the Tribunal which made it, and the stage 2 final determination will be by the original Judge or Tribunal provided, in both cases, that that is practicable. Unlike r. 63 which deals with the signing of a judgment or reasons in the absence of the Judge, and which identifies the circumstances in which it might be impossible or impracticable for that to be done, namely death, incapacity, or absence—r. 72(3) gives no clues as to when it would be appropriate to ask another Judge to deal with the application. However, in practice they are likely to be the same as it is clearly preferable at both stages for the trial Judge to do so. If that proves impracticable then the President, or a Regional Employment Judge (in Scotland the Vice President) shall appoint another Judge to consider the application if the Judge was sitting alone and may appoint themselves (reg. 8(2)). Where the decision under challenge was that of a full Tribunal the President, Vice President, or Regional Employment Judge may direct that the remaining members of the Tribunal deal with the application or reconstitute the Tribunal 'in whole or in part'.

5. The Tribunal's own initiative

Rule 73 deals with reconsideration of judgments by the Tribunal of its own ini- **10.40** tiative, formerly old r. 36(2), and the contrast in language between the two provisions raises some interesting questions of interpretation. That changes to the way a Tribunal may reconsider its own judgments have been made is clear: the extent of those changes much less so. The 2004 Rules carried a provision similar to that in new r. 72(3) which enables a reconsideration made on application by a party to be carried out by a Judge or Tribunal other than the Judge or Tribunal which made the decision, where it is not practicable for the first Judge or Tribunal to do so. However, old r. 36(2) provided that where the decision was being reviewed on the initiative of the Tribunal 'the review must be carried out by the same Tribunal or Employment Judge who made the original decision' without exception. This requirement is absent from r. 73 and there is no direct or obvious indirect reference back to r. 72(3) (only r. 72(2) being referred to) leaving the question of who may carry out a reconsideration under this Rule at large.

10.41   As with applications to reconsider, a two-stage process is involved: the initial proposal to reconsider and the final reconsideration itself. At least four possibilities arise:

- that only the Tribunal which gave the original judgment may make the proposal to reconsider and carry out the final reconsideration;
- *pace* r. 72(1), where the original decision was that of a full Tribunal the initial proposal may be that of the Employment Judge which chaired the Tribunal but the final reconsideration must be that of the full Tribunal;
- where that is not practicable (at either stage) a substitute may be appointed as in r. 72(3); and
- that a substitute may be appointed (at either stage) even absent issues of practicability.

10.42   Two interpretations of the rule seem equally available. The first is that as r. 72(3) applies expressly (and therefore exclusively) to *applications* for reconsideration, the exemption from the reconsideration having to be by the original Judge or Tribunal does not apply to reconsiderations which do not arise from applications by parties (i.e. those made on the Tribunal's initiative) which in consequence can only be by the original Judge or Tribunal. The second is that the omission of the quoted words previously found in r. 36(2) was intentional and intended to make at least the initial stage of this process—the proposal to reconsider—open to any Judge. This interpretation is supported by the reference in r. 70 to a review of the Tribunal's own initiative reflecting a request from the EAT which may need to be considered when the original Judge is not available and by the opening words of r. 73 'The Tribunal' which is not defined in r. 1 but tends to be used in the Rules when reference is being made to the Tribunals collectively rather than 'a Tribunal' (which is defined) and which tends to apply to a specific Tribunal. It seems that no assistance can be derived from the fact that the final reconsideration shall be in accordance with r. 72(2) as that speaks only of process, r. 72(3) dealing with by whom the reconsideration is to be carried out. Rule 72(2) is not expressly subject to r. 72(3) and does not obviously have to be read with it.

10.43   It is unsatisfactory that such an important aspect of the self-reconsideration provisions should be left unstated. But it may well have been left unstated because it was thought to be too obvious to require statement. The second interpretation suggested in the previous paragraph could have serious implications for judicial independence as it could lead to over assiduous Regional Employment Judges (and Vice-Presidents) not merely privately drawing to the attention of a junior judicial colleague flaws in their reasoning, but writing to the parties explaining how the REJ proposes to put it right! The solution to the difficulty, it is suggested, is that the starting point is that the original Tribunal (so not just the Judge who chaired a full Tribunal) is the Tribunal which is to both make the initial proposal and to conduct the final reconsideration. However (as with all other rules) this is subject to the overriding objective in r. 2, which may require the rule to be interpreted in a way similar to r. 72(3) but only where such an interpretation is not inimical to the prime concern of protecting judicial independence. That of course gives rise to the obvious question, if that interpretation is correct, isn't r. 72(3) redundant when it comes to disposing of reconsiderations made on application? The answer, it is suggested, is 'no': where it is not practicable for the original Judge to undertake a reconsideration under r. 73, and to substitute another Judge in the manner permitted by r. 72(3) would infringe the principle of judicial independence, then a reconsideration can only take place on application by a party.

Although r. 73 only expressly adopts the stage 2 procedure for disposing of the **10.44** reconsideration itself, it seems that in practice the stage 1 process must also be followed to the extent that the rule does not provide for it. Whereas old r. 36(2)(a) provided that a notice must be sent to the parties explaining 'in summary' the grounds on which it is proposed to review the decision 'and give them an opportunity to give reasons why there should be no review', r. 73 only requires that the parties be informed 'of the reasons why the decision is being reconsidered...'. However, by adopting the stage 2 process of r. 72(2) the implication must be that the notice must invite representations, as r. 72(2) provides that the original decision shall be reconsidered at a hearing unless 'having regard to any response to the notice provided under paragraph (1)' the Employment Judge considers that a hearing is not necessary in the interests of justice. The requirement now is to 'inform the parties of the reasons why the decision is being reconsidered' which appears to require rather more detail than an explanation 'in summary'. However, following *Oni v. NHS Leicester City* (above) the Tribunal should be careful not to express itself in such a way as to indicate that it had already made up its mind on the issue.

A very important change from the 2004 Rules is that there is now no time-limit **10.45** within which a Tribunal can review its own judgments although the time-limit of fourteen days for sending the notice in old r. 36(2)(b) was probably extendable under old r. 10(2)(e).

11

COSTS, PREPARATION TIME, AND WASTED COSTS ORDERS—RULES 74–84

A. OVERVIEW

11.01 Some important changes are made to the costs regime, the three elements of which are brought together into a single section of the Rules, for the purposes of simplification and to ensure they are more easily understood. The most significant changes are:

- A costs order may now be made in favour of a party in respect of costs incurred by that party while legally represented even if they are not legally represented at the hearing. This rectifies a major injustice which caused great hardship to parties who had been legally represented up to the hearing but could not

135

afford to pay for representation at the hearing. The only order which could have been made in those circumstances, a preparation time award in respect of work done by that party's legal or other advisors relating to the conduct of the proceedings up to but not including the hearing, which was likely to have been derisory in comparison with the amount of costs actually incurred, has not been reproduced in the new Rules.

- Employment Judges may now carry out detailed assessments of costs themselves where the amount exceeds £20,000 rather than remit the task to the county court or, in Scotland, the Sheriff Court.
- The £10,000 ceiling on a preparation time order is removed.
- The prohibition on making both a costs order and a preparation time order in the same proceedings is modified.

11.02   An ambiguity has crept into the rule governing the amount of costs which can be awarded where the parties have agreed the terms of an order.

B. DEFINITIONS

1. Generally

11.03   Rule 74, although headed 'Definitions' is only a partial definition provision as two important definitions, those of wasted costs and preparation time, are found elsewhere (r. 80 in respect of the former, and rr. 75(2) and 79 in respect of the latter). The definitions used in the 2004 Rules are unchanged in substance but with one important addition. The old definition of costs (in Scotland, expenses) formerly found at r. 38(3) is now r. 74(1). 'Legally represented' formerly r. 38(5) is now r. 74(2) but with the definition of 'general qualification' in s. 71(3)(c) of the Courts and Legal Services Act 1990 being set out in full.

2. 'Represented by a lay person'

11.04   The new and important definition, which recognizes that under the 2004 Rules it was generally considered that only legal costs could be ordered, is that of 'Represented by a lay person' being a paid representative who does not fulfil any of the definitions of 'legally represented'. As the words in the definition are 'who charges for representation in the proceedings' an organization which supplies representation as part of a membership package or overall consultancy retainer but which does not charge for representation in a particular case, will be outside the scope of the definition and, in consequence, of the scope of r. 78(2), so that no costs order can be made. A preparation time order would however be available as such a representative would be an advisor for the purposes of r. 75(2). Whether organizations such as Law Centres and CABs, which provide representation without fee but at a cost to themselves are entitled to claim that cost is not expressly dealt with in the Rules but as the definition of costs is 'fees, charges,

disbursements or expenses incurred by *or on behalf of* the receiving party...'
[emphasis added] it would seem that a costs order could be made to cover the
cost to the representative of providing free representation.

3. Costs orders

Rule 75(1) redefines a costs order to take into account the changes that have   **11.05**
occurred since the 2004 Rules. There are now three limbs: the costs incurred by
the receiving party whilst legally represented or while represented by a lay representative (r. 75(1)(a)); a Tribunal fee paid by the receiving party (r. 75(1)(b)); and
payment to another party or a witness in respect of 'expenses incurred, or to be
incurred, for the purpose of, or in connection with, an individual's attendance
as a witness at the Tribunal'. Note the absence of the word 'reasonable' from
this last provision although from r. 78(1)(d) the power to make an award is only
in respect of 'necessary and reasonably incurred expenses'. The reason for the
omission of the words '(the receiving party)' in r. 75(1)(c) is unclear. The phrase
occurs in the previous sub-paragraphs to emphasize that the cost being reim-
bursed is a cost incurred by the receiving party, and so its absence may indicate
that the payment of witness expenses to a party may be ordered in respect of
expenses incurred by one of that party's witnesses even though the party has no
enforceable obligation to reimburse the witness.

4. Preparation time orders

Rule 75(2) defines a preparation time order in terms similar to that employed in   **11.06**
old r. 42(1) and (3) but omits the qualification of old r. 42(2) that such an order
can only be made if the receiving party is not legally represented at the hearing.
Although old r. 46 is preserved in r. 75(3) (subject to a qualification discussed in
the next paragraph)—so that it is still not possible to make both a costs order
and a preparation time order in favour of the same party in the same proceedings—this omission would enable the Tribunal to make a preparation time order
in favour of a party who was legally represented at the hearing in the unlikely
event of that being the more favourable order. Preparation time includes not
only the time of the party but of his or her employees or advisors but excludes
time spent at 'any final hearing'. Thus the time spent at case management discussions and preliminary hearings can be included in a preparation time order.

By virtue of an amendment to s. 13 ETA by s. 21(3) of the Enterprise and   **11.07**
Regulatory Reform Act 2013, a preparation time order and a costs order may
now be made in favour of the same party where the costs order is one under
r. 75(1)(b) in respect of a Tribunal fee or under r. 75(1)(c) in respect of witness
expenses. Rule 75(3) reflects this change but otherwise preserves the fundamental
rule that a costs order and a preparation time order cannot be made in the same
proceedings in favour of the same party. It also preserves the effect of old r. 46(2)
which enabled a Tribunal to determine at an early stage in the proceedings that

either a costs or preparation time order will be made but to defer the decision as to which it shall be until the conclusion of the proceedings.

C. COSTS ORDERS AND PREPARATION TIME ORDERS

1. When orders may be made

(a) *The new provisions*

11.08 The basic principles on which such orders are to be made remain largely unchanged, the only change of note in the language of the rule being the introduction of the words '(or part)' into r. 76(1) which otherwise reflects old r. 40(2) and (3). It is probable that no change in the law is achieved as there has always had to be a causative connection between the conduct complained of and the costs incurred (although not a 'precise causal link': *Barnsley MBC v. Yerrakalva* [2012] IRLR 78 CA *per* Mummery LJ, para. 41) which would have enabled a Tribunal to award costs where only part but not the whole of the proceedings had been conducted in the proscribed manner if that conduct had led to identifiable costs being incurred.

11.09 There may however be an important but almost certainly unintended change in the law through retaining old Rules concepts in the face of new definitions. The 2004 Rules provided that a costs order could be made if the bringing of the proceedings had been misconceived, which was defined (old reg. 2) as 'includes having no reasonable prospect of success'. In r. 76(1)(b) this becomes that an order for costs may be made where the Tribunal considers that 'any claim or response had no reasonable prospect of success.' What this overlooks is that, unlike the 2004 Rules, the 2013 Rules draw a distinction between a claim, which means 'any proceedings before a Tribunal making a complaint' and a complaint which is, roughly, a cause of action (see r. 1 and paras. 4.03 and 4.04). On a literal interpretation this would appear to mean that unless all of the complaints in a claim form are deemed to be misconceived then no order for costs can be made. However, the problem is overcome by a purposive interpretation of the sub-paragraph which recognizes the use of the word 'any' in front of the word 'claim' rather than the definite article as indicating that here the word 'claim' is used in a non-technical sense to mean any complaint or contention. Such an interpretation would almost certainly reflect the purpose of the Rule.

(b) *The task of the Tribunal*

11.10 The task of the Tribunal is threefold. The first step is that if the Tribunal is of the opinion that one of the conditions in sub-paragraphs (a) or (b) of r. 76(1)— the so-called threshold conditions—is met, then the Tribunal 'shall', that is must, consider whether to make a costs or preparation time order. It was held in *Oni v. NHS Leicester City* [2013] ICR 91 EAT that this does not require the Tribunal as part of its decision on the merits to consider (and to express a view on) whether a threshold condition has been met where the issue of costs is not before it. A Tribunal has no power to make an award of costs of its own initiative other than in respect of witness expenses (r. 76(5)). However, if the Tribunal considers that a threshold condition is met, there is no obligation to make an order: 'A Tribunal may make a costs order...'—it is a matter for the exercise of the Tribunal's discretion. In fact there are two discretions to be exercised, something which is perhaps clearer from old r. 40(2) than r. 76. The first is whether to make a costs order at all; the second is as to the amount the paying party should pay as there is no requirement for an all or nothing approach—a costs order is an order 'in respect of the costs' that the receiving party has occurred, not of the costs (r. 75(1)(a)).

11.11 No appeal will lie against the exercise of the Tribunal's discretion unless the Tribunal's reasons disclose an error of legal principle, or failure to give proper consideration to all of the relevant circumstances, or was obviously wrong (*Dean & Dean (A Firm) v. Dionissiou-Moussaoui* [2011] EWCA Civ 1332). In *Barnsley MBC v. Yerrakalva* (above) the Employment Tribunal's decision that the claimant pay the whole of the respondent's costs was overturned on appeal and an order that she pay half the costs substituted because although the claimant had been untruthful and in consequence one of the threshold conditions had been met, the Tribunal had failed to take into account its own significant criticisms of the respondent's conduct of the litigation and the effect it had had on the costs they had incurred—that it had 'gone over the top' in defending the claim.

11.12 'The vital point in exercising the discretion to order costs is to look at the whole picture of what happened in the case and to ask whether there has been unreasonable conduct by the claimant in bringing and conducting the case and, in doing so, to identify the conduct, what was unreasonable about it and what effects it had' (*Yerrakalva* para. 41, *per* Mummery LJ). There was no requirement for the Tribunal 'to determine whether or not there was a precise causal link between the unreasonable conduct in question and the specific costs being claimed' but it was equally not the case that causation was irrelevant or that the circumstances had to be separated into sections and each section analysed separately so as to lose sight of the totality of the relevant circumstances. A *Calderbank*[1] type offer (that is, an offer made without prejudice save as to costs) is a factor which an Employment Tribunal can take into account when exercising its discretion to award costs but a failure to beat a *Calderbank* offer does not by itself lead to an order for costs being made (*Kopel v. Safeway Stores Ltd* [2003] IRLR 753 EAT).

11.13 That costs orders are exceptional has in the past often reflected the reluctance of Tribunals, particularly of the lay members but also of some Judges, to make costs orders. It should not do so. The Underhill Review suggests that this is an area where Presidential guidance might be issued under r. 7 to encourage the

---

[1] *Calderbank v. Calderbank* [1976] Fam 93.

making of more orders. Costs orders should be exceptional only because, as Burton P. pointed out in *Royal Mail Group Plc v. Sharma* (UKEAT/0839/04), the conduct which triggers a threshold condition is, fortunately, the exception. Thus a finding that the central contention in a claim is based on a falsehood should normally result in an award of costs (*Daleside Nursing Home Ltd v. Matthews* UKEAT/0519/08) although there is no legal principle that where the claimant has lied, costs should follow. In *HCA International Ltd v. May-Bheemul* UKEAT/0477/10 it was held that a lie on its own will not necessarily be sufficient to found an award for costs. The Tribunal must always examine the context and look at the nature, gravity and effect of the lie in determining the unreasonableness of the conduct.

(c) *The threshold conditions*

11.14 '*Vexatiously*'. A claim is vexatious if it is brought in the knowledge that it is hopeless and 'not with any expectation of recovering compensation but out of spite to harass (the claimant's) employers or for some other improper motive' (*ET Marler Ltd v. Robertson* [1974] ICR 72 NIRC).

11.15 '*Otherwise unreasonably*'. There does not appear to be direct appellate authority on what this short phrase means although in *Osannaya v. Queen Mary University of London* UKEAT/0225/11 HH Judge McMullen said (at para. 19) that it required a high threshold to be crossed. That, it is suggested, is plainly right. The word 'otherwise' links the word 'unreasonably' with the words which precede it indicating that they fall to be interpreted *eujsdem generis*, that is as being of a piece; of the same kind. Thus conduct which is merely not reasonable does not cross the threshold. Only conduct which is so unreasonable as to be equated with the vexatious pursuit of the proceedings or abusive or disruptive behaviour is sufficient. Put another way, vexatiously, abusively, and disruptively are examples of the kind of unreasonable conduct required for the threshold to be crossed. It would not normally be appropriate to order a party to pay costs because of the manner in which their representative had conducted the proceedings unless it was clear that the representative's conduct was adopted by the party, such as by declining to dispense with their services after the consequences of failing to do so had been pointed out by the Tribunal.

11.16 The late withdrawal of a claim is not by itself unreasonable: it may indicate that the claimant is acting responsibly. The claimant's conduct of the proceedings has to be looked at overall.

11.17 '*No reasonable prospect of success*'. This is an objective test. The question whether the party knew their claim or response had no reasonable prospect of success is relevant only for the exercise of the Tribunal's discretion whether to award costs, not whether the threshold condition is met. It is in this context that a Tribunal should consider what a party knew or should have known had they gone about matters sensibly (*Cartiers Superfoods Ltd v. Laws* [1978] IRLR 315 EAT).

(d) *When threshold conditions do not apply*

Rule 76(2) restates old r. 40(4) and (1) (in that order) and provides that a costs **11.18** or preparation time order may be made where a party is in breach of an order or practice direction or the hearing has been postponed or adjourned on the application of a party. In this latter case it may be the party who has applied for the postponement or adjournment who is entitled to their costs if the application is necessitated by the conduct of the other party, although there is no requirement for the other party to have behaved 'otherwise unreasonably'. The Tribunal's discretion is at large. The same is true in respect of witness expenses which the Tribunal may order of its own initiative (r. 76(5)) or on the application of the witness.

(e) *Costs and fees*

Rule 76(4) enables the Tribunal to order the payment of the winning party's fees **11.19** without the need for a threshold condition to be met, even if the claim, employer's contract claim, or application of the kind listed in column 1 of Schedule 1 to the Fees Order in respect of which the fee was paid was only partially successful. An order under this provision can therefore be made following a successful application if the party making the application has paid a fee.

2. When a costs order shall be made

Rule 76(3) replaces old r. 39 and requires the Tribunal to make a costs order (but, **11.20** it is suggested, only if an application is made as the words 'on its own initiative' do not appear in the paragraph) where the final hearing of an unfair dismissal claim has to be postponed or adjourned because the claimant having expressed a wish to be re-engaged or reinstated not less than seven days prior to the hearing, the respondent has failed to adduce, without special reason, 'reasonable evidence as to the availability of the job from which the claimant was dismissed or of comparable or suitable employment'. The rule as originally drafted enabled the Tribunal to make 'such an order', the words employed in para. (2) of the rule, which refer back to para. (1) making it clear that the Tribunal could make either a costs or preparation time order. These have been replaced by DBIS lawyers in the final version of the Rules with the words 'order the respondent to pay the costs incurred'. Why the power to make a preparation time order is excluded, if that is the intention, is wholly unclear. Whether it is the intention is open to some doubt as the wording employed is less clear than the obvious alternative 'the Tribunal shall make a costs order against the respondent'. Nonetheless the rule as currently drafted would make it very difficult for the Tribunal to make a preparation time order in these circumstances although that was clearly not the intention of the Underhill group and injustice will undoubtedly result in some cases.

3. Procedure

11.21 Rule 77 replaces, in very much simpler form, old r. 38(7)–(9) but without any change in the procedure. The rule requires a costs application to be made within twenty-eight days of the date on which the decision final determining the proceedings against the party applying was sent to the parties, although the time can be extended under r. 5. An application can also be made at the hearing, a point which was explicit in old r. 38(7) but must be implied in r. 77. There is no requirement to hold a hearing of the costs application even if one is requested but it would normally be prudent to do so if the paying party has requested one and the Judge is minded to make an order. There is also no express provision for rejecting an application which a Judge believes to have no reasonable prospect of success without first referring it to the other party, but none is probably required as the power would seem to be inherent in respect of any application for an order by virtue of the overriding objective.

4. The amount of a costs order

(a) *Basic orders*

11.22 Rule 78 replaces old r. 41 with some additions to reflect recent changes in the Tribunal's procedures generally and with an important change of substance. There are five orders available to the Tribunal but in some cases, more than one order can be made. Where the costs do not exceed £20,000 or the application is limited to that amount, the Tribunal may order the costs without the need for a detailed assessment of the kind required by r. 78(1)(b)—although it would almost certainly be an improper exercise of the Tribunal's discretion just to award the amount claimed without any scrutiny unless the paying party agreed: the Tribunal should satisfy itself that the amount claimed is not excessive. The most important change comes in sub-para. (1)(b) where the costs will, or are likely to, exceed £20,000. In the past all such awards had to be referred to the county court (in Scotland the Sheriff Court) for a detailed assessment in accordance with the CPR (in Scotland, to be taxed). Now the detailed assessment can be carried out by 'an' Employment Judge using the same principles. Thus the Judge doing the detailed assessment need not be the Judge who heard the case.

(b) *Fees and witness expenses*

11.23 Rule 78(1)(c) and (d) permit the Tribunal to make orders for the repayment of the whole or part of a Tribunal fee and expenses necessarily and reasonably incurred by a witness for the purpose of or in connection with their attendance as a witness. In each case the order is to be in a specified amount. In the case of fees expressly and in the case of witness expenses by implication, the order may be for less than the full cost incurred. Both of these orders could be made in the same proceedings but would not normally need to be made in favour of the same party where a costs order had been made under sub-paragraphs (a) or (b) as such orders should include reimbursement of fees and witness expenses. Under the 2004 Rules there was no power to award witness expenses where a preparation time order had been made but this gap has been closed by s. 21(3) of the Enterprise and Regulatory Reform Act 2013 which amends s. 13A ETA.

(c) Consent orders

Rule 78(1)(e) seems to give the Tribunal the usual discretion to refuse to make **11.24** an order where the parties have agreed terms, whereas its equivalent under the old Rules (r. 41(b)) clearly did not, providing that the costs order 'shall be' for the sum agreed. This apparent change may however be illusory as the word 'may' appears only in the opening words of r. 78(1)—'A costs order may'—indicating that the Tribunal may only make one of the five potential orders which follow. The concluding words of r. 78(1)(e) 'be made in that amount' could be interpreted as mandatory, lacking as they do the word 'may' in front of them. This ambiguity is unfortunate but a case can be made for giving the Tribunal power to refuse its consent where, for example, an unrepresented party has struck what appears to be a manifestly bad bargain with a well represented opponent. Rule 78(3) provides, for the avoidance of doubt, that the amount of costs ordered under paras. (1)(b)–(e) may exceed £20,000.

(d) Lay representatives

Rule 78(2) is new and compliments r. 74(3) which permits costs orders to be made **11.25** in favour of lay representatives. It provides that where a costs order includes an amount in respect of fees charged by a lay representative, the hourly rate which may be used to calculate those fees 'shall be no higher than' the amount applicable for calculating preparation time orders. This would appear to allow the Tribunal to award less than the preparation time rate irrespective of the amount claimed which seems to create room for penalizing poor representation. However, the purpose of the provision seems only to be to place a cap on the hourly rate which can be awarded.

5. The amount of a preparation time order

Rule 79 reproduces the effect of old r. 45 but with the removal of the previ- **11.26** ous ceiling of £10,000 on the amount which can be awarded. Rule 79(1) creates a rudimentary means of assessing the multiplicand, that is, the hours spent in preparation time as defined in r. 75(2). There would appear to be nothing to prevent a Tribunal increasing the multiplicand if it felt that the receiving party had significantly underestimated the time spent, but the intention is presumably that the power of assessment in r. 79(1)(b) will be used to reduce the amount claimed where it seems excessive. The multiplier is fixed by r. 79(2) as £33 per hour from 29 July 2013 to 5 April 2014 rising by £1.00 on each 6 April thereafter.

D. WASTED COSTS

1. When a wasted costs order may be made

11.27   Old r. 48 now becomes new rr. 80–82 with one change (possibly two changes) of substance. Rule 80(1) repeats the definition of wasted costs in old r. 48(3) which is derived from s. 51(7) of the Supreme Court Act 1981. In *Ridehalgh v. Horsefeld* (and other conjoined appeals) [1994] Ch 205; [1994] 3 WLR 462 CA guidance was given on the exercise by courts of their jurisdiction to make wasted costs orders. Given the common statutory origin of the definitions, that guidance would also apply in Employment Tribunals. For a commentary on the power see CPR 48.7 [2B]–[4]. The regime in the Employment Tribunal however differs in two important respects from the CPR and it would in consequence be dangerous to read CPR 48.7 into, or rely on it as an aid in applying, r. 80. The regime in the Tribunal (r. 80(2)) is more restrictive than in the county court where it can apply to any 'legal or other representative'—an expression which includes lay representatives not acting for reward. In the Employment Tribunal it only applies to a representative acting 'in pursuit of profit with regard to the proceedings'. Thus a solicitor genuinely acting pro bono would not be amenable to an order under this Rule although a lay representative appearing as part of a membership package rather than for a specific fee might be. The definition of 'in pursuit of profit' has been widened from that in old r. 48(4) to include acting on a contingency fee basis as well as a conditional fee arrangement.

11.28   The regime is however broader than CPR 48.7 in that a wasted costs order can be triggered by the conduct of an employee of the party's legal or other representative, not just the representative personally. This appears to place the legal entity which ultimately provides the representation on the same footing as the individual appearing in the Tribunal or having the personal conduct of the proceedings for the purposes of a wasted costs order which avoids the difficulty which would otherwise arise where the person actually conducting the proceedings does not have the means to satisfy the order. Note that a barrister is immune from a wasted costs order in respect of advocacy in open court but not for conduct immediately relevant to the exercise of that right (*Medcalf v. Weatherill* [2003] 1 AC 120; [2002] 3 All ER 721 HL).

11.29   Rule 80(3) repeats in substance old r. 48(5) and leaves unresolved a problem which the latter created. A wasted costs order may be made in favour of a party 'whether or not that party is legally represented'. Where a party who is not legally represented succeeds in a claim they may only recover from the other party a preparation time payment calculated in accordance with r. 79. But the definition of wasted costs (now in r. 81) does not include preparation time. It therefore seems that a party who is not legally represented and who has incurred costs as the result, for example, of improper, unreasonable, or negligent conduct by the other party's representative, may legitimately claim at a higher hourly rate than that provided for by r. 79(2) provided it can be justified, for example by showing that they have been prevented from earning a higher hourly rate through their own business as a result of having to spend time on the proceedings. The rule also provides (as did old r. 48(5)) that an order may be made in favour of a party against their own representative and may not be made against a representative who is representing a party in their capacity as an employee of that party. This would not of course preclude the making of a costs order against that party under r. 76(1)(a) on the grounds of unreasonable conduct of the proceedings.

2. Effect of a wasted costs order

Rule 81 reproduces the effect of old r. 48(1) and (7). The whole or part of the **11.30** costs wasted can be ordered to be repaid or disallowed. It is necessary for a causal link to be established between the costs wasted and the conduct complained of, although merely to show that the costs would not have been incurred but for the conduct is not sufficient (*Byrne v. Sefton Health Authority* (2001) unreported, *The Times*, 28 November, CA). The order must specify the amount of the costs to be paid, repaid or disallowed.

3. Procedure

Rule 82 expressly provides that the Tribunal may make a wasted costs order of **11.31** its own initiative. While this was probably permissible under old r. 48, the rule was silent on the point. However it is suggested that the advice in CPR 48.7 [5] applies with equal force in the Tribunal, that 'normally, save in the most obvious cases, the court should leave it to the aggrieved party to apply for a wasted costs order'. The time for making an application is twenty-eight days after the date on which the judgment finally determining the proceedings as against the party applying was sent to the parties, but time can be extended under r. 5. The representative must be given a reasonable opportunity to make representations but there seems to be no absolute right to make them orally: it is for the Tribunal to decide whether there should be a hearing. The Tribunal must inform the representative's client of any proceedings and any order under this rule.

In deciding whether to order a hearing of an application the Tribunal should **11.32** have regard to the overriding objective and to the further costs likely to be incurred compared with those sought to be recovered. While the decision in *Oni v. NHS Leicester City* (see para. 11.10) might appear to create a problem if a Judge or Tribunal has expressed themselves forcefully about the conduct of a representative during a hearing, it was held in *Re P (Barrister) (Wasted costs order)* (2001), unreported, *The Times*, 31 July, CA (Crim Div) that the fact that a Judge has expressed views on a barrister's conduct during the trial will not 'itself' give rise to an appearance of bias and the Judge should not decline to consider an application for wasted costs. It is in the public interest that he or she should do so in order to dispose of the matter economically and quickly. Nonetheless, there may be cases where it would be seriously unfair for the trial Judge to hear the application: *Re Freudiana Holdings Ltd* [1994] NPC 89 where a claim was dismissed after 165 days of hearing. The normal rule must be that the Judge or Tribunal which heard the case should hear the wasted costs application. Where the Tribunal proposes to make a wasted costs order of its own initiative, it is an obvious requirement, although not spelled out in the Rule, that the representative be told clearly what it is that they have done wrong and what the consequences are said to be.

E. ALLOWANCES

11.33 Rule 83 brings together provisions previously found in three rules. It provides that where a Tribunal makes an award of costs, preparation time, or wasted costs it may also order the payment to the Secretary of State of the whole or part of any allowance paid by the Secretary of State to any assessor appointed for the purposes of the proceedings, an independent expert required to prepare a report on the question of whether the work of the claimant and that of a comparator was of equal value under s. 131(2) EA, and to 'any person for the purposes of, or in connection with, that person's attendance at the Tribunal'. The wording of the rule rather confusingly merges s. 5(2) and (3) ETA and in so doing creates some uncertainty. Whilst the section makes a clear distinction between assessors and independent experts on the one hand, to whom the Secretary of State may pay 'fees and allowances' (s. 5(2)) and on the other, 'any other person' to whom the Secretary of State may pay allowances 'for the purposes of or in connection with, their attendance at Employment Tribunals' the rule does not, appearing instead to limit the award the Tribunal can make in all cases to payments made for the purposes of or in connection with attendance at the Tribunal. It therefore seems that a Tribunal no longer has power to order reimbursement to the Secretary of State of a fee paid to an independent expert for the preparation of a report, particularly if the expert does not attend to give evidence.

11.34 Although the rule does not say so, it would not appear to be necessary for any causal connection to be identified between the conduct giving rise to the making of the preparation time, costs, or wasted costs order and the incurring of the allowance by the Secretary of State. It would appear merely to be an option available to the Tribunal should the relevant threshold condition for the making of the principle order be satisfied. Such orders are very rarely made in practice.

F. ABILITY TO PAY

11.35 Rule 84 combines provisions formerly found in each of the three 'costs' rules. While it appears to give the Tribunal a completely unfettered discretion whether to have any regard to the paying party's ability to pay, some recent decisions of the EAT have purported to put a restrictive gloss on the rule. In *Doyle v. North West London Hospitals NHS Trust* UKEAT/0271/11 it was said at para. 14: 'It seems to us that there must be some circumstances (for example where a claimant is completely unrepresented) where in the face of an application for costs the Tribunal ought to raise the issue of means itself.' The EAT allowed an appeal against a whole costs award which was likely to exceed £100,000 where the issue of means had not been raised on the claimant's behalf, the claimant being represented by her partner who was also an experienced barrister. However, in an appeal heard before *Doyle* which was not drawn to the attention of the court in *Doyle*, HH Judge McMullen QC said that: 'The tribunal is required, if the matter is raised, to consider ability to pay. If the matter is not raised, there is no authority imposing a legal duty on the judge to raise the question, even with a litigant in person. I do not consider that there is (such a duty)' (*Osannaya v. Queen Mary University of London* UKEAT/0144/11, at para. 20).

In *Oni v. NHS Leicester City* (above) HH Judge Richardson, having declined **11.36** to resolve the conflict between *Doyle* and *Osonnaya* observed that whether or not it is obligatory to do so as a matter of law, *Doyle* shows the wisdom of the Tribunal raising, at the very least in a case where the costs are substantial, the question of means. However, on remitting the case back for reconsideration he did not order that the Tribunal should take into account the claimant's means, only that if the claimant wished it to do so she must complete county court Form EX 140 (statement of means) and lodge it prior to the rehearing, which suggests that he felt there was no freestanding obligation on the Tribunal to consider means if it was not raised. *Doyle* notwithstanding, the better view is that there is no obligation on a Tribunal to raise the issue of means if it is not raised by the paying party. If it is raised it must be dealt with in the reasons.

In *Jilley v. Solihuill Mental Health NHS Trust* (UKEAT/0584/06) Judge **11.37** Richardson said that the rule '...gives to the Tribunal a discretion whether to take into account the paying party's ability to pay. If it decided not to do so it should explain why. If it decides to take into account ability to pay, it should set out its findings about ability to pay, say what impact this has had on its decision whether to award costs or on the amount and explain why...A succinct statement of how the Tribunal has dealt with the matter and why it has done so are generally essential.' In *Purohit v. Hospira (UK) Ltd and anor* UKEAT/0182/12 Judge Richardson sent back for further consideration a decision on costs in which the Tribunal had said that it had not been told about any savings or investments which the claimant had when she had expressly said that she had none, on the grounds that the Tribunal had failed to 'properly' take into account the material on the claimant's means before it.

In *Howman v. The Queen Elizabeth Hospital Kings Lynn* UKEAT/0509/12 **11.38** per Keith J, the EAT set aside an order that the claimant pay the respondents costs on an indemnity basis on the grounds that the Tribunal had failed to take into account (that is, to fully think through the implications of the order in the light of) the claimant's inability to pay the costs (of which it seems the Tribunal was fully aware) and the effect of the order which would have required him to sell his home. 'In the final analysis, if the Tribunal decides to have regard to someone's ability to pay in deciding what order for costs it should make, what it needs to do is balance the need to compensate the litigant who has unreasonably been put to expense against the other litigants ability to pay. The latter does not necessarily trump the former, but it may do.' However, in *Vaughan v. London Borough of Lewisham* (UKEAT/0533/12) which was handed down before the judgment in *Howman,* it was held that there is nothing to prevent a Tribunal making a whole costs order against an impecunious party where the circumstances otherwise warrant it even where no deposit had been ordered. Whether to attempt to enforce the order now or later in the event of the party having a windfall is a matter for the receiving party.

11.39   The resolution to this conflict is to be found in *Arrowsmith v. Nottingham Trent University* [2012] ICR 159 CA, at para. 37 (to which Keith J referred in *Howman* but seemed to regard as not binding because *Jilley* had not been drawn to the Court's attention): 'the fact that [the employee's] ability to pay was...limited did not...require the Tribunal to assess a sum [for costs] that was confined to an amount that [the employee] could pay'.

11.40   In the absence of an express power in the Rules to do so, it would not be appropriate for a Tribunal to make the enforcement of an order for costs conditional on obtaining the leave of the Tribunal.

12

DELIVERY OF DOCUMENTS AND MISCELLANEOUS—RULES 85–93 AND 95–106

A. DELIVERY OF DOCUMENTS—RULES 85–92

1. Overview

12.01 Rules 85–90 replace in simpler language and more easily navigable form old r. 60 'Notices etc', in particular by splitting delivery to the Tribunal (r. 85) and delivery to parties (r. 86). Old r. 60(7) is omitted, presumably in the interests of saving costs. It required any application which might involve payment out of the National Insurance Fund (that is claims for monetary payments where the respondent was or might be insolvent) to be copied to the Secretary of State. It was only in relatively rare cases that the Secretary of State wished to intervene. Some new provisions are introduced concerning irregular service (r. 91) and copying correspondence sent to the Tribunal (r. 92).

2. Delivery to the Tribunal

12.02 Rule 85(1) says that documents 'may be delivered to the Tribunal' by three methods but this should be interpreted as meaning 'may only' be delivered by one of the methods identified, namely, by post, direct delivery, or 'electronic communication' (as defined in s. 15(1) of the Electronic Communications Act 2000 read with the Communications Act 2003). This is not the same as the methods which the Tribunal 'holds itself out' as being those by which it will receive documents (*Tyne & Wear Autistic Society v. Smith* [2005] IRLR 336; [2005] ICR 663 EAT). The Tribunal does not hold itself out as being willing to receive a document by means of a form of electronic communication which it does not possess. Rule 85(2) is introduced to enable Presidential practice directions to restrict the ways in which a claim form can be presented, necessitated principally to restrict presentation to those means by which the fee can also be paid or a remission application made. For further commentary on this issue see paras. 4.05–4.08. Rule 85(3) amplifies, but does not change, the effect of, old r. 60(3). The Tribunal can require a particular means of communication to be used or not used.

3. Delivery to parties

12.03 Rule 86(1) also begins 'documents may be delivered to a party' by a similar list of means plus personal service, but here the rule is not mandatory. Although r. 86 does not say so, it is subject to r. 91 ('irregular service') which enables the Tribunal to treat a document as delivered to a person by another means if satisfied that it or its substance has in fact come to the attention of that person. Rules 85 and 86 apply to delivery of documents by parties as well as the Tribunal. Rule 86(1)(d), which permits personal delivery, has what appears to be a drafting anomaly. It only permits personal service on a party 'if no representative has been named in the claim form or response' and only on representatives 'named in the claim form or response'. It therefore appears to preclude personal service on a party who originally named a representative but is no longer represented or on a representative who has been instructed since the claim or response was entered. Service in breach of the rule could however be cured by virtue of r. 91. A document can be served 'on the occasion of a hearing' on any person identified by the party as representing them at that hearing.

Rule 86(2) provides that where a document is sent by post or hand-delivered or **12.04** sent by means of electronic communication 'it shall be delivered to the address given in the claim form or response (which shall be the address of the party's representative, if one is named) or to a different address as notified in writing by the party in question'. This is therefore about sending documents to parties at the address which they have given, not which another party has given for them. However, although the rule does not appear to provide for it, it will be taken as requiring the claim form to be sent to the address for the respondent given on the claim form. There is, perhaps surprisingly, no express provision anywhere in the Rules to that effect. If a party has given both a postal address and an electronic address both may be used, unless the party specifies in writing that a particular address should or should not be used (r. 86(3)).

Rule 86(2) highlights the omission of an equivalent to old r. 60(4)(h)(ii) which **12.05** specifically provided for delivery to a party at 'any other known address or place of business in the United Kingdom, or, if the party is a corporate body, the body's registered or principal office in the United Kingdom' in cases where a notice sent to the address given by the other party was returned. It seems likely that no such provision was deemed necessary given the existing statutory requirements with regard to service on corporate bodies and the power to order substituted service generally (r. 89 see below at para. 12.08).

4. Delivery to non-parties

Rule 87 replaces old r. 60(4)(h)(i) with similar effect while introducing the concept **12.06** of a non-party having given in advance an address for service to the Tribunal. This is presumably intended to cover a situation where a non-party is seeking to become a party or to be allowed to participate in proceedings under r. 34. It may possibly (given that at the time they make the nomination they will not necessarily be a party) accommodate the practice of some regions in which regular respondents such as local authorities have nominated an address for service of all proceedings against them, irrespective of the address given on the claim form. In any event, there is nothing in the Rules to prohibit such a practice. Rule 87 appears to apply only to the Tribunal and not to other parties.

5. Special cases

12.07 Rule 88 sensibly replaces the lengthy list of addresses for the Secretary of State, the Law Officers, and the Counsel General of the Welsh Assembly given in old r.60(4)(a)–(f) to be used in cases where they are not parties, with a requirement for such addresses to be issued by practice direction.

6. Substituted service

12.08 Rule 89 replaces old r. 60(7) with some change of wording but not of effect. Whereas the old rule provided for substituted service 'in such manner as the President or Regional Employment Judge/Vice President may deem fit in any case he considers appropriate', r. 89 merely provides for it 'in such manner as appears appropriate'. Any case considered appropriate now becomes a case where no address for service in accordance with rr. 85–88 is known or it appears that service at such address is unlikely to come to the attention of the addressee.

12.09 The rule gives a very broad discretion and in consequence there is no warrant for importing into the rule the more restrictive provisions of CPR 6.15. In particular it seems clear that under r. 89 the President or Regional Employment Judge/Vice President may make such an order of their own initiative and indeed are much more likely to do so than on application. However, the wording of r. 89 suggests that, unlike CPR 6.15(2), in the Tribunal orders for substituted service can only be prospective, not retrospective. However, see r. 91 (para. 12.12 below) for something akin to a retrospective order.

7. Date of delivery

12.10 Rule 90 mirrors old r. 61(2) and adopts the usual time rules for presuming delivery. In the 'ordinary course of post' is a flexible concept which is not defined in the Rules. It is currently taken to mean two working days for first class letters and four for second. The rule applies to r. 85 as well as r. 86 which means deemed dates of delivery now apply to documents sent by post to the Tribunal 'unless the contrary is proved'. This is almost certainly new as old r. 61(2) was always taken in practice to apply only to documents sent by the Tribunal to parties although it did not expressly say so. There are worrying implications here, not least for Tribunal staff. A party seeking relief from sanction following non-compliance with an unless order may allege that their response to the order was posted so that by virtue of r. 90(a) it is deemed to have been received in time and in consequence there was no breach of the order. This may result in the other party seeking to call as witnesses members of the Tribunal staff in order to prove that it was not received.

12.11 There is no doubt that deemed delivery has no place in the concept of presentation of either claim or response: presentation is only achieved on actual receipt. Proof of posting at a time when the ordinary course of post should have ensured timeous receipt is of course an important consideration should the claim form eventually be received out of time and the question of whether it was reasonably practicable for it to have been presented in time arises.

8. Irregular service

Rule 91 is a new provision which sensibly permits the Tribunal to treat as validly delivered any document sent to a person in a manner which does not comply with rr. 86–88, if satisfied that the document 'or its substance' has in fact come to that person's attention. This is the nearest the Tribunal rules get to permitting substituted service retrospectively, but it falls some way short of such an order because of the need to be satisfied that the irregular service was in fact effective. It is only necessary for the 'substance' of the document to have come to the person's attention which means that service can have been effective even if the document itself only reaches a third party who communicates its substance to the intended recipient. 'Substance' presumably means the operative parts of the document e.g. the date time and place of a hearing. **12.12**

9. Correspondence with the Tribunal: copying to other parties

Rule 92 is essentially a new provision as the 2004 Rules only required 'applica- **12.13** tions in proceedings' to be copied, although the Tribunal routinely copied all correspondence received where this had not already been done by the party. It is very simple in operation, replicating none of the complexity and rigidity of old r. 11. The rule now extends to all communications sent to the Tribunal other than an application under r. 31 for a witness order. Although there is no express exemption from the general requirement to copy for any subsequent correspond- ence in connection with the application or the witness order itself if granted (or for correspondence challenging a refusal to grant an order), in practice the Tribunal has tended not to copy such correspondence to the other parties. The rule therefore seems likely to be interpreted as not requiring 'follow up' cor- respondence concerning an application for a witness order to be copied. In any event, the Tribunal may 'order' a departure from the requirement to copy any item of correspondence to all other parties 'where it considers it in the interests of justice to do so'. The word was originally 'permit' rather than order which was more apposite as the Tribunal will often be acting informally of its own initiative and it would be disproportionate to require a formal order to be issued each time a departure from the rule is allowed. This provision avoids the problem which would otherwise arise where one party makes an urgent application by email but the other party has not disclosed an email address. Although extremely unusual in Employment Tribunal proceedings, the last sentence of r. 92 would enable an *ex parte* application to be made for a case management order other than a wit- ness order in appropriate circumstances. Such an application would have to be supported by cogent reasons.

B. MISCELLANEOUS—RULES 93 AND 95–106

1. Overview

12.14 These rules (excluding r. 94 'national security proceedings' which is dealt with separately in Chapter 13) bring together subjects previously largely dealt with in rr. 51–59 and parts of r. 60 of the 2004 Rules. They also bring into the main body of the Rules, and apply them with minimum modification to, appeals against assessment to industrial training levy (para. 12.25), appeals against Health and Safety Act prohibition and improvement notices (paras. 12.27–12.31), and appeals against unlawful act notices (para. 12.32). In so doing fundamental changes are made to the procedure for levy appeals and controversial changes to the costs rule for Health and Safety Act appeals.

2. ACAS

12.15 Rule 93 replaces old r. 21 (with considerable amendment) and r. 2(2)(d). Whereas old r. 21 required copies of all documents, orders, judgments, written reasons, and notices to be sent to ACAS, r. 93(1)(a) requires only that a copy of the claim form and response be sent. The Tribunal has routinely copied at least most correspondence to ACAS and it is not clear whether this will now cease given the much narrower scope of r. 93. There is certainly no requirement for it under the Rules. Rule 93(2) gives the right to an ACAS representative to attend any preliminary hearing (subject to r. 50 'Privacy and restrictions on disclosure' and r. 94 'National security'). This gives a conciliator (and anyone else who could reasonably be regarded as representing ACAS) the right to attend a hearing such as a 'case management discussion' under r. 53(1)(a) which would otherwise be held in private.

3. Interim relief proceedings

12.16 Rule 95 follows old r. 18A in treating interim relief hearings as preliminary hearings to which rr. 53–56 apply. However it introduces a new restriction, that the Tribunal shall not hear oral evidence unless it directs otherwise. By virtue of r. 43, the use of the word 'oral' is presumably intended to indicate that documentary evidence may be adduced without the prior permission of the Tribunal but no witnesses may be called nor written witness statements tendered (as the witness would be liable to cross-examination and would therefore be giving oral evidence) without the permission of the Tribunal which, in order to avoid the risk of a postponement, should be obtained in advance of the hearing.

4. Proceedings involving the National Insurance Fund

Rule 96 repeats the effect of old r. 51. Although the Secretary of State is still **12.17** entitled to appear and be heard at any hearing which may involve a payment out of the NIF and be treated as a party to those proceedings, the absence of a provision similar to old r. 64(7) means that he will no longer be routinely notified of such proceedings.

5. Collective agreements

Rule 97 replaces with no changes of substance, old r. 52. By virtue of ss. 145 **12.18** and 148 of the Equality Act 2010 'collective agreement' has the meaning given in s. 178 of the Trade Union and Labour Relations (Consolidation) Act 1992.

6. Devolution issues

Rule 98 reproduces the effect of old r. 56 in simpler language avoiding repetition. **12.19** On being notified that a devolution issue arises, the Law Officers in Scotland and the Counsel General to the Welsh Assembly have fourteen days in which to notify the Tribunal that they wish to be treated as a party 'so far as the proceedings relate to the devolution issue'. The time-limit can be extended under r. 5.

7. Transfer of proceedings between Scotland and England and Wales

Rule 99 replicates the effect of old r. 57. However, neither rule accurately reflects **12.20** the practice of the Tribunal in that successive Presidents have reserved to themselves the making and granting of requests for transfer. Nonetheless a party seeking to transfer a case from one jurisdiction to the other should in the first instance apply to the Vice President if the case is proceeding in Scotland, or the Regional Employment Judge of the region in which it is proceeding in England or Wales. The Vice President or REJ may refuse the application but if minded to grant it must refer the file to their President with a request that it be transferred. Note that only claims which could have been started in either jurisdiction by virtue of r. 8(2) can be transferred under this rule. A claim presented in the wrong country must be rejected. Note also that if the transfer is to be done at the Tribunal's own initiative there is no requirement to give notice to the parties of the intention to transfer, a change brought about by the 2004 Rules.

8. References to the Court of Justice of the European Union

Rule 100 replaces old r. 58 with the references to the name and article number **12.21** of the governing treaty updated. It is not open to a party to make, or to require the Tribunal to make, a reference to the CJEU. Only the Tribunal may make a reference as a step in the proceedings to obtain the ruling of the Court on a question of European law, that ruling being binding on the Tribunal and on the courts of all Member States. It is considered good practice for the Tribunal to make such a reference if it appears that one is necessary rather than leave it to an appellate court. The procedure for making a reference is the subject of guidance issued periodically by the CJEU. The current guidance can be found in: 'Recommendations to National Courts and Tribunals in relation to the initiation of preliminary ruling proceedings', *Official Journal*, 2012/C 338/01.

9. Transfer of proceedings from a court

12.22 Rule 101 replaces old r. 59 with no change of effect. It applies the Tribunal's Rules of Procedure in their entirety to any proceedings transferred to the Tribunal from a Court. The only cases likely to be transferred are claims involving equal pay.

10. Vexatious litigants

12.23 Rule 102 replaces, in much simpler form, old r. 60(4). However, whereas under the old rule there was a mandatory requirement to send to the Attorney General or Lord Advocate certain documents relating to the Tribunal proceedings, r. 102 merely says that the Tribunal 'may' provide 'any information' or document requested. The Solicitor General is added to the Law Officers who may make the request.

11. Information to the Commission for Equality and Human Rights

12.24 Rule 103 replaces, again in much simpler form, old r. 61(8), (9) and (10). The rule is self-explanatory.

12. Levy appeals

12.25 Rule 104 applies the Rules of Procedure to appeals against assessments to levy under the Industrial Training Act 1982, subject to the modification that references to a claim and claimant are to be read as references to a levy appeal and to the appellant in such an appeal. Under the 2004 Rules levy appeals had their own discrete rules regime in Schedule 3. The most radical departures from a procedure which has remained unchanged since the inception of Employment (then Industrial) Tribunals under the Industrial Training Act 1964 are that such appeals are now to be presented direct to the Tribunal rather than sent in the first instance to the Industry Training Board which made the assessment to training levy in question, and the Board is now required to enter a response to the appeal. If the Board should fail to do so r. 21 would apply creating the possibility of an appeal succeeding by default. It is not clear to what extent if at all the Industry Training Boards are aware of and prepared for this change and it seems very likely that, at least in the short term, notices of assessment to levy will be issued with out of date information about how to appeal. A further change is that whereas under the 2004 Rules if the Board required further information about the appeal it sent a notice to the appellant who was obliged to reply within twenty-one days, under the 2013 Rules the Board would have to apply for a case management order under r. 29.

The amount of the levy and the time-limit for appealing against an assessment **12.26** to levy are laid down in annual statutory instruments made under s. 12(6) of the 1982 Act. The time-limit is normally one month from the date of service of the notice which, unless the contrary is proved, is in the normal course of post i.e. two days after posting by first class post or four days by second class post. There is no longer a specific form for making a levy appeal. Formerly, the notice of appeal had to be 'substantially in accordance with' the form annexed to the Rules. No such form is annexed to the 2013 Rules and by virtue of reg. 12(2)(b) it is not necessary to use the prescribed form. A fee is payable (Type A) by the appellant on presenting the appeal and when the appeal is listed for hearing.

13. Health and Safety Act notice appeals

(a) *Fees*

It is uncontroversial that a State may, in appropriate circumstances and given **12.27** appropriate safeguards, impose a fee on a citizen seeking access to the courts to exercise a civil right. It is unheard of for a State to require a citizen the subject of criminal charges to pay a fee if he wishes to defend himself against those charges in a public court. The status of a citizen wishing to appeal against an improvement notice issued under s. 21 or a prohibition notice issued under s. 22 of the Health and Safety at Work etc Act 1974 seems closer to the latter than the former given the penal nature of the notices—the imposition by agents of the State of a sanction which is likely to have, possibly very significant, financial implications for a business if unappealed—and the criminal consequences of disobeying such a notice (up to two years' imprisonment and or an unlimited fine if convicted on indictment: 1974 Act, Schedule 3A). It is therefore a matter of considerable surprise to find that appeals against such notices appear in Table 2 of Schedule 2 to the Fees Order meaning that the appellant is required to pay both a Type A 'claim' fee and a hearing fee. Whether this requirement would survive a challenge on Human Rights grounds under Art. 6 of the Convention (or possibly Art. 1 of the First Protocol) must be a matter of some doubt. Further discussion of this possibility lies outside the scope of this volume however.

(b) *Costs*

The difficulties for appellants created by the requirement to pay a fee to gain **12.28** access to the Tribunal are compounded by a change in the costs rules applying to Health and Safety appeals. This change has been made as a result of DBIS policy. The Appeals against Improvement and Prohibition Notices Rules formed Schedule 4 to the 2004 Rules. The costs regime was r. 10. Rule 10(1) provided only that: 'A Tribunal...may make an order...that a party...make a payment in respect of the costs incurred by another party'. The remainder of the rule mirrored the corresponding provisions of the general costs regime. Thus, in the case of Health and Safety Act appeals there were no threshold requirements (e.g. that the position of the appellant or respondent was misconceived) which had to be met for an order to be made. Although the rule meant that costs were at the discretion of the Tribunal, in practice they tended to follow the event.

12.29 It is understood that the reason for the change, which makes the costs regime of Schedule 1 (discussed above at paras. 11.03–11.25) also the costs regime for Health and Safety Act appeals, is that DBIS can see no difference from a policy point of view between such appeals and more conventional Tribunal proceedings. This is little short of astonishing. A successful appellant in a Health and Safety Act appeal will now not only be required to pay a fee for the privilege of defending themselves against the notice, they will be unable to recover their legal costs unless the Tribunal is satisfied (very roughly) that no reasonable Inspector would have issued the notice in the first place. For the reasons discussed in the preceding paragraph this cannot be right. The fact that the Tribunal could order the repayment of the claim and hearing fees under r. 76(4) if the appeal was successful is likely to be of little consolation.

(c) *Other provisions*

12.30 As required by s. 24(2) of the 1974 Act, r. 105(1) creates the time-limit for presenting an appeal. It is twenty-one days from the date of service of the notice on the appellant, which may be extended by such further period as the Tribunal considers reasonable if it is satisfied that it was not reasonably practicable for the appeal to have been presented in time. The date of service is two days after posting if the notice was sent by first class post or four days if by second class post. There are now no other specific Health and Safety Act notice appeal rules, none being required as the rules in Schedule 4 to the 2004 Rules (apart from the costs rule) replicated provisions in the Act or in the main Rules of Procedure. Rule 105(2) provides that, subject to references to claim and claimant being read as references to an appeal and an appellant in an appeal and to the respondent as being the inspector who issued the notice, the entirety of the Rules now applies to such appeals.

12.31 It is not necessary to use the prescribed form to commence a Health and Safety Act notice appeal (reg. 12(2)(b)). There is no longer a specific requirement for the notice of appeal to include the date of the notice being appealed against, the address of the premises concerned, the details of the requirements or directions appealed against and the grounds for the appeal, but a notice of appeal which lacked such information would be at risk of rejection under r. 12 on the grounds that it was in a form which could not sensibly be responded to. The respondent must now enter a response to the appeal (as with the notice of appeal it is not necessary for the prescribed form to be used) and if they fail to do so the possibility of the appeal being disposed of by default under r. 21 arises.

Note, as discussed in para. 10.33, it no longer appears to be possible to apply for a reconsideration of a decision to reject or allow an application to suspend the operation of a prohibition notice pending the final appeal under s. 24(3)(b) of the 1974 Act.

14. Unlawful act notice appeals

Rule 106 applies the Rules of Procedure to appeals against unlawful act notices, **12.32** that is, notices issued under s. 21 of the Equality Act 2006, varied only so that references in the Rules to a claim and claimant shall be read as references to an appeal and an appellant in an appeal, and references to the respondent shall be read as references to the Commission for Equality and Human Rights. In the 2004 Rules such appeals had their own Rules of Procedure in Schedule 5 which disapplied certain provisions of Schedule 1 in relation to them. While many of the formerly disapplied provisions will be inappropriate to unlawful act notice appeals, one change of potential significance is that r. 50 ('Privacy and restrictions on disclosure') now applies to them whereas old r. 50 ('Restricted reporting orders') did not.

Rule 3 of old Schedule 5 included in the minimum requirements for a notice of **12.33** appeal against an unlawful act notice, details of the requirements which are being appealed and the grounds for the appeal. While these are no longer required as such, by virtue of r. 10(1)(b) there can be little doubt that any notice of appeal which does not include at least the former will be rejected under r. 12(1)(b) on the grounds that it cannot sensibly be responded to or as an abuse of process. By virtue of reg. 12(2)(b) it is not necessary to use the prescribed claim form as the notice of appeal. The Commission will now be required to enter a formal response to the notice of appeal (although not necessarily on the prescribed form) and r. 21 applies if they neglect to do so.

13

NATIONAL SECURITY PROCEEDINGS[1]—RULE 94 AND SCHEDULE 2

A. OVERVIEW

Rule 94 and Schedule 2 relating to national security cases have been brought **13.01** into line with the over all style of the new Rules. The changes also reflect developments in the handling of national security cases in the civil courts and tribunals generally since Employment Tribunal rules on national security first appeared in 2001, and the case law relating to the conduct of such cases. The new rules were drafted by members of the Tribunal's judiciary experienced in the handling of such cases, civil servants, and members of the security services. In one respect, discussed below, the rules do not reflect established practice and it seems likely that established practice will prevail (see para. 13.11 below). It should be noted that r. 94 and Schedule 2 do not provide a self-contained regime

---

[1] With acknowledgement and thanks to Judge Elizabeth Potter, REJ of the London Central region, for contributing the material for this chapter.

for national security proceedings. As r. 1(1) of Schedule 2 makes clear, the rules in that Schedule apply so as to modify the Rules of Procedure in Schedule 1 in proceedings where a direction is given under r. 94(1) or an order made under r. 94(2). Rule 94(10) requires the Tribunal to ensure that in exercising its functions, information is not disclosed contrary to the interests of national security.

B. RULE 94

1. Ministerial direction

13.02 The basic structure of r. 94 mirrors the old r. 54. Under r. 94(1) a Minister may, in respect of particular Crown employment proceedings, where he considers 'it would be expedient in the interests of national security', direct a Tribunal to:

(a) conduct all or part of the proceedings in private;

(b) exclude a person from all or part of the proceedings;

(c) take steps to conceal the identity of a witness to the proceedings.

Such a direction may be made whether or not the Minister is a party to the proceedings (r. 94(8)). For the meaning of 'Crown employment proceedings' see s. 10(8) ETA. 'Minister' means 'Minister of the Crown' (r. 1(1)).

Under old r. 54 only a claimant or the claimant's representative could be excluded from all or part of the proceedings. Any person can now be excluded under r. 94(1)(b). This reflects the possibility that a respondent or its representative may need to be excluded, for example in a situation where the claimant is doing work that is security sensitive under a government contract and the management of the respondent and/or its legal advisers are not security vetted to deal with sensitive aspects of the claimant's work.

2. Tribunal order

13.03 Rule 94(2) enables a Tribunal, where it considers it expedient in the interests of national security in respect of any proceedings, to order anything which can be directed by a Minister to be done under r. 94(1). It may also order a person not to disclose any documents or their contents which have been provided for the purposes of the proceedings to any other person, i.e. to all other persons, or to all other persons subject to specified exceptions. A Minister may choose to ask the Tribunal to make an order under r. 94(2) whether or not the Minister is a party to the proceedings (r. 94(4)), rather than making a direction under r. 94(1). When considering such an application the Tribunal may consider material provided to it by the Minister or a party without providing copies to the other parties (r. 94(3); and see para. 13.06) and may make any order which could be made under r. 94(1) for the proceedings generally in respect of the application (r. 94(5)). Rule 94(2) retains the fundamental obligation and safeguard set out in old r. 54(2) that any order made must be kept under review. In *Farooq v. Commissioner of Police of the Metropolis* (UKEAT/0542/07) it was said that, in order to give grounds for review or reconsideration there had to be a change in circumstances or for it to become apparent that there had been a failure to consider some fundamental point of law.

If the Tribunal refuses an application under r. 94(2) it may, if it considers **13.04** it expedient in the interests of national security, by order take steps to keep secret all or part of its written reasons and the reasons will not, in any event, be entered in the register (r. 94(9) and Schedule 2, para. 6(2)).

3. Circumstances warranting an order

The meaning of the words 'expedient in the interests of national security' **13.05** was considered in *AB v. Secretary of State for Defence* [2010] ICR 54 EAT which emphasized that any exception to the strong rule of open justice has to be cogently justified. The particular nature of 'the interests of national security' does however mean that where real risks to the lives of members of the armed forces or the security services or others are established, those risks must weigh heavily in the balance against the principle of open justice. The case cautions against the making of orders for private hearings too early in proceedings: '...it must be better in principle to decide whether to make an order at all only at the stage where the tribunal is in a position to do so on full information...'. Therefore in practice an application under r. 94(2) at an early stage of the proceedings may result only in an initial order limited to the preparatory phase of the case relating to the claim and response and any further information about either disclosure and the appointment of a special advocate. Whether parts of the full hearing are to be in private can be determined closer to the hearing when the issues and evidence are more clearly understood and when the special advocate (see paras. 13.09–13.14 below) has been appointed to represent the interests of the excluded person.

4. Delayed submission and copying of response

Rules 94(6) and (7) reflect the fact that frequently a respondent or Minister seeks **13.06** a national security order as a pre-condition for the presentation of a detailed response. Therefore where a Minister has made a direction under r. 94(1) or an application under r. 94(4) for an order under r. 94(2) for a person to be excluded from all or part of the proceedings, the Tribunal is not to send a copy of the response to that person pending the decision on the application (r. 94(6)) and the Minister may apply for an extension of the twenty-eight day time-limit under r. 16 for presenting a response (r. 94(7)).

5. Preliminary judicial consideration of sensitive material

13.07 Rule 94(3) is a new provision enabling an Employment Judge to consider material, without providing it to any other person, for the purposes of deciding whether to make an order under r. 94(2). A respondent, or a Minister if not a party, may choose to provide to the Employment Judge security sensitive material to demonstrate the necessity of an order. The emphasis in *AB v. Secretary of State for Defence* (above) on the need for cogent justification for any exception to the rule of open justice makes it imperative that the Judge can be shown sensitive relevant material before deciding whether to make an order. It would be inconsistent with the national security interest for that material to be provided to the person in respect of whom an exclusion order is being sought where the thrust of the application is that the nature of such material is the justification for the application.

C. SCHEDULE 2

1. Witness orders and disclosure of documents

13.08 Rules 31 and 32 are modified by r. 3 of Schedule 2. Where a person has been excluded under either r. 94(1) or (2) and the Tribunal is considering whether to make an order for disclosure of documents or a witness order, a Minister, whether or not a party to the proceedings, may object to the order being made, or, if already made, may apply to have it set aside, and the Minister's objection or application shall be heard in private.

2. The special advocate

(a) *Background*

13.09 At para. 2.38 of the Green Paper on Justice and Security of October 2011[2] the government made a commitment to bring the Employment Tribunal Rules into line with other special advocate regimes which had been introduced since the Employment Tribunal Rules of Procedure 2001. Comparison with the Special Immigration and Asylum Commission (Procedure) Rules 2003[3] and the Civil Procedure (Amendment No. 3) Rules 2011[4] relating to proceedings under the Terrorism Prevention and Investigation Measures Act 2011 shows the consistent approach being adopted across courts and tribunals to the use of special advocates. Appellate decisions under those Rules are therefore likely to be informative of the correct approach under Schedule 2.

---

[2] Cm 8194.
[3] SI 2003/1034.
[4] SI 2011/2970 (L. 21).

(b) *Appointment of the special advocate*

The appointment of a special advocate in Employment Tribunal proceedings **13.10** is not automatic. It is not uncommon in a national security case for the claimant and their representatives to be people who have been vetted for the purposes of their employment and who are as fully aware of the need to protect the interests of national security as the respondent. In such circumstances a private hearing will be in the interests of national security but there is no need for any party or representative to be excluded from the hearing or from sight of any of the evidence. However, if a direction is given under r. 94(1), or an order made under r. 94(2) to exclude 'a party' from all or part of the proceedings, r. 4(1) of Schedule 2 requires the Tribunal to inform the Attorney General in England and Wales or the Advocate General in Scotland who has the discretion to appoint a special advocate to represent the interests of the excluded person. It seems from r. 4(2) that the term 'a party' is here used loosely as by virtue of r. 4(2)(a) a special advocate may be appointed if 'a person's representative is excluded'.

(c) *Role of the special advocate*

Although r. 2 of Schedule 2 provides that the Tribunal shall not send a copy of **13.11** the response to any excluded person, it is expected that the principle of open justice will result in the continuation of the current practice of having two versions of the response where a person has been excluded. An open version which deals with aspects of the case that can be disclosed to them will be sent to the excluded person. A closed version will be provided to the special advocate representing the interests of the excluded person, dealing with the parts of the proceedings from which that person is excluded. Rule 4(10) of Schedule 2 provides that the term 'party' in certain of the rules in Schedule 1 shall include a special advocate appointed in the proceedings.

As provided in r. 4(5) of Schedule 2, the special advocate may communi- **13.12** cate directly or indirectly with the excluded person at any time before receiving 'closed material' from a Minister. 'Closed material' is material which a Minister believes to have national security sensitivity which makes it inappropriate for the excluded person to see. It may include the closed response to a claim, documents, and witness evidence. At the point the special advocate is shown that material he is said to have gone into 'closed'. His ability to communicate about the proceedings is tightly controlled from that point on. Rule 4(6) provides that after receiving the closed material the special advocate must not communicate with any person about any matter connected with the proceedings, except in accordance with paras. (7) or (9) or an order of the Tribunal. The special advocate therefore has only a limited initial opportunity after his appointment to talk to the person who is to be excluded and to understand their case and evidence. He or she may not thereafter take instructions on the closed material.

Rule 4(7) provides that after 'going into closed' the special advocate can **13.13** communicate freely about the proceedings with the Tribunal, the Minister or his representative, the relevant Law Officer and any other person, except for the excluded person or his representative, with whom it is necessary for administrative purposes to communicate about matters not connected with the substance of the proceedings. However if the special advocate wishes to communicate with the excluded person or with any other person outside the terms of r. 4(7), he has to apply to the Tribunal under r. 4(8) to authorize him to do so. If such an application is made, the Tribunal is obliged to notify the Minister and the Minister may, within a period specified by the Tribunal, give notice of objection to the proposed communication. Rule 4(9) further provides that once the special advocate has received closed material the excluded person may only communicate with the special advocate in writing and the special advocate may not reply beyond sending a written acknowledgement of receipt to 'the legal representative', presumably the excluded person's legal representative.

13.14   These detailed provisions in relation to communication with the special advocate reflect the concerns of Mitting J in *Rahman v. (1) Commissioner of Police of the Metropolis, (2) Secretary of State for the Home Department* (UKEATPA/00 76/09: UKEAT/0125/10) where it was noted that the provisions of Schedule 2 in the 2004 Employment Tribunal Rules were out of line with Rules of Procedure regarding special advocates in other courts and tribunals, which prohibited any communication with the excluded person without the express permission of the court. Mitting J suggested that the fact that Schedule 2 was the first closed material procedure to be approved by Parliament meant that it was less satisfactory than those that had come later and he struggled to interpret the Schedule to give substantially the same degree of protection for a respondent as 'standard' closed procedure rules 'to avoid what Parliament had considered to be the undesirable consequence of leaving it to the special advocate alone to make a judgment about what he may communicate to an excluded person after he has seen closed material'.

3. Hearings

13.15   Rule 5 of Schedule 2 emphasizes that the norm in a national security case is open justice, a hearing in public. Orders under r. 50 or r. 94 of Schedule 1 may provide for some or all of the hearing to be in private. However *AB v. Secretary of State for Defence* (see above) demonstrates in practical terms the narrow scope to be given to privacy on national security grounds. In that case the EAT concluded that it was expedient in the interests of national security for any part of the hearing which dealt with the claimant's service overseas as a member of a military unit to be held in private because of the risk of operational prejudice. However, so far as possible, his treatment following his return to the United Kingdom should be dealt with in public.

4. Reasons in National Security proceedings

Where there has been an order made under r. 94 of Schedule 1, special pro-   **13.16**
visions exist in relation to the terms of the written reasons produced by the
Tribunal and their entry on the Register, which distinguish r. 94 cases from
hearings conducted in private under r. 50. Under r. 6 of Schedule 2, the written reasons given in accordance with r. 62 of Schedule 1 must first be sent
by the Tribunal to the relevant Minister. A new provision (r. 6(1)) is that the
Minister is allowed a period of forty-two days to decide whether it is expedient in the interests of national security to make a direction under r. 6(3) that
the reasons shall not be disclosed to specified persons either at all or only
in an edited format to be prepared by the Tribunal but omitting specified
information. Under r. 6(5) where a Minister has directed that there should be
edited reasons, the edited reasons are entered on the Register. However under
r.6(6) where the Minister has directed that no reasons be sent to specified persons then no reasons will be entered on the Register but the reasons are to be
sent to the persons identified in r. 6(7).

14

FEES

A. OVERVIEW

The drafting of the Fees Order (with which the Underhill group was not involved) **14.01** leaves much to be desired.[1] There are many gaps and anomalies and the remission provisions have numerous ambiguities and uncertainties. The remission regime is likely to be short-lived given the current consultation on a new fees remission scheme which will apply across all civil courts and fee-paying tribunals. The relationship between the Fees Order and the Rules is also problematic, particularly rr. 11 and 40, neither of which were drafted by the Underhill group. These are

---

[1] It was conceded by the government in the Scottish judicial review proceedings brought by Fox and Partners (see para 1.03) that the designation of equal pay claims as Type A claims was a drafting error.

discussed at paras. 4.18 and 7.91 respectively. While the main commentary on the Fees Order is in this chapter, further commentary is at para 1.03 and elsewhere where appropriate throughout the book (see TABLE OF LEGISLATION). The Fees Order itself is at Appendix 2.

14.02   Whether the gaps in the Fees Order are also due to drafting defects or a matter of government policy is moot, but given the nature of at least some of them, the latter seems the more likely explanation. The following are perhaps the most important omissions; others are dealt with in the commentary below:

- Unlike the county court, there is no mechanism[2] for appealing a decision to reject a remission application or only partially reduce a fee. It is possible that r. 40(5) of the Rules of Procedure may allow a challenge in the nature of an appeal to be made to all fees other than claim fees, but that too is poorly drafted and its ambit and intentions are uncertain (see paras. 7.95 and 7.96). Anecdotally, errors in the county courts when dealing with remission applications are not infrequent.

- Unlike the county court, there is no 'tapering' provision reducing the claim or hearing fee where the amount claimed is small. In consequence in some purely monetary claims the claim fee alone will exceed the amount claimed. There is a serious risk that this will deter some claimants from bringing claims, which would be an infringement of the principle of effectiveness where the claim derives from EU law, e.g. any claim under the Working Time Regulations 1998. To the extent that fees for bringing an equivalent claim in the county court or the sheriff court are lower, the EU law principle of equivalence would also appear to be infringed.

- There is no provision for return of the claim fee where the claim is rejected, even where the reason for rejection is want of jurisdiction or because the claimant lacks entitlement to bring the claim, despite the fact that the claim in such circumstances is effectively a nullity. This objection is not met, even partially, by the adoption of Standard Operating Procedures (SOPs) which, as a matter of administrative discretion,[3] authorize the return of the fee in some limited circumstances—where the claim is rejected for not being on the prescribed form or for not including the minimum information. SOPs have no force of law and are not public documents.

- There is no provision dealing with amendments to claim forms which add a Type B claim to existing Type A claims.

- The period within which a fee must be paid following a notice to pay is not dealt with in the Order (art. 4 and Schedule 3, para. 9(2)). Such a notice will be sent in the case of all applications where a fee is payable, with a notice of

---

[2] Either in the Order itself or the SOPs (see footnote 3) which guide staff on its implementation
[3] SOPs are signed off by the Jurisdictional Board or the Fees Project Board of which both Presidents are members.

hearing, or where a remission application is unsuccessful or only partially successful. The period will be set by the SOPs at twenty-one days in all cases. The Order does not provide any mechanism to apply for an extension of time and nor do the SOPs. Although it is understood that the administration takes the contrary view, r. 5 of the Rules of Procedure does not offer any assistance, as the twenty-one-day period is not a time-limit specified by the Rules. The only remedy seems to be an application under r. 40(5) to reinstate the claim or response after it has been automatically dismissed if the fee is not paid in time.

- Nothing is said about claims re-submitted after rejection. By virtue of art. 4(1) (a) of the Order a second fee would appear to be payable in such cases.

- Nothing is said about claims accepted upon reconsideration. Where the reason for acceptance is that the original decision to reject was wrong, it would seem that no further fee could be payable. The position is less clear in cases where the original decision was correct but the defect has since been rectified. However, it still seems that no further fee should be payable.

- There is no provision for a refund or partial refund of a hearing fee if a claim is withdrawn or settled which removes an incentive to settle or withdraw a weak claim. It is understood that the SOPs will not provide for the refund of the difference between a Type B hearing fee and a Type A hearing fee if the claim contains complaints of both types but the Type B claim is withdrawn before the hearing, but after the hearing fee has been paid.

- There is no provision for the refund of a hearing fee or for the requirement to pay a hearing fee being suspended or cancelled where a judgment is or may be issued under r. 21. This is a particular problem where the claim is of a type which is listed for hearing on receipt of the claim form, e.g. pure unfair dismissal claims and monetary claims. There will inevitably be cases where the claimant is sent the notice to pay the hearing fee and the compliance date is either shortly before or shortly after the twenty-eight day period for entering the response. If the fee is payable shortly before the end of the twenty-eight day period the claimant would appear to have no option but to pay it and to ask the Tribunal to order the respondent to re-pay it as part of the r. 21 judgment. Given the relatively low success rate of claimants seeking to enforce Tribunal awards, many claimants will be throwing good money after bad. Where the time for payment expires after the twenty-eight day period and no response has been presented or the claim is admitted, the need for a hearing ceases (or is likely to cease) yet claimants will still have to pay the hearing fee or their claim will be dismissed under r. 40(2) (a). There is a simple solution to this problem, namely for the administration not to send the notice to pay the hearing fee until a response form resisting the claim is received, but it is understood that the SOPs do not address this. Moreover, given the delay in some Tribunal offices in dealing with correspondence, there would be many instances in purely monetary claims where significantly fewer than twenty-one days are left between the response being processed and the hearing date—meaning that the fee might not be paid before the date fixed for the hearing: so the hearing would have to be postponed.

14.03   Although not an omission as such, there appears to be no recognition of the problems likely to be caused to claimants faced with having to comply with a three-month time-limit for presenting a claim. Such claimants must complete the lengthy (80-page) and notoriously complicated county court remission form which, it is understood, the Tribunal will adopt (although the Order gives no warrant for its adoption). Given that under the remission regime the party's disposable income is to be assessed in the month in which the fee becomes payable, claimants who receive significant termination payments shortly after a month's end will want to wait at least a month before applying to enable their financial position to stabilize, particularly if they are unable to apply for a qualifying benefit (see para. 14.20) immediately. A significant increase in satellite litigation, specifically preliminary hearings, to deal with out-of-time points where the claimant has been unable to complete the remission form and obtain the necessary documentary evidence in good time; or where, to have completed it in time would have been seriously disadvantageous to the claimant in terms of entitlement to remission, seems inevitable.

B. INTERPRETATION

1. 'Fee group'

14.04 The importance of a fee group is that, effectively, lower rates of fees are prescribed for a group than if individual members of the group were each required to pay separate fees. Because of the way this term is defined in art. 2, it is likely to be of relatively limited applicability. In relation to an issue fee, the group means those persons named as claimants in the claim form. In relation to a hearing fee, it is the group of persons each of whom was named in the claim form and is also 'named as claimant' in the notice of hearing. The major problem is with the hearing fee. Apart from the logistical anomaly that in practice only the lead claimant is named in the notice of hearing (so the title of the proceedings might be 'Smith and others': which suggests that, strictly speaking, a fee group can never exist for this purpose)— it would appear that where claims are consolidated after receipt of the claim forms, the resultant agglomeration is not a fee group. In consequence, unless the lead cases mechanism of r. 36 is applied to the consolidated claims, each claimant in the consolidated group will have to pay a separate hearing fee or submit a separate remission application. No provision is made for lead cases as such although in practice the person designated as the lead claimant would no doubt look to other claimants in the group for a contribution to any fees incurred.

2. 'Final hearing'

Despite the fact that this term is defined in r. 57, that definition is not expressly **14.05** adopted. Nonetheless it seems reasonably clear that the meaning in the Fees Order is the same as in the Rules and in consequence, no fee is payable for a preliminary hearing as that hearing only 'may' rather than 'will' determine liability. A concession to this effect was made in the Scottish judicial review proceedings.

C. FEES

1. Fee-charging occasions

A fee is payable in respect of a claim where the claim form was presented on **14.06** or after 29 July 2013, the date on which the Fees Order came into force (arts. 1 and 15) or in the case of an appeal to the EAT where the notice of appeal was received after that date (art. 16), on the following occasions:

- on presentation of a claim form (which includes notices of appeal presented to the Tribunal: art. 4(1)(a));
- on the date specified in a notice for securing the final hearing of the claim or appeal (art. 4(1)(b));
- on making one of the applications listed in column 1 of Schedule 1 (art. 4(2));
- by the respondent on the date specified in a notice in respect of a judicial mediation (art. 4(3));
- on a date specified in a notice following the lodging of an appeal to the EAT (art. 13). Notwithstanding the wording of art. 13, the government conceded during the Scottish judicial review proceedings that only one fee is payable irrespective of the number of appellants; and
- on a date specified in a notice for securing the oral hearing at which the appeal is to be finally disposed of (art. 14).

Four kinds of application carry a fee: **14.07**

- an application for a reconsideration of a default judgment;
- an application for a reconsideration of a judgment following a final hearing;
- an application to dismiss a claim following withdrawal; and
- an application to present an employer's contract claim 'as part of the response to the employee's contract claim'.

None are without difficulty.

(a) *Default judgments*

14.08 The phrase, and seemingly the concept, 'default judgment' are absent from the 2013 Rules of Procedure and there is no separate regime for reconsideration of a judgment under r. 21. It is suggested that the Order has to be construed strictly as it is a taxing provision by nature, and in consequence a strong case can be made that no fee is chargeable for the reconsideration of a judgment made under r. 21 which, as discussed at paras. 5.17–5.22 seems to provide for something falling rather short of the default judgment provision (old r. 8) in the 2004 Rules.

(b) *Judgment following a final hearing*

14.09 There is no provision for the payment of a fee for the reconsideration of a judgment following a preliminary hearing even if in consequence of that hearing the claim is at an end. There is no provision for the fee to be refunded in the event that an application to reconsider a judgment following a final hearing is successful on the grounds that there was either an administrative or judicial error involved in the judgment which has been set aside or varied. It seems wrong in principle for either party to have to bear the cost of the reconsideration application if, for example, the claim had been dismissed at the original hearing in the absence of the claimant but it was not discovered until after the application fee had been paid that the notice of hearing had been incorrectly addressed.

(c) *Applications to dismiss following withdrawal*

14.10 Such an application may not be possible under the Rules! See para. 9.13 for further commentary.

(d) *Employer's contract claims*

14.11 Strictly interpreted, this provision suggests that the fee is only payable where the employer's contract claim is included in the response. While r. 23 appears to impose as a mandatory requirement that such a claim be included in the employer's response, as discussed at paras. 5.32 and 5.33, it is very likely that in some, possibly limited, circumstances such a claim may legitimately be brought at a later date. The question then arises whether it is made as part of the response. The answer is probably 'yes', as the application to bring the claim after the response has been presented would be by way of an application to amend the response to include the employer's contract claim. There is an obvious asymmetry in play here and there is no immediately apparent reason why an employer's contract claim should not be treated in the same way as the employee's contract claim with the employer being required to pay the fee on presentation. There would be no question of the response being rejected if the fee was not paid, only the employer's contract claim.

2. Hearing fee anomalies

(a) *Remedy hearings under r. 21*

Strictly speaking this is not an anomaly but it seems wrong in principal for a **14.12** claimant to have to pay a full hearing fee for a remedy hearing under r. 21, both because such hearings are inevitably short and because of the risk that the claimant will be unable to enforce the subsequent judgment. It is to be hoped that Judges will use the alternative option of asking a claimant to clarify the amount of a monetary claim, or provide justification for such parts of it as need justifying, as a paper exercise, with hearings being used only as a last resort or where the claim is more in the nature of one for damages such as an unfair dismissal or a discrimination claim. But in these latter cases, where appropriate, particularizing the remedy sought in the claim form and restricting the claim to that amount would also avoid the need for a remedy hearing.

(b) *Costs hearings*

Where a claimant withdraws a claim and the respondent seeks a costs hearing, **14.13** who is responsible for the hearing fee? If a fee for the final hearing has already been paid there would appear to be no difficulty as the original hearing (or a postponement of it) would become the costs hearing. But if no fee has been paid there is no power under the Fees Order to ask the respondent to pay a hearing fee—art. 4(1)(b) makes it clear that the claimant is responsible for any hearing fee. It is highly unlikely that any claimant is going to pay a fee for such a costs hearing and without a fee there can be no hearing. This is recognized by the administration as a lacuna in the Order and the approach likely to be adopted is to treat the situation as an exceptional circumstance for the purposes of para. 8 of Schedule 3 to the Order and for the fee to be waived. Whether this is to be a standing arrangement or only following an application by the respondent in a particular case is unclear. What is clear is that there is no power to charge the respondent.

(c) *Employer's contract claims*

Exactly the same problem appears to arise if the claimant withdraws the claim **14.14** before the hearing fee has been paid but an employer's contract claim is outstanding and the employer wishes to pursue it to a hearing. In practice it is likely that the employer will have to apply for a hearing together with a waiver of the fee under para. 8 of Schedule 3. In the event that the waiver application is refused the employer would appear to have no mechanism for securing a hearing and as the employer's contract claim is treated in at least some respects as a claim for the purposes of the Rules, to withdraw it would risk triggering the automatic dismissal of the claim under r. 52 thereby creating a cause of action estoppel preventing the respondent from pursuing the claim elsewhere (see Chapter 9 for further commentary).

(d) *Delaying payment*

14.15 It is likely that there will be circumstances in which the claimant wishes to delay paying the hearing fee for perfectly sensible reasons such as that settlement seems likely or they may be about to obtain employment which changes their expectations about the value of the claim. The administration's view is that the claimant can apply for an extension of time for payment which will be considered by a Judge under r. 5 or r. 41. That seems clearly wrong. Rule 5 only applies to time-limits 'specified in these Rules [that is the Rules of Procedure] or in any decision'. Even if the administration's view that the notice to pay provisions envisage a two-stage process, the second being in effect an 'unless' notice under r. 40(1), is correct (see paras. 7.92 and 7.93), the time for payment is fixed neither by the Rules nor the Order but by administrative decision as part of the SOPs. It is therefore not amenable to r. 5. The general power for the Tribunal to regulate its own procedure in r. 41 appears to be limited to hearings (see paras. 8.04–8.06). There is therefore apparently no mechanism available for solving this problem. However, a solution, albeit a rather unsatisfactory one, may be available because of another part of the SOPs. If an application to postpone a hearing is made and granted before the time for payment expires, the notice to pay will be rescinded. But this has two disadvantages: the respondent will have the right to object to the application (which tactically they may wish to do in order to apply pressure to settle); and if the settlement negotiations fail, the hearing date has been lost which might lead to a delay of many months before the case can be heard.

3. The amount

14.16 There are two levels of fee, Type A claims and Type B claims. Type A claims are those listed in Table 2 of Schedule 2: Type B claims are everything else over which the Tribunal has jurisdiction (arts. 6 and 7). Type B fees are higher (see Schedule 1 for fees payable for applications and Table 3 of Schedule 2 for claim and hearing fees in the case of single claimants or Table 4 in the case of fee groups). Complaints of unfair dismissal and all complaints of discrimination[4] (that is of less favourable treatment) in its broad, non-technical sense, are Type B claims. Irrespective of the number of complaints in a claim form, only one fee is payable, the Type A fee if all complaints are of Type A, the Type B fee if any of the complaints are of Type B (arts. 9 and 11(2)). The amount payable by a fee group must not exceed the amount of the fee which the group collectively would have to pay as single claimants after taking account of any member of the group entitled to remission (art. 10). This appears to mean that if in a fee group of ten, nine are entitled to full remission, the fee payable on presentation of a Type A claim becomes £160 rather than £320. Where eight are entitled to full remission and one to 50 per cent, the remission the fee would appear to become

---

[4] Apart from equal pay claims as the result of a drafting error.

£240. In the case of an application the fee is the same irrespective of the number of claims in the claim form or number of claimants (art. 11(1)).

4. Adjustments

(a) *Overpayments*

The Order does not deal with adjustments to fees where mistakes are made by Tribunal clerks. Some limited concessions are made in the SOPs. The initial level of fee payable on a claim form will be determined by a clerk at one of the two central processing facilities. Clerks currently vet all claims and give them juris-dictional codes for statistical purposes. Mistakes are not uncommon and it is very likely that similar mistakes of diagnosis will be made with regard to fees. If a Type B claim fee is paid when only a Type A fee was payable, a refund of the difference will only be made if the error is recognized at or before the ini-tial consideration stage (see Chapter 6). However it is not clear from the SOPs whether a refund will be made in all such cases or whether it remains discretion-ary. Although Judges have traditionally been reluctant to deal with issues of coding of case files, regarding it as a purely administrative matter, it will for this reason now become an important part of the initial consideration process. **14.17**

(b) *Underpayments*

A similar policy will apply to underpayments but with some interestingly ben-eficial side effects. If the claim originally only contained Type A complaints, no additional fee will be requested if a Type B claim is added later by amendment, at least if the amendment is made after initial consideration, but art. 4(1)(a) would appear to prevent it in any event. If after initial consideration it is identi-fied at a preliminary hearing that the claim form does actually include a Type B claim even though only a Type A fee has been charged, no additional fee will be sought. **14.18**

5. Fee group—failure to pay fee

In theory art. 12 is an important and sensible provision, enabling a member of a fee group to secure their own position if the group as a whole fails to pay a fee (almost always the hearing fee) by the due date. However, it only works if the rather dubious 'two-stage' interpretation of r. 40 discussed at paras. 7.92 and 7.93 is correct. Art. 12(1) provides that where a fee remains unpaid after the date specified in the notice requiring payment, any member of the fee group 'before the date on which the claim to which the fee relates is liable to be struck out for non-payment' may notify the Lord Chancellor that they are no longer part of the fee group. If they do, they shall be treated as a single claimant for the pur-poses of the claim (art. 12(2)). The more natural reading of r. 40, it is suggested, is that there is only one stage and in consequence the two relevant dates—the date on which the notice expires and the date 'on which the claim is liable to be **14.19** struck out for non-payment', are the same. Moreover, there is no question of the claim being 'liable to be struck out'. By virtue of r. 40(2)(a) upon the expiration of the period in the notice to pay 'the claim shall be dismissed without further order'—in other words, dismissal is automatic. In consequence, on the more natural reading of r. 40, at precisely the same moment that the right to opt out of the group becomes exercisable, the right is lost because the claim is dismissed. The best that the claimant wishing to opt out of the group can hope for is that an application under r. 40(5) to reinstate the claim will succeed. However, r. 40(5) does not expressly address the case where only one or some of a group of claimants wishes to apply for a claim to be reinstated. The overriding objective (r. 2) would suggest that the rule should be interpreted so as to accommodate such an application.

D. REMISSIONS—SCHEDULE 3

1. Full remission—qualifying benefits

14.20 No fee is payable if at the time when the fee would be payable, the party (that is the person liable to pay the fee) is in receipt of one of the qualifying benefits listed in para. 2(2) of the Schedule. There is nothing in the Schedule which addresses the not uncommon situation where a party has applied for a qualifying benefit but the application has either not been dealt with during the limitation period for their Tribunal claim or has been refused but the benefit is subsequently awarded on appeal. While the most likely outcome is that the party will be unable to afford to pay the claim fee and will either abandon the claim or present the claim after the time-limit has expired thus creating more satellite litigation, if a fee was paid and proceedings commenced, it is not clear whether para. 10 'Refunds' would apply. The difficulty is that the enquiry under para. 10 focuses on the time the fee was paid. If the belated award of the qualifying benefit was retrospective to the date of the application for the benefit then it is at least arguable that at the time the fee was paid none was payable by virtue of para. 2 and a refund should be made. However, should the party apply for and be refused a refund, the Schedule affords no right of appeal and none is likely to be created in practice.

2. Full remission—gross annual income

14.21 No fee is payable if the party's gross annual income, or that of the couple of which the party is part, does not exceed the amount set out in the table in para. 3. 'Gross annual income' is defined as the total annual income for the preceding twelve months from all sources other than excluded benefits as defined in para. 1. Presumably 'total annual income' means total annual gross income and would appear to include one-off items of a windfall nature. It also seems that if the party's partner in the couple is in receipt of a qualifying benefit but the party is not, not only does that not entitle the party to remission of a fee (para. 6(1)) the benefit also appears to count as income of the couple.

For this purpose a 'couple' is defined as:[5] **14.22**

(a) a man and woman who are married to each other, or two people of the same sex who are civil partners of each other, and who are neither—
  (i) separated under a court order; nor
  (ii) separated in circumstances in which the separation is likely to be permanent;

(b) a man and a woman who are not married to each other but are living together as husband and wife;

(c) two people of the same sex who are not civil partners of each other but are living together as if they were civil partners.

3. The 'partner' problem

'Partner' means a person with whom the party lives as a couple (Schedule 3, **14.23** para. 1). There is an important but unaddressed problem in connection with assessment based on gross annual income which also arises (together with another problem) where the remission application is based on disposable monthly income rather than annual income, namely that of the impecunious party whose partner's income takes the couple beyond the qualifying threshold for remission but who refuses, or is unable, to fund the litigation. The impecunious party appears to have no right in law to compel their partner to come to their aid. If this prevents the party from pursuing their claim, in cases where the right of action derives from EU law the Order would seem to infringe the principle of effectiveness. It may also be indirectly discriminatory against women if, as was certainly the case historically, they tend to have lower incomes than their partners. Such a party's only recourse would appear to be to apply to the Lord Chancellor for remission under para. 8 'Remission in exceptional circumstances'.

4. Full and part remission—disposable monthly income

For the purposes of determining whether a party is entitled to remission the **14.24** 'income of a partner' is to be included as income of the party (para. 6). In the case of gross annual income under para. 3 that is not a problem because the paragraph specifically provides for the 'gross annual income' of the couple to be taken into account. However in the case of disposable monthly income, while para. 5 refers to the 'gross monthly income' of the party, para. 6(1) only provides that 'the income' of the partner is included as income of the party. The difficulty

---

[5] Section 3(5A) of the Tax Credits Act 2002 as inserted by para 144 of Schedule 24 to the Civil Partnership Act 2004.

here is that while the terms 'gross annual income' and 'gross monthly income' are defined so as to not to include the excluded benefits as defined in para. 1, the 'income of a partner' is not defined at all and so it is not obvious that if the partner is in receipt of an excluded benefit this has to be left out of account. There is little doubt that if the partner is in receipt of a qualifying benefit as defined in para. 2, that counts as being income of the party, and it also seems likely that if the partner is in receipt of an excluded benefit, that also counts as income of the party. Whether this was the intention or whether the reference to 'income' rather than 'gross monthly income' is just poor drafting, is difficult to say.

14.25 At first sight there appears to be a typographical error in para. 4 as one would expect the figure of £200 in para. 4(2)(b) to be £210. But although the paragraph results in an anomaly at the margin between two bands, this appears to be intentional. The paragraph works in this way: if the party's disposable monthly income calculated in accordance with para. 5 is £210, the maximum fee payable is £50: if it is £211 the maximum fee is £55. It appears that in order to be required to pay a Type A claim fee in full, a party's disposable income would have to be £420 per month and £600 for a Type B claim. To pay the hearing fee in full, the disposable income would have to be £560 for a Type A claim and £2000 for a Type B claim.

5. Disposable income

14.26 Paragraph 5 defines how to calculate disposable monthly income. As the calculation relates to a specific month, namely the month in which the fee becomes payable, rather than a typical or average month, the reference to income must be taken to be income received rather than income normally receivable if there is a difference. As it seems likely that 'disposable monthly income' includes such things as redundancy payments and notice pay, most claimants will delay making an application for remission until the month after employment has terminated or the payment received if later. The Schedule makes no provision for penalizing a party who under-declares income or overstates the specified outgoings, either in terms of the proceedings or otherwise. Given s. 42(8) of the Tribunals, Courts and Enforcement Act 2007, any excess fee would be recoverable as a civil debt but there would seem to be no other sanction except possibly to strike the claim out under r. 37(1)(b) if it could be established that the party had acted fraudulently.

6. Applications

14.27 Paragraph 7(1) provides that a party is only relieved of liability to pay a fee if that party makes an application for remission 'in accordance with this paragraph'. The paragraph is however silent as to how an application is to be made! It deals with two issues only: when it is to be made, namely at the time when the fee would otherwise be payable, and the evidence which must be produced to support it. It is understood that the intention is that the existing county court remission application form is to be used but there is no warrant for its use in the Order. Much more importantly, there is no warrant for rejecting a remission application not made on that form. Paragraph 7 provides that certain documentary evidence must be provided where full remission is applied for (under para. 7(3)) and for different documentary evidence where full or partial remission is applied for (under para. 7(4)). In para. 7(4)(a) the requirement is for the party to provide documentary evidence of 'such of the party's gross monthly income' as derives from certain sources.

It is understood that in the case of claim forms submitted online accompanied **14.28** by a remission application, claimants will be sent a notice requiring them to produce the evidence by a certain date, presumably within twenty-one days. 'Party' is defined as the individual who would be responsible for the fee if remission were not granted. There is therefore no specific requirement for documentary evidence of the income of a partner to be provided even though, by virtue para. 6(1), such income is 'to be included as income of a party'. It may be that this wording is believed to be sufficient to require the production of documentary evidence of a partner's earnings, but that view seems to be wrong. Nothing is said about whether original documents must be provided nor whether scanned documents will be accepted.

7. Exceptional circumstances

Paragraph 8 provides that a fee may be reduced or remitted 'where the Lord **14.29** Chancellor is satisfied that there are exceptional circumstances which justify doing so'. Unfortunately the paragraph gives no clue about the nature of circumstances which might be regarded as exceptional, whether they must have pertained at the time the fee was paid or may have come into existence afterwards, or when the application must be made, nor how to make the application or where to direct it. From para. 10(2) it seems that the exceptional circumstances must relate to the time the fee was paid and, inferentially, that the application should be made at the time the fee was payable (thus suggesting that absent the exceptional circumstances a fee would be payable) or within six months of the date the fee was paid, subject to the possibility of this time being extended under para. 10(4). Mistakes in dealing with remission applications are, regrettably, unlikely to be exceptional, nor are delays in dealing with applications for, or successful appeals from refusal to award, a qualifying benefit.

8. Refunds

Paragraph 10(1) provides for the refund of fees where a party was in fact enti- **14.30** tled to full or partial remission but failed to provide the documentary evidence at the time. If an application for a refund is made within six months of the fee being paid (para. 10(3)) and the necessary documentary evidence provided, 'the fee must be refunded'. The time can be extended if the Lord Chancellor considers that there is a good reason for the application being made after the end of the six-month period (para. 10(4)). Note that there is no specific requirement for a full remission application to be made, only for the necessary documentary evidence to be provided—although this may be intended to include a completed remission form.

APPENDIX 1

2013 No. 1237
EMPLOYMENT TRIBUNALS
The Employment Tribunals (Constitution and Rules of Procedure) Regulations 2013

Made 28th May 2013
Laid before Parliament 31st May 2013
Coming into force
for the purpose of regulations 1, 3 and 11 1st July 2013
for all other purposes 29th July 2013

The Secretary of State, in exercise of the powers conferred by section 24(2) of the Health and Safety at Work etc. Act 1974,[1] sections 1(1), 4(6) and (6A), 7(1), (3), (3ZA), (3A), (3AA), (3AB), (3B), (3C) and (5), 7A(1) and (2), 7B(1) and (2), 9(1) and (2), 10(2), (5), (6) and (7), 10A(1), 11(1), 12(2), 13, 13A, 19, and 41(4) of the Employment Tribunals Act 1996,[2]

---

[1] 1974 c. 37.

[2] 1996 c. 17; by virtue of section 1 of the Employment Rights (Dispute Resolution) Act 1998 (c. 8) industrial tribunals were renamed employment tribunals and references to 'industrial tribunal' and 'industrial tribunals' in any enactment were substituted with 'employment tribunal' and 'employment tribunals'. Section 4(6) was amended by the Employment Rights (Dispute Resolution) Act 1998, Schedule 1, paragraph 12(4), and by the Tribunals, Courts and Enforcement Act 2007 (c. 15), Schedule 8, paragraphs 35 and 37. Section 4(6A) was inserted by the Employment Rights (Dispute Resolution) Act 1998, section 3(6), and amended by the Tribunals, Courts and Enforcement Act 2007, Schedule 8, paragraphs 35 and 37. Section 7(3)(f)(i) was repealed by the Employment Rights (Dispute Resolution) Act 1998, Schedule 1, paragraph 14(2); section 7(3)(ia) was inserted by the Employment Act 2002 (c. 22), section 24(1); and section 7(3)(h) was amended by the Equality Act 2010 (c. 15), Schedule 26, paragraphs 27 and 29. Section 7(3ZA) was inserted by the Employment Act 2002, section 25. Section 7(3A) to (3C) was inserted by the Employment Rights (Dispute Resolution) Act 1999, section 2, and section 7(3A) was then substituted by the Employment Act 2002, section 26. Section 7(3AA) and (3AB) was inserted by the Employment Act 2008 (c. 24), section 4. Section 7A was inserted by the Employment Act 2002, section 27, and section 7A(1) was amended by the Tribunals Courts and Enforcement Act 2007, Schedule 8, paragraphs 35 and 41. Section 7B was inserted by the Tribunals, Courts and Enforcement Act 2007, Schedule 8, paragraphs 35 and 42. Sections 10 and 10A were substituted by the Employment Relations Act 1999 (c. 26), Schedule 8, paragraph 3, and section 10(6) was then substituted by the Employment Relations Act 2004 (c. 24), section 36. Section 12 was amended by the Equality Act 2010, Schedule 26, paragraphs 27 and 30. Section 13 was amended by the Employment Act 2002, section 22(1). Section 13(2) was amended by the Employment Relations Act 1999, section 44, Schedule 4, paragraph 4 of Part III, and Schedule 9. Section 13A was inserted by the Employment Act 2002, section 22(2). Section 19(1)

183

paragraph 37 of Schedule 6 to the Scotland Act 1998,[3] and paragraph 32 of Schedule 9 to the Government of Wales Act 2006,[4] makes the following Regulations.

The Secretary of State has consulted with the Administrative Justice and Tribunals Council, and that Council has consulted with the Scottish Committee and the Welsh Committee, in accordance with paragraph 24 of Schedule 7 to the Tribunals, Courts and Enforcement Act 2007.[5]

Citation and commencement

1.— (1) These Regulations may be cited as the Employment Tribunals (Constitution and Rules of Procedure) Regulations 2013 and the Rules of Procedure contained in Schedules 1, 2 and 3 may be referred to, respectively, as—
 (a) the Employment Tribunals Rules of Procedure 2013;
 (b) the Employment Tribunals (National Security) Rules of Procedure 2013; and
 (c) the Employment Tribunals (Equal Value) Rules of Procedure 2013.
 (2) This regulation and regulations 3 and 11 come into force on 1st July 2013 and the remainder of these Regulations (including the Schedules) come into force on 29th July 2013.

Revocation

2. Subject to the savings in regulation 15 the Employment Tribunals (Constitution and Rules of Procedure) Regulations 2004[6] are revoked.

Interpretation

3. Except in the Schedules which are subject to the definitions contained in the Schedules, in these Regulations—

'2004 Regulations' means the Employment Tribunals (Constitution and Rules of Procedure) Regulations 2004;
'appointing office holder' means, in England and Wales, the Lord Chancellor, and in Scotland, the Lord President;
'Employment Tribunals Act' means the Employment Tribunals Act 1996;
'Lord President' means the Lord President of the Court of Session;
'national security proceedings' means proceedings in relation to which a direction is given, or an order is made, under rule 94 of Schedule 1;
'President' means either of the two presidents appointed from time to time in accordance with regulation 5(1);
'Regional Employment Judge' means a person appointed or nominated in accordance with regulation 6(1) or (2);
'Senior President of Tribunals' means the person appointed in accordance with section 2 of the Tribunals, Courts and Enforcement Act 2007;

---

was renumbered as such by the Employment Act 2002, section 24(4), and was amended by sections 24(3), 53 and 54 of, and Schedule 7, paragraph 23(1) and (3), and Schedule 8 to, that Act.
 [3] 1998 c. 46.
 [4] 2006 c. 32.
 [5] 2007 c. 15.
 [6] S.I. 2004/1861.

'Tribunal' means an employment tribunal established in accordance with regulation 4 and, in relation to any proceedings, means the Tribunal responsible for the proceedings in question, whether performing administrative or judicial functions;

'Vice President' means a person appointed or nominated in accordance with regulation 6(3) or (4).

Establishment of employment tribunals

4. There are to be tribunals known as employment tribunals.

President of Employment Tribunals

5.— (1) There shall be a President of Employment Tribunals, responsible for Tribunals in England and Wales, and a President of Employment Tribunals, responsible for Tribunals in Scotland, appointed by the appointing office holder.

(2) A President shall be—

(a) a person who satisfies the judicial-appointment eligibility condition within the meaning of section 50 of the Tribunals, Courts and Enforcement Act 2007 on a 5-year basis;

(b) an advocate or solicitor admitted in Scotland of at least five years standing; or

(c) a member of the Bar of Northern Ireland or solicitor of the Supreme Court of Northern Ireland of at least five years standing.

(3) A President may at any time resign from office by giving the appointing officer holder notice in writing to that effect.

(4) The appointing officer holder may remove a President from office on the ground of inability or misbehaviour, or if the President is adjudged to be bankrupt or makes a composition or arrangement with his creditors.

(5) Where a President is unable to carry out the functions set out in these Regulations, those functions may be discharged by a person nominated by the appointing office holder (save that any nomination in relation to England and Wales shall be made by the Lord Chief Justice following consultation with the Senior President of Tribunals, rather than by the Lord Chancellor).

(6) The Lord Chief Justice may nominate a judicial office holder (as defined in section 109(4) of the Constitutional Reform Act 2005)[7] to exercise his functions under this regulation.

Regional Employment Judges and the Vice President

6.— (1) The Lord Chancellor may appoint Regional Employment Judges.

(2) The President (England and Wales) or the Regional Employment Judge for an area may nominate an Employment Judge to discharge the functions of the Regional Employment Judge for that area.

(3) The Lord President may appoint a Vice President.

(4) The President (Scotland) or the Vice President may nominate an Employment Judge to discharge the functions of the Vice President.

---

[7] 2005 c. 4; section 109 was amended by the Tribunals, Courts and Enforcement Act 2007, Schedule 8, paragraph 63.

(5) Appointments and nominations under this regulation shall be from the full-time Employment Judges on the panel referred to in regulation 8(2)(a).

Responsibilities of the Presidents, Regional Employment Judges and Vice President

7.— (1) The President shall, in relation to the area for which the President is responsible, use the resources available to—
  (a) secure, so far as practicable, the speedy and efficient disposal of proceedings;
  (b) determine the allocation of proceedings between Tribunals; and
  (c) determine where and when Tribunals shall sit.

(2) The President (England and Wales) may direct Regional Employment Judges, and the President (Scotland) may direct the Vice President, to take action in relation to the fulfilment of the responsibilities in paragraph (1) and the Regional Employment Judges and Vice President shall follow such directions.

Panels of members for tribunals

8.— (1) There shall be three panels of members for the Employment Tribunals (England and Wales) and three panels of members for the Employment Tribunals (Scotland).

(2) The panels of members shall be—
  (a) a panel of chairmen who satisfy the criteria set out in regulation 5(2) and are appointed by the appointing office holder (in these Regulations (including the Schedules) referred to as 'Employment Judges');
  (b) a panel of persons appointed by the Lord Chancellor after consultation with organisations or associations representative of employees; and
  (c) a panel of persons appointed by the Lord Chancellor after consultation with organisations or associations representative of employers.

(3) Members of the panels shall hold and vacate office in accordance with the terms of their appointment, but may resign from office by written notice to the person who appointed them under paragraph (2), and any member who ceases to hold office shall be eligible for reappointment.

(4) The President may establish further specialist panels of members referred to in paragraph (2) and may select persons from those panels to deal with proceedings in which particular specialist knowledge would be beneficial.

Composition of tribunals

9.— (1) Where proceedings are to be determined by a Tribunal comprising an Employment Judge and two other members, the President, Vice President or a Regional Employment Judge shall select—
  (a) an Employment Judge; and
  (b) one member from each of the panels referred to in regulation 8(2)(b) and (c),
  and for all other proceedings shall select an Employment Judge.

(2) The President, Vice President or a Regional Employment Judge may select him or herself as the Employment Judge required under paragraph (1).

(3) The President, Vice President or a Regional Employment Judge may select from the appropriate panel a substitute for a member previously selected to hear any proceedings.

(4) This regulation does not apply in relation to national security proceedings (see regulation 10(2)).

National security proceedings—panel of members and composition of tribunals

10.— (1) The President shall select—
   (a) a panel of persons from the panel referred to in regulation 8(2)(a);
   (b) a panel of persons from the panel referred to in regulation 8(2)(b); and
   (c) a panel of persons from the panel referred to in regulation 8(2)(c),
who may act in national security proceedings.

(2) Where proceedings become national security proceedings, the President, Vice President or a Regional Employment Judge shall—
   (a) select an Employment Judge from the panel referred to in paragraph (1)(a) and may select him or herself; and
   (b) where the proceedings are to be determined by a Tribunal comprising an Employment Judge and two other members, select in addition one member from each of the panels referred to in sub-paragraphs (b) and (c) of paragraph (1).

Practice directions

11.— (1) The President may make, vary or revoke practice directions about the procedure of the Tribunals in the area for which the President is responsible, including—
   (a) practice directions about the exercise by Tribunals of powers under these Regulations (including the Schedules); and
   (b) practice directions about the provision by Employment Judges of mediation, in relation to disputed matters in a case that is the subject of proceedings, and may permit an Employment Judge to act as mediator in a case even though they have been selected to decide matters in that case.

(2) Practice directions may make different provision for different cases, different areas, or different types of proceedings.

(3) Any practice direction made, varied or revoked shall be published by the President in an appropriate manner to bring it to the attention of the persons to whom it is addressed.

Power to prescribe

12.— (1) The Secretary of State may prescribe—
   (a) one or more versions of a form which shall be used by claimants to start proceedings in a Tribunal;
   (b) one or more versions of a form which shall be used by respondents to respond to a claim before a Tribunal; and
   (c) that the provision of certain information on the prescribed forms is mandatory.

(2) It is not necessary to use a form prescribed under paragraph (1) if the proceedings are—
   (a) referred to a Tribunal by a court;
   (b) proceedings in which a Tribunal will be exercising its appellate jurisdiction; or

(c) proceedings brought by an employer under section 11 of the Employment Rights Act 1996.[8]

(3) The Secretary of State shall publish the prescribed forms in an appropriate manner to bring them to the attention of prospective claimants, respondents and their advisers.

Application of Schedules 1 to 3

13.— (1) Subject to paragraph (2), Schedule 1 applies to all proceedings before a Tribunal except where separate rules of procedure made under the provisions of any enactment are applicable.

(2) Schedules 2 and 3 apply to modify the rules in Schedule 1 in relation, respectively, to proceedings which are—

(a) national security proceedings; or

(b) proceedings which involve an equal value claim (as defined in rule 1 of Schedule 3).

Register and proof of judgments

14.— (1) The Lord Chancellor shall maintain a register containing a copy of all judgments and written reasons issued by a Tribunal which are required to be entered in the register under Schedules 1 to 3.

(2) The Lord Chancellor shall delete any entry in the register six years from the date of judgment.

(3) A document purporting to be certified by a member of staff of a Tribunal to be a true copy of an entry of a judgment in the register shall, unless the contrary is proved, be sufficient evidence of the document and its contents.

Transitional provisions

15.— (1) Subject to paragraphs (2) and (3), these Regulations and the Rules of Procedure contained in Schedules 1 to 3 apply in relation to all proceedings to which they relate.

(2) Where a respondent receives from a Tribunal a copy of the claim form before 29th July 2013, rules 23 to 25 of Schedule 1 do not apply to the proceedings and rule 7 of Schedule 1 to the 2004 Regulations continues to apply.

(3) Where in accordance with Schedules 3 to 5 of the 2004 Regulations, a notice of appeal was presented to a Tribunal before 29th July 2013, Schedule 1 does not apply to the proceedings and Schedule 3, 4 or 5, as appropriate, of the 2004 Regulations continues to apply.

Jo Swinson
Parliamentary Under Secretary of State for Employment Relations and
Consumer Affairs
Department for Business, Innovation and Skills
28th May 2013

---

[8] 1996 c. 18.

SCHEDULE 1 REGULATION 13(1)

THE EMPLOYMENT TRIBUNALS RULES OF PROCEDURE

Introductory and General

1. Interpretation
2. Overriding objective
3. Alternative dispute resolution
4. Time
5. Extending or shortening time
6. Irregularities and non-compliance
7. Presidential Guidance

Starting a Claim

8. Presenting the claim
9. Multiple claimants
10. Rejection: form not used or failure to supply minimum information
11. Rejection: absence of Tribunal fee or remission application
12. Rejection: substantive defects
13. Reconsideration of rejection
14. Protected disclosure claims: notification to a regulator

The Response to the Claim

15. Sending claim form to respondents
16. Response
17. Rejection: form not used or failure to supply minimum information
18. Rejection: form presented late
19. Reconsideration of rejection
20. Applications for extension of time for presenting response
21. Effect of non-presentation or rejection of response, or case not contested
22. Notification of acceptance

Employer's Contract Claim

23. Making an employer's contract claim
24. Notification of employer's contract claim
25. Responding to an employer's contract claim

Initial Consideration of Claim Form and Response

26. Initial consideration
27. Dismissal of claim (or part)
28. Dismissal of response (or part)

Case Management Orders and Other Powers

Rules Common to All Kinds of Hearing

Withdrawal

Preliminary Hearings

Final Hearing

Decisions and Reasons

Reconsideration of Judgments

Costs Orders, Preparation Time Orders and Wasted Costs Orders

Delivery of Documents

Miscellaneous

Introductory and General

Interpretation

1.— (1) In these Rules—

'ACAS' means the Advisory, Conciliation and Arbitration Service referred to in section 247 of the Trade Union and Labour Relations (Consolidation) Act 1992;[9]
'claim' means any proceedings before an Employment Tribunal making a complaint;
'claimant' means the person bringing the claim;
'Commission for Equality and Human Rights' means the body established under section 1 of the Equality Act 2006;[10]
'complaint' means anything that is referred to as a claim, complaint, reference, application or appeal in any enactment which confers jurisdiction on the Tribunal;
'Employment Appeal Tribunal' means the Employment Appeal Tribunal established under section 87 of the Employment Protection Act 1975[11] and continued in existence under section 135 of the Employment Protection (Consolidation) Act 1978[12] and section 20(1) of the Employment Tribunals Act;
'electronic communication' has the meaning given to it by section 15(1) of the Electronic Communications Act 2000;[13]
'employee's contract claim' means a claim brought by an employee in accordance with articles 3 and 7 of the Employment Tribunals Extension of Jurisdiction (England and Wales)

---

[9] 1992 c. 52.
[10] 2006 c. 3.
[11] 1975 c. 71; section 87 was repealed by the Employment Protection (Consolidation) Act 1978 (c. 44), Schedule 17.
[12] 1978 c. 44; section 135 was repealed by the Employment Tribunals Act 1996 (c. 17), Schedule 3, Part I.
[13] 2000 c. 7; section 15(1) was amended by the Communications Act 2003 (c. 21), Schedule 17, paragraph 158.

Order 1994[14] or articles 3 and 7 of the Employment Tribunals Extension of Jurisdiction (Scotland) Order 1994;[15]

'employer's contract claim' means a claim brought by an employer in accordance with articles 4 and 8 of the Employment Tribunals Extension of Jurisdiction (England and Wales) Order 1994[16] or articles 4 and 8 of the Employment Tribunals Extension of Jurisdiction (Scotland) Order 1994;[17]

'Employment Tribunal' or 'Tribunal' means an employment tribunal established in accordance with regulation 4, and in relation to any proceedings means the Tribunal responsible for the proceedings in question, whether performing administrative or judicial functions;

'Employment Tribunals Act' means the Employment Tribunals Act 1996;[18]

'Equality Act' means the Equality Act 2010;[19]

'full tribunal' means a Tribunal constituted in accordance with section 4(1) of the Employment Tribunals Act;[20]

'Health and Safety Act' means the Health and Safety at Work etc. Act 1974;[21]

'improvement notice' means a notice under section 21 of the Health and Safety Act;

'levy appeal' means an appeal against an assessment to a levy imposed under section 11 of the Industrial Training Act 1982;[22]

'Minister' means Minister of the Crown;

'prescribed form' means any appropriate form prescribed by the Secretary of State in accordance with regulation 12;

'present' means deliver (by any means permitted under rule 85) to a tribunal office;

'President' means either of the two presidents appointed from time to time in accordance with regulation 5(1);

'prohibition notice' means a notice under section 22 of the Health and Safety Act;[23]

'Regional Employment Judge' means a person appointed or nominated in accordance with regulation 6(1) or (2);

'Register' means the register of judgments and written reasons kept in accordance with regulation 14;

'remission application' means any application which may be made under any enactment for remission or part remission of a Tribunal fee;

'respondent' means the person or persons against whom the claim is made;

'Tribunal fee' means any fee which is payable by a party under any enactment in respect of a claim, employer's contract claim, application or judicial mediation in an Employment Tribunal;

---

[14] S.I. 1994/1623; by virtue of section 1 of the Employment Rights (Dispute Resolution) Act 1998 (c. 8) industrial tribunals were renamed employment tribunals and references to 'industrial tribunal' and 'industrial tribunals' in any enactment were substituted with 'employment tribunal' and 'employment tribunals'. By virtue of the destination table to the Employment Tribunals Act 1996, the reference in article 3(a) to 'section 131(2) of the 1978 Act' should be read as section 3(2) of the Employment Tribunals Act 1996. Article 7 was amended by S.I. 2011/1133.

[15] S.I. 1994/1624; by virtue of the destination table to the Employment Tribunals Act 1996 the reference in article 3(a) to 'section 131(2) of the 1978 Act' should be read as section 3(2) of the Employment Tribunals Act 1996. Article 7 was amended by S.I. 2011/1133.

[16] Article 8 was amended by S.I. 2011/1133.

[17] Article 8 was amended by S.I. 2011/1133.

[18] 1996 c. 17.

[19] 2010 c. 15.

[20] Section 4(1)(b) was substituted by the Employment Rights (Dispute Resolution) Act 1998, section 4, from a date to be appointed.

[21] 1974 c. 37.

[22] 1982 c. 10. Section 11 was amended by the Employment Act 1989 (c. 38), Schedule 4, paragraph 10; there are other amending instruments but none is relevant.

[23] Section 22 was amended by the Consumer Protection Act 1987 (c. 43), Schedule 3, paragraph 2.

'tribunal office' means any office which has been established for any area in either England and Wales or Scotland and which carries out administrative functions in support of the Tribunal, and in relation to particular proceedings it is the office notified to the parties as dealing with the proceedings;

'unlawful act notice' means a notice under section 21 of the Equality Act 2006;[24]

'Vice President' means a person appointed or nominated in accordance with regulation 6(3) or (4);

'writing' includes writing delivered by means of electronic communication.

(2) Any reference in the Rules to a Tribunal applies to both a full tribunal and to an Employment Judge acting alone (in accordance with section 4(2) or (6) of the Employment Tribunals Act).[25]

(3) An order or other decision of the Tribunal is either—

(a) a 'case management order', being an order or decision of any kind in relation to the conduct of proceedings, not including the determination of any issue which would be the subject of a judgment; or

(b) a 'judgment', being a decision, made at any stage of the proceedings (but not including a decision under rule 13 or 19), which finally determines—

(i) a claim, or part of a claim, as regards liability, remedy or costs (including preparation time and wasted costs); or

(ii) any issue which is capable of finally disposing of any claim, or part of a claim, even if it does not necessarily do so (for example, an issue whether a claim should be struck out or a jurisdictional issue).

Overriding objective

2. The overriding objective of these Rules is to enable Employment Tribunals to deal with cases fairly and justly. Dealing with a case fairly and justly includes, so far as practicable—

(a) ensuring that the parties are on an equal footing;

(b) dealing with cases in ways which are proportionate to the complexity and importance of the issues;

(c) avoiding unnecessary formality and seeking flexibility in the proceedings;

(d) avoiding delay, so far as compatible with proper consideration of the issues; and

(e) saving expense.

A Tribunal shall seek to give effect to the overriding objective in interpreting, or exercising any power given to it by, these Rules. The parties and their representatives shall assist the Tribunal to further the overriding objective and in particular shall co-operate generally with each other and with the Tribunal.

Alternative dispute resolution

3. A Tribunal shall wherever practicable and appropriate encourage the use by the parties of the services of ACAS, judicial or other mediation, or other means of resolving their disputes by agreement.

---

[24] 2006 c. 3; section 21 was amended by the Equality Act 2010 (c. 15), Schedule 26, paragraph 67.

[25] Section 4(2) and (6) was amended by the Tribunals, Courts and Enforcement Act 2007 (c. 15), Schedule 8, paragraphs 35 and 37.

Time

4.— (1) Unless otherwise specified by the Tribunal, an act required by these Rules, a practice direction or an order of a Tribunal to be done on or by a particular day may be done at any time before midnight on that day. If there is an issue as to whether the act has been done by that time, the party claiming to have done it shall prove compliance.

(2) If the time specified by these Rules, a practice direction or an order for doing any act ends on a day other than a working day, the act is done in time if it is done on the next working day. 'Working day' means any day except a Saturday or Sunday, Christmas Day, Good Friday or a bank holiday under section 1 of the Banking and Financial Dealings Act 1971.[26]

(3) Where any act is required to be, or may be, done within a certain number of days of or from an event, the date of that event shall not be included in the calculation. (For example, a response shall be presented within 28 days of the date on which the respondent was sent a copy of the claim: if the claim was sent on 1st October the last day for presentation of the response is 29th October).

(4) Where any act is required to be, or may be, done not less than a certain number of days before or after an event, the date of that event shall not be included in the calculation. (For example, if a party wishes to present representations in writing for consideration by a Tribunal at a hearing, they shall be presented not less than 7 days before the hearing: if the hearing is fixed for 8th October, the representations shall be presented no later than 1st October).

(5) Where the Tribunal imposes a time limit for doing any act, the last date for compliance shall, wherever practicable, be expressed as a calendar date.

(6) Where time is specified by reference to the date when a document is sent to a person by the Tribunal, the date when the document was sent shall, unless the contrary is proved, be regarded as the date endorsed on the document as the date of sending or, if there is no such endorsement, the date shown on the letter accompanying the document.

Extending or shortening time

5. The Tribunal may, on its own initiative or on the application of a party, extend or shorten any time limit specified in these Rules or in any decision, whether or not (in the case of an extension) it has expired.

Irregularities and non-compliance

6. A failure to comply with any provision of these Rules (except rule 8(1), 16(1), 23 or 25) or any order of the Tribunal (except for an order under rules 38 or 39) does not of itself render void the proceedings or any step taken in the proceedings. In the case of such non-compliance, the Tribunal may take such action as it considers just, which may include all or any of the following—

(a) waiving or varying the requirement;

---

[26] 1971 c. 80.

(b) striking out the claim or the response, in whole or in part, in accordance with rule 37;

(c) barring or restricting a party's participation in the proceedings;

(d) awarding costs in accordance with rules 74 to 84.

Presidential Guidance

7. The Presidents may publish guidance for England and Wales and for Scotland, respectively, as to matters of practice and as to how the powers conferred by these Rules may be exercised. Any such guidance shall be published by the Presidents in an appropriate manner to bring it to the attention of claimants, respondents and their advisers. Tribunals must have regard to any such guidance, but they shall not be bound by it.

Starting a Claim

Presenting the claim

8.— (1) A claim shall be started by presenting a completed claim form (using a prescribed form) in accordance with any practice direction made under regulation 11 which supplements this rule.

(2) A claim may be presented in England and Wales if—

(a) the respondent, or one of the respondents, resides or carries on business in England and Wales;

(b) one or more of the acts or omissions complained of took place in England and Wales;

(c) the claim relates to a contract under which the work is or has been performed partly in England and Wales; or

(d) the Tribunal has jurisdiction to determine the claim by virtue of a connection with Great Britain and the connection in question is at least partly a connection with England and Wales.

(3) A claim may be presented in Scotland if—

(a) the respondent, or one of the respondents, resides or carries on business in Scotland;

(b) one or more of the acts or omissions complained of took place in Scotland;

(c) the claim relates to a contract under which the work is or has been performed partly in Scotland; or

(d) the Tribunal has jurisdiction to determine the claim by virtue of a connection with Great Britain and the connection in question is at least partly a connection with Scotland.

Multiple claimants

9. Two or more claimants may make their claims on the same claim form if their claims are based on the same set of facts. Where two or more claimants wrongly include claims on the same claim form, this shall be treated as an irregularity falling under rule 6.

Rejection: form not used or failure to supply minimum information

10.— (1) The Tribunal shall reject a claim if—
(a) it is not made on a prescribed form; or
(b) it does not contain all of the following information—
    (i) each claimant's name;
    (ii) each claimant's address;
    (iii) each respondent's name;
    (iv) each respondent's address.

(2) The form shall be returned to the claimant with a notice of rejection explaining why it has been rejected. The notice shall contain information about how to apply for a reconsideration of the rejection.

Rejection: absence of Tribunal fee or remission application

11.— (1) The Tribunal shall reject a claim if it is not accompanied by a Tribunal fee or a remission application.

(2) Where a claim is accompanied by a Tribunal fee but the amount paid is lower than the amount payable for the presentation of that claim, the Tribunal shall send the claimant a notice specifying a date for payment of the additional amount due and the claim, or part of it in respect of which the relevant Tribunal fee has not been paid, shall be rejected by the Tribunal if the amount due is not paid by the date specified.

(3) If a remission application is refused in part or in full, the Tribunal shall send the claimant a notice specifying a date for payment of the Tribunal fee and the claim shall be rejected by the Tribunal if the Tribunal fee is not paid by the date specified.

(4) If a claim, or part of it, is rejected, the form shall be returned to the claimant with a notice of rejection explaining why it has been rejected.

Rejection: substantive defects

12.— (1) The staff of the tribunal office shall refer a claim form to an Employment Judge if they consider that the claim, or part of it, may be—
(a) one which the Tribunal has no jurisdiction to consider; or
(b) in a form which cannot sensibly be responded to or is otherwise an abuse of the process.

(2) The claim, or part of it, shall be rejected if the Judge considers that the claim, or part of it, is of a kind described in sub-paragraphs (a) or (b) of paragraph (1).

(3) If the claim is rejected, the form shall be returned to the claimant together with a notice of rejection giving the Judge's reasons for rejecting the claim, or part of it. The notice shall contain information about how to apply for a reconsideration of the rejection.

Reconsideration of rejection

13.— (1) A claimant whose claim has been rejected (in whole or in part) under rule 10 or 12 may apply for a reconsideration on the basis that either—

(a) the decision to reject was wrong; or

(b) the notified defect can be rectified.

(2) The application shall be in writing and presented to the Tribunal within 14 days of the date that the notice of rejection was sent. It shall explain why the decision is said to have been wrong or rectify the defect and if the claimant wishes to request a hearing this shall be requested in the application.

(3) If the claimant does not request a hearing, or an Employment Judge decides, on considering the application, that the claim shall be accepted in full, the Judge shall determine the application without a hearing. Otherwise the application shall be considered at a hearing attended only by the claimant.

(4) If the Judge decides that the original rejection was correct but that the defect has been rectified, the claim shall be treated as presented on the date that the defect was rectified.

Protected disclosure claims: notification to a regulator

14. If a claim alleges that the claimant has made a protected disclosure, the Tribunal may, with the consent of the claimant, send a copy of any accepted claim to a regulator listed in Schedule 1 to the Public Interest Disclosure (Prescribed Persons) Order 1999.[27] 'Protected disclosure' has the meaning given to it by section 43A of the Employment Rights Act 1996.[28]

The Response to the Claim

Sending claim form to respondents

15. Unless the claim is rejected, the Tribunal shall send a copy of the claim form, together with a prescribed response form, to each respondent with a notice which includes information on—

(a) whether any part of the claim has been rejected; and

(b) how to submit a response to the claim, the time limit for doing so and what will happen if a response is not received by the Tribunal within that time limit.

Response

16.— (1) The response shall be on a prescribed form and presented to the tribunal office within 28 days of the date that the copy of the claim form was sent by the Tribunal.

(2) A response form may include the response of more than one respondent if they are responding to a single claim and either they all resist the claim on the same grounds or they do not resist the claim.

(3) A response form may include the response to more than one claim if the claims are based on the same set of facts and either the respondent resists all of the claims on the same grounds or the respondent does not resist the claims.

---

[27] S.I. 1999/1549, amended by the Energy Act 2004 (c. 20), and S.I. 2003/1993, 2004/3265, 2005/2035, 2005/2464, 2005/3172, 2008/531, 2008/2831, 2009/462, 2009/2457, 2009/2748, 2010/7, 2010/671, 2011/2581, 2012/462, 2012/725, 2012/1641, 2012/1479, 2012/2400.

[28] 1996 c. 18; section 43A was inserted by the Public Interest Disclosure Act 1996 (c. 23), section 1.

Rejection: form not used or failure to supply minimum information

17.— (1) The Tribunal shall reject a response if—
  (a) it is not made on a prescribed form; or
  (b) it does not contain all of the following information—
      (i)   the respondent's full name;
      (ii) the respondent's address;
      (iii) whether the respondent wishes to resist any part of the claim.

(2) The form shall be returned to the respondent with a notice of rejection explaining why it has been rejected. The notice shall explain what steps may be taken by the respondent, including the need (if appropriate) to apply for an extension of time, and how to apply for a reconsideration of the rejection.

Rejection: form presented late

18.— (1) A response 3shall be rejected by the Tribunal if it is received outside the time limit in rule 16 (or any extension of that limit granted within the original limit) unless an application for extension has already been made under rule 20 or the response includes or is accompanied by such an application (in which case the response shall not be rejected pending the outcome of the application).

(2) The response shall be returned to the respondent together with a notice of rejection explaining that the response has been presented late. The notice shall explain how the respondent can apply for an extension of time and how to apply for a reconsideration.

Reconsideration of rejection

19.— (1) A respondent whose response has been rejected under rule 17 or 18 may apply for a reconsideration on the basis that the decision to reject was wrong or, in the case of a rejection under rule 17, on the basis that the notified defect can be rectified.

(2) The application shall be in writing and presented to the Tribunal within 14 days of the date that the notice of rejection was sent. It shall explain why the decision is said to have been wrong or rectify the defect and it shall state whether the respondent requests a hearing.

(3) If the respondent does not request a hearing, or the Employment Judge decides, on considering the application, that the response shall be accepted in full, the Judge shall determine the application without a hearing. Otherwise the application shall be considered at a hearing attended only by the respondent.

(4) If the Judge decides that the original rejection was correct but that the defect has been rectified, the response shall be treated as presented on the date that the defect was rectified (but the Judge may extend time under rule 5).

Applications for extension of time for presenting response

20.— (1) An application for an extension of time for presenting a response shall be presented in writing and copied to the claimant. It shall set out the reason why the extension is sought and shall, except where the time limit has not yet expired, be accompanied by a draft of the response which the respondent wishes to present or an explanation of why that is not possible and if the respondent wishes to request a hearing this shall be requested in the application.

(2) The claimant may within 7 days of receipt of the application give reasons in writing explaining why the application is opposed.

(3) An Employment Judge may determine the application without a hearing.

(4) If the decision is to refuse an extension, any prior rejection of the response shall stand. If the decision is to allow an extension, any judgment issued under rule 21 shall be set aside.

Effect of non-presentation or rejection of response, or case not contested

21.— (1) Where on the expiry of the time limit in rule 16 no response has been presented, or any response received has been rejected and no application for a reconsideration is outstanding, or where the respondent has stated that no part of the claim is contested, paragraphs (2) and (3) shall apply.

(2) An Employment Judge shall decide whether on the available material (which may include further information which the parties are required by a Judge to provide), a determination can properly be made of the claim, or part of it. To the extent that a determination can be made, the Judge shall issue a judgment accordingly. Otherwise, a hearing shall be fixed before a Judge alone.

(3) The respondent shall be entitled to notice of any hearings and decisions of the Tribunal but, unless and until an extension of time is granted, shall only be entitled to participate in any hearing to the extent permitted by the Judge.

Notification of acceptance

22. Where the Tribunal accepts the response it shall send a copy of it to all other parties.

Employer's Contract Claim

Making an employer's contract claim

23. Any employer's contract claim shall be made as part of the response, presented in accordance with rule 16, to a claim which includes an employee's contract claim. An employer's contract claim may be rejected on the same basis as a claimant's claim may be rejected under rule 12, in which case rule 13 shall apply.

Notification of employer's contract claim

24. When the Tribunal sends the response to the other parties in accordance with rule 22 it shall notify the claimant that the response includes an employer's contract claim and include information on how to submit a response to the claim, the time limit for doing so, and what will happen if a response is not received by the Tribunal within that time limit.

Responding to an employer's contract claim

25. A claimant's response to an employer's contract claim shall be presented to the tribunal office within 28 days of the date that the response was sent to the claimant. If no response is presented within that time limit, rules 20 and 21 shall apply.

Initial Consideration of Claim Form and Response

Initial consideration

26.— (1) As soon as possible after the acceptance of the response, the Employment Judge shall consider all of the documents held by the Tribunal in relation to the claim, to confirm whether there are arguable complaints and defences within the jurisdiction of the Tribunal (and for that purpose the Judge may order a party to provide further information).

(2) Except in a case where notice is given under rule 27 or 28, the Judge conducting the initial consideration shall make a case management order (unless made already), which may deal with the listing of a preliminary or final hearing, and may propose judicial mediation or other forms of dispute resolution.

Dismissal of claim (or part)

27.— (1) If the Employment Judge considers either that the Tribunal has no jurisdiction to consider the claim, or part of it, or that the claim, or part of it, has no reasonable prospect of success, the Tribunal shall send a notice to the parties—

    (a) setting out the Judge's view and the reasons for it; and

    (b) ordering that the claim, or the part in question, shall be dismissed on such date as is specified in the notice unless before that date the claimant has presented written representations to the Tribunal explaining why the claim (or part) should not be dismissed.

(2) If no such representations are received, the claim shall be dismissed from the date specified without further order (although the Tribunal shall write to the parties to confirm what has occurred).

(3) If representations are received within the specified time they shall be considered by an Employment Judge, who shall either permit the claim (or part) to proceed or fix a hearing for the purpose of deciding whether it should be permitted to do so. The respondent may, but need not, attend and participate in the hearing.

(4) If any part of the claim is permitted to proceed the Judge shall make a case management order.

Dismissal of response (or part)

28.— (1) If the Employment Judge considers that the response to the claim, or part of it, has no reasonable prospect of success the Tribunal shall send a notice to the parties—

    (a) setting out the Judge's view and the reasons for it;

(b) ordering that the response, or the part in question, shall be dismissed on such date as is specified in the notice unless before that date the respondent has presented written representations to the Tribunal explaining why the response (or part) should not be dismissed; and

(c) specifying the consequences of the dismissal of the response, in accordance with paragraph (5) below.

(2) If no such representations are received, the response shall be dismissed from the date specified without further order (although the Tribunal shall write to the parties to confirm what has occurred).

(3) If representations are received within the specified time they shall be considered by an Employment Judge, who shall either permit the response (or part) to stand or fix a hearing for the purpose of deciding whether it should be permitted to do so. The claimant may, but need not, attend and participate in the hearing.

(4) If any part of the response is permitted to stand the Judge shall make a case management order.

(5) Where a response is dismissed, the effect shall be as if no response had been presented, as set out in rule 21 above.

Case Management Orders and Other Powers

Case management orders

29. The Tribunal may at any stage of the proceedings, on its own initiative or on application, make a case management order. The particular powers identified in the following rules do not restrict that general power. A case management order may vary, suspend or set aside an earlier case management order where that is necessary in the interests of justice, and in particular where a party affected by the earlier order did not have a reasonable opportunity to make representations before it was made.

Applications for case management orders

30.— (1) An application by a party for a particular case management order may be made either at a hearing or presented in writing to the Tribunal.

(2) Where a party applies in writing, they shall notify the other parties that any objections to the application should be sent to the Tribunal as soon as possible.

(3) The Tribunal may deal with such an application in writing or order that it be dealt with at a preliminary or final hearing.

Disclosure of documents and information

31. The Tribunal may order any person in Great Britain to disclose documents or information to a party (by providing copies or otherwise) or to allow a party to inspect such material as might be ordered by a county court or, in Scotland, by a sheriff.

Requirement to attend to give evidence

32. The Tribunal may order any person in Great Britain to attend a hearing to give evidence, produce documents, or produce information.

Evidence from other EU Member States

33. The Tribunal may use the procedures for obtaining evidence prescribed in Council Regulation (EC) No. 1026/2001 of 28 May 2001 on cooperation between the courts of the Member States in the taking of evidence in civil or commercial matters.[29]

Addition, substitution and removal of parties

34. The Tribunal may on its own initiative, or on the application of a party or any other person wishing to become a party, add any person as a party, by way of substitution or otherwise, if it appears that there are issues between that person and any of the existing parties falling within the jurisdiction of the Tribunal which it is in the interests of justice to have determined in the proceedings; and may remove any party apparently wrongly included.

Other persons

35. The Tribunal may permit any person to participate in proceedings, on such terms as may be specified, in respect of any matter in which that person has a legitimate interest.

Lead cases

36.— (1) Where a Tribunal considers that two or more claims give rise to common or related issues of fact or law, the Tribunal or the President may make an order specifying one or more of those claims as a lead case and staying, or in Scotland sisting, the other claims ('the related cases').

(2) When the Tribunal makes a decision in respect of the common or related issues it shall send a copy of that decision to each party in each of the related cases and, subject to paragraph (3), that decision shall be binding on each of those parties.

(3) Within 28 days after the date on which the Tribunal sent a copy of the decision to a party under paragraph (2), that party may apply in writing for an order that the decision does not apply to, and is not binding on the parties to, a particular related case.

(4) If a lead case is withdrawn before the Tribunal makes a decision in respect of the common or related issues, it shall make an order as to—

(a) whether another claim is to be specified as a lead case; and

(b) whether any order affecting the related cases should be set aside or varied.

Striking out

37.— (1) At any stage of the proceedings, either on its own initiative or on the application of a party, a Tribunal may strike out all or part of a claim or response on any of the following grounds—

(a) that it is scandalous or vexatious or has no reasonable prospect of success;

---

[29] OJ L 174, 27.6.01, p1.

   (b) that the manner in which the proceedings have been conducted by or on behalf of the claimant or the respondent (as the case may be) has been scandalous, unreasonable or vexatious;

   (c) for non-compliance with any of these Rules or with an order of the Tribunal;

   (d) that it has not been actively pursued;

   (e) that the Tribunal considers that it is no longer possible to have a fair hearing in respect of the claim or response (or the part to be struck out).

   (2) A claim or response may not be struck out unless the party in question has been given a reasonable opportunity to make representations, either in writing or, if requested by the party, at a hearing.

   (3) Where a response is struck out, the effect shall be as if no response had been presented, as set out in rule 21 above.

Unless orders

38.— (1) An order may specify that if it is not complied with by the date specified the claim or response, or part of it, shall be dismissed without further order. If a claim or response, or part of it, is dismissed on this basis the Tribunal shall give written notice to the parties confirming what has occurred.

   (2) A party whose claim or response has been dismissed, in whole or in part, as a result of such an order may apply to the Tribunal in writing, within 14 days of the date that the notice was sent, to have the order set aside on the basis that it is in the interests of justice to do so. Unless the application includes a request for a hearing, the Tribunal may determine it on the basis of written representations.

   (3) Where a response is dismissed under this rule, the effect shall be as if no response had been presented, as set out in rule 21.

Deposit orders

39.— (1) Where at a preliminary hearing (under rule 53) the Tribunal considers that any specific allegation or argument in a claim or response has little reasonable prospect of success, it may make an order requiring a party ('the paying party') to pay a deposit not exceeding £1,000 as a condition of continuing to advance that allegation or argument.

   (2) The Tribunal shall make reasonable enquiries into the paying party's ability to pay the deposit and have regard to any such information when deciding the amount of the deposit.

   (3) The Tribunal's reasons for making the deposit order shall be provided with the order and the paying party must be notified about the potential consequences of the order.

   (4) If the paying party fails to pay the deposit by the date specified the specific allegation or argument to which the deposit order relates shall be struck out. Where a response is struck out, the consequences shall be as if no response had been presented, as set out in rule 21.

   (5) If the Tribunal at any stage following the making of a deposit order decides the specific allegation or argument against the paying party for substantially the reasons given in the deposit order—

   (a) the paying party shall be treated as having acted unreasonably in pursuing that specific allegation or argument for the purpose of rule 76, unless the contrary is shown; and

(b) the deposit shall be paid to the other party (or, if there is more than one, to such other party or parties as the Tribunal orders),

otherwise the deposit shall be refunded.

(6) If a deposit has been paid to a party under paragraph (5)(b) and a costs or preparation time order has been made against the paying party in favour of the party who received the deposit, the amount of the deposit shall count towards the settlement of that order.

Non-payment of fees

40.— (1) Subject to rule 11, where a party has not paid a relevant Tribunal fee or presented a remission application in respect of that fee the Tribunal will send the party a notice specifying a date for payment of the Tribunal fee or presentation of a remission application.

(2) If at the date specified in a notice sent under paragraph (1) the party has not paid the Tribunal fee and no remission application in respect of that fee has been presented—

(a) where the Tribunal fee is payable in relation to a claim, the claim shall be dismissed without further order;

(b) where the Tribunal fee is payable in relation to an employer's contract claim, the employer's contract claim shall be dismissed without further order;

(c) where the Tribunal fee is payable in relation to an application, the application shall be dismissed without further order;

(d) where the Tribunal fee is payable in relation to judicial mediation, the judicial mediation shall not take place.

(3) Where a remission application is refused in part or in full, the Tribunal shall send the claimant a notice specifying a date for payment of the Tribunal fee.

(4) If at the date specified in a notice sent under paragraph (3) the party has not paid the Tribunal fee, the consequences shall be those referred to in sub-paragraphs (a) to (d) of paragraph (2).

(5) In the event of a dismissal under paragraph (2) or (4) a party may apply for the claim or response, or part of it, which was dismissed to be reinstated and the Tribunal may order a reinstatement. A reinstatement shall be effective only if the Tribunal fee is paid, or a remission application is presented and accepted, by the date specified in the order.

Rules Common to All Kinds of Hearing

General

41. The Tribunal may regulate its own procedure and shall conduct the hearing in the manner it considers fair, having regard to the principles contained in the overriding objective. The following rules do not restrict that general power. The Tribunal shall seek to avoid undue formality and may itself question the parties or any witnesses so far as appropriate in order to clarify the issues or elicit the evidence. The Tribunal is not bound by any rule of law relating to the admissibility of evidence in proceedings before the courts.

Written representations

42. The Tribunal shall consider any written representations from a party, including a party who does not propose to attend the hearing, if they are delivered to the Tribunal and to all other parties not less than 7 days before the hearing.

Witnesses

43. Where a witness is called to give oral evidence, any witness statement of that person ordered by the Tribunal shall stand as that witness's evidence in chief unless the Tribunal orders otherwise. Witnesses shall be required to give their oral evidence on oath or affirmation. The Tribunal may exclude from the hearing any person who is to appear as a witness in the proceedings until such time as that person gives evidence if it considers it in the interests of justice to do so.

Inspection of witness statements

44. Subject to rules 50 and 94, any witness statement which stands as evidence in chief shall be available for inspection during the course of the hearing by members of the public attending the hearing unless the Tribunal decides that all or any part of the statement is not to be admitted as evidence, in which case the statement or that part shall not be available for inspection.

Timetabling

45. A Tribunal may impose limits on the time that a party may take in presenting evidence, questioning witnesses or making submissions, and may prevent the party from proceeding beyond any time so allotted.

Hearings by electronic communication

46. A hearing may be conducted, in whole or in part, by use of electronic communication (including by telephone) provided that the Tribunal considers that it would be just and equitable to do so and provided that the parties and members of the public attending the hearing are able to hear what the Tribunal hears and see any witness as seen by the Tribunal.

Non-attendance

47. If a party fails to attend or to be represented at the hearing, the Tribunal may dismiss the claim or proceed with the hearing in the absence of that party. Before doing so, it shall consider any information which is available to it, after any enquiries that may be practicable, about the reasons for the party's absence.

Conversion from preliminary hearing to final hearing and vice versa

48. A Tribunal conducting a preliminary hearing may order that it be treated as a final hearing, or vice versa, if the Tribunal is properly constituted for the purpose and if it is satisfied that neither party shall be materially prejudiced by the change.

Majority decisions

49. Where a Tribunal is composed of three persons any decision may be made by a majority and if it is composed of two persons the Employment Judge has a second or casting vote.

Privacy and restrictions on disclosure

50.— (1) A Tribunal may at any stage of the proceedings, on its own initiative or on application, make an order with a view to preventing or restricting the public disclosure of any aspect of those proceedings so far as it considers necessary in the interests of justice or in order to protect the Convention rights of any person or in the circumstances identified in section 10A of the Employment Tribunals Act.

(2) In considering whether to make an order under this rule, the Tribunal shall give full weight to the principle of open justice and to the Convention right to freedom of expression.

(3) Such orders may include—

(a) an order that a hearing that would otherwise be in public be conducted, in whole or in part, in private;

(b) an order that the identities of specified parties, witnesses or other persons referred to in the proceedings should not be disclosed to the public, by the use of anonymisation or otherwise, whether in the course of any hearing or in its listing or in any documents entered on the Register or otherwise forming part of the public record;

(c) an order for measures preventing witnesses at a public hearing being identifiable by members of the public;

(d) a restricted reporting order within the terms of section 11 or 12 of the Employment Tribunals Act.

(4) Any party, or other person with a legitimate interest, who has not had a reasonable opportunity to make representations before an order under this rule is made may apply to the Tribunal in writing for the order to be revoked or discharged, either on the basis of written representations or, if requested, at a hearing.

(5) Where an order is made under paragraph (3)(d) above—

(a) it shall specify the person whose identity is protected; and may specify particular matters of which publication is prohibited as likely to lead to that person's identification;

(b) it shall specify the duration of the order;

(c) the Tribunal shall ensure that a notice of the fact that such an order has been made in relation to those proceedings is displayed on the notice board of the Tribunal with any list of the proceedings taking place before the Tribunal, and on the door of the room in which the proceedings affected by the order are taking place; and

(d) the Tribunal may order that it applies also to any other proceedings being heard as part of the same hearing.

(6) 'Convention rights' has the meaning given to it in section 1 of the Human Rights Act 1998.[30]

---

[30] 1998 c. 42.

Withdrawal

End of claim

51. Where a claimant informs the Tribunal, either in writing or in the course of a hearing, that a claim, or part of it, is withdrawn, the claim, or part, comes to an end, subject to any application that the respondent may make for a costs, preparation time or wasted costs order.

Dismissal following withdrawal

52. Where a claim, or part of it, has been withdrawn under rule 51, the Tribunal shall issue a judgment dismissing it (which means that the claimant may not commence a further claim against the respondent raising the same, or substantially the same, complaint) unless—

    (a) the claimant has expressed at the time of withdrawal a wish to reserve the right to bring such a further claim and the Tribunal is satisfied that there would be legitimate reason for doing so; or

    (b) the Tribunal believes that to issue such a judgment would not be in the interests of justice.

Preliminary Hearings

Scope of preliminary hearings

53.— (1) A preliminary hearing is a hearing at which the Tribunal may do one or more of the following—

    (a) conduct a preliminary consideration of the claim with the parties and make a case management order (including an order relating to the conduct of the final hearing);

    (b) determine any preliminary issue;

    (c) consider whether a claim or response, or any part, should be struck out under rule 37;

    (d) make a deposit order under rule 39;

    (e) explore the possibility of settlement or alternative dispute resolution (including judicial mediation).

    (2) There may be more than one preliminary hearing in any case.

    (3) 'Preliminary issue' means, as regards any complaint, any substantive issue which may determine liability (for example, an issue as to jurisdiction or as to whether an employee was dismissed).

Fixing of preliminary hearings

54. A preliminary hearing may be directed by the Tribunal on its own initiative following its initial consideration (under rule 26) or at any time thereafter or as the result of an application by a party. The Tribunal shall give the parties reasonable notice of the date of the hearing and in the case of a hearing involving any preliminary issues at least 14 days notice shall be given and the notice shall specify the preliminary issues that are to be, or may be, decided at the hearing.

Constitution of tribunal for preliminary hearings

55. Preliminary hearings shall be conducted by an Employment Judge alone, except that where notice has been given that any preliminary issues are to be, or may be, decided at the hearing a party may request in writing that the hearing be conducted by a full tribunal in which case an Employment Judge shall decide whether that would be desirable.

When preliminary hearings shall be in public

56. Preliminary hearings shall be conducted in private, except that where the hearing involves a determination under rule 53(1)(b) or (c), any part of the hearing relating to such a determination shall be in public (subject to rules 50 and 94) and the Tribunal may direct that the entirety of the hearing be in public.

Final Hearing

Scope of final hearing

57. A final hearing is a hearing at which the Tribunal determines the claim or such parts as remain outstanding following the initial consideration (under rule 26) or any preliminary hearing. There may be different final hearings for different issues (for example, liability, remedy or costs).

Notice of final hearing

58. The Tribunal shall give the parties not less than 14 days' notice of the date of a final hearing.

When final hearing shall be in public

59. Any final hearing shall be in public, subject to rules 50 and 94.

Decisions and Reasons

Decisions made without a hearing

60. Decisions made without a hearing shall be communicated in writing to the parties, identifying the Employment Judge who has made the decision.

Decisions made at or following a hearing

61.— (1) Where there is a hearing the Tribunal may either announce its decision in relation to any issue at the hearing or reserve it to be sent to the parties as soon as practicable in writing.

(2) If the decision is announced at the hearing, a written record (in the form of a judgment if appropriate) shall be provided to the parties (and, where the proceedings were referred to the Tribunal by a court, to that court) as soon as practicable. (Decisions

concerned only with the conduct of a hearing need not be identified in the record of that hearing unless a party requests that a specific decision is so recorded.)

(3) The written record shall be signed by the Employment Judge.

Reasons

62.— (1) The Tribunal shall give reasons for its decision on any disputed issue, whether substantive or procedural (including any decision on an application for reconsideration or for orders for costs, preparation time or wasted costs).

(2) In the case of a decision given in writing the reasons shall also be given in writing. In the case of a decision announced at a hearing the reasons may be given orally at the hearing or reserved to be given in writing later (which may, but need not, be as part of the written record of the decision). Written reasons shall be signed by the Employment Judge.

(3) Where reasons have been given orally, the Employment Judge shall announce that written reasons will not be provided unless they are asked for by any party at the hearing itself or by a written request presented by any party within 14 days of the sending of the written record of the decision. The written record of the decision shall repeat that information. If no such request is received, the Tribunal shall provide written reasons only if requested to do so by the Employment Appeal Tribunal or a court.

(4) The reasons given for any decision shall be proportionate to the significance of the issue and for decisions other than judgments may be very short.

(5) In the case of a judgment the reasons shall: identify the issues which the Tribunal has determined, state the findings of fact made in relation to those issues, concisely identify the relevant law, and state how that law has been applied to those findings in order to decide the issues. Where the judgment includes a financial award the reasons shall identify, by means of a table or otherwise, how the amount to be paid has been calculated.

Absence of Employment Judge

63. If it is impossible or not practicable for the written record or reasons to be signed by the Employment Judge as a result of death, incapacity or absence, it shall be signed by the other member or members (in the case of a full tribunal) or by the President, Vice President or a Regional Employment Judge (in the case of a Judge sitting alone).

Consent orders and judgments

64. If the parties agree in writing or orally at a hearing upon the terms of any order or judgment a Tribunal may, if it thinks fit, make such order or judgment, in which case it shall be identified as having been made by consent.

When a judgment or order takes effect

65. A judgment or order takes effect from the day when it is given or made, or on such later date as specified by the Tribunal.

Time for compliance

66. A party shall comply with a judgment or order for the payment of an amount of money within 14 days of the date of the judgment or order, unless—
  (a) the judgment, order, or any of these Rules, specifies a different date for compliance; or
  (b) the Tribunal has stayed (or in Scotland sisted) the proceedings or judgment.

The Register

67. Subject to rules 50 and 94, a copy shall be entered in the Register of any judgment and of any written reasons for a judgment.

Copies of judgment for referring court

68. Where the proceedings were referred to the Tribunal by a court a copy of any judgment and of any written reasons shall be provided to that court.

Correction of clerical mistakes and accidental slips

69. An Employment Judge may at any time correct any clerical mistake or other accidental slip or omission in any order, judgment or other document produced by a Tribunal. If such a correction is made, any published version of the document shall also be corrected. If any document is corrected under this rule, a copy of the corrected version, signed by the Judge, shall be sent to all the parties.

Reconsideration of Judgments

Principles

70. A Tribunal may, either on its own initiative (which may reflect a request from the Employment Appeal Tribunal) or on the application of a party, reconsider any judgment where it is necessary in the interests of justice to do so. On reconsideration, the decision ('the original decision') may be confirmed, varied or revoked. If it is revoked it may be taken again.

Application

71. Except where it is made in the course of a hearing, an application for reconsideration shall be presented in writing (and copied to all the other parties) within 14 days of the date on which the written record, or other written communication, of the original decision was sent to the parties or within 14 days of the date that the written reasons were sent (if later) and shall set out why reconsideration of the original decision is necessary.

Process

72.— (1) An Employment Judge shall consider any application made under rule 71. If the Judge considers that there is no reasonable prospect of the original decision being varied or revoked (including, unless there are special reasons, where substantially the same application has already been made and refused), the application shall be refused and the Tribunal shall inform the parties of the refusal. Otherwise the Tribunal shall send a notice to the parties setting a time limit for any response to the application by the other parties and seeking the views of the parties on whether the application can be determined without a hearing. The notice may set out the Judge's provisional views on the application.

(2) If the application has not been refused under paragraph (1), the original decision shall be reconsidered at a hearing unless the Employment Judge considers, having regard to any response to the notice provided under paragraph (1), that a hearing is not necessary in the interests of justice. If the reconsideration proceeds without a hearing the parties shall be given a reasonable opportunity to make further written representations.

(3) Where practicable, the consideration under paragraph (1) shall be by the Employment Judge who made the original decision or, as the case may be, chaired the full tribunal which made it; and any reconsideration under paragraph (2) shall be made by the Judge or, as the case may be, the full tribunal which made the original decision. Where that is not practicable, the President, Vice President or a Regional Employment Judge shall appoint another Employment Judge to deal with the application or, in the case of a decision of a full tribunal, shall either direct that the reconsideration be by such members of the original Tribunal as remain available or reconstitute the Tribunal in whole or in part.

Reconsideration by the Tribunal on its own initiative

73. Where the Tribunal proposes to reconsider a decision on its own initiative, it shall inform the parties of the reasons why the decision is being reconsidered and the decision shall be reconsidered in accordance with rule 72(2) (as if an application had been made and not refused).

Costs Orders, Preparation Time Orders and Wasted Costs Orders

Definitions

74.— (1) 'Costs' means fees, charges, disbursements or expenses incurred by or on behalf of the receiving party (including expenses that witnesses incur for the purpose of, or in connection with, attendance at a Tribunal hearing). In Scotland all references to costs (except when used in the expression 'wasted costs') shall be read as references to expenses.

(2) 'Legally represented' means having the assistance of a person (including where that person is the receiving party's employee) who—

(a) has a right of audience in relation to any class of proceedings in any part of the Senior Courts of England and Wales, or all proceedings in county courts or magistrates' courts;

(b) is an advocate or solicitor in Scotland; or

(c) is a member of the Bar of Northern Ireland or a solicitor of the Court of Judicature of Northern Ireland.

(3) 'Represented by a lay representative' means having the assistance of a person who does not satisfy any of the criteria in paragraph (2) and who charges for representation in the proceedings.

Costs orders and preparation time orders

75.— (1) A costs order is an order that a party ('the paying party') make a payment to—

(a) another party ('the receiving party') in respect of the costs that the receiving party has incurred while legally represented or while represented by a lay representative;

(b) the receiving party in respect of a Tribunal fee paid by the receiving party; or

(c) another party or a witness in respect of expenses incurred, or to be incurred, for the purpose of, or in connection with, an individual's attendance as a witness at the Tribunal.

(2) A preparation time order is an order that a party ('the paying party') make a payment to another party ('the receiving party') in respect of the receiving party's preparation time while not legally represented. 'Preparation time' means time spent by the receiving party (including by any employees or advisers) in working on the case, except for time spent at any final hearing.

(3) A costs order under paragraph (1)(a) and a preparation time order may not both be made in favour of the same party in the same proceedings. A Tribunal may, if it wishes, decide in the course of the proceedings that a party is entitled to one order or the other but defer until a later stage in the proceedings deciding which kind of order to make.

When a costs order or a preparation time order may or shall be made

76.— (1) A Tribunal may make a costs order or a preparation time order, and shall consider whether to do so, where it considers that—

(a) a party (or that party's representative) has acted vexatiously, abusively, disruptively or otherwise unreasonably in either the bringing of the proceedings (or part) or the way that the proceedings (or part) have been conducted; or

(b) any claim or response had no reasonable prospect of success.

(2) A Tribunal may also make such an order where a party has been in breach of any order or practice direction or where a hearing has been postponed or adjourned on the application of a party.

(3) Where in proceedings for unfair dismissal a final hearing is postponed or adjourned, the Tribunal shall order the respondent to pay the costs incurred as a result of the postponement or adjournment if—

(a) the claimant has expressed a wish to be reinstated or re-engaged which has been communicated to the respondent not less than 7 days before the hearing; and

(b) the postponement or adjournment of that hearing has been caused by the respondent's failure, without a special reason, to adduce reasonable evidence as to the availability of the job from which the claimant was dismissed or of comparable or suitable employment.

(4) A Tribunal may make a costs order of the kind described in rule 75(1)(b) where a party has paid a Tribunal fee in respect of a claim, employer's contract claim or application and that claim, counterclaim or application is decided in whole, or in part, in favour of that party.

(5) A Tribunal may make a costs order of the kind described in rule 75(1)(c) on the application of a party or the witness in question, or on its own initiative, where a witness has attended or has been ordered to attend to give oral evidence at a hearing.

Procedure

77. A party may apply for a costs order or a preparation time order at any stage up to 28 days after the date on which the judgment finally determining the proceedings in respect of that party was sent to the parties. No such order may be made unless the paying party has had a reasonable opportunity to make representations (in writing or at a hearing, as the Tribunal may order) in response to the application.

The amount of a costs order

78.— (1) A costs order may—
   (a) order the paying party to pay the receiving party a specified amount, not exceeding £20,000, in respect of the costs of the receiving party;
   (b) order the paying party to pay the receiving party the whole or a specified part of the costs of the receiving party, with the amount to be paid being determined, in England and Wales, by way of detailed assessment carried out either by a county court in accordance with the Civil Procedure Rules 1998, or by an Employment Judge applying the same principles; or, in Scotland, by way of taxation carried out either by the auditor of court in accordance with the Act of Sederunt (Fees of Solicitors in the Sheriff Court) (Amendment and Further Provisions) 1993,[31] or by an Employment Judge applying the same principles;
   (c) order the paying party to pay the receiving party a specified amount was reimbursement of all or part of a Tribunal fee paid by the receiving party;
   (d) order the paying party to pay another party or a witness, as appropriate, a specified amount in respect of necessary and reasonably incurred expenses (of the kind described in rule 75(1)(c)); or
   (e) if the paying party and the receiving party agree as to the amount payable, be made in that amount.
   (2) Where the costs order includes an amount in respect of fees charged by a lay representative, for the purposes of the calculation of the order, the hourly rate applicable for the fees of the lay representative shall be no higher than the rate under rule 79(2).
   (3) For the avoidance of doubt, the amount of a costs order under sub-paragraphs (b) to (e) of paragraph (1) may exceed £20,000.

The amount of a preparation time order

79.— (1) The Tribunal shall decide the number of hours in respect of which a preparation time order should be made, on the basis of—
   (a) information provided by the receiving party on time spent falling within rule 75(2) above; and
   (b) the Tribunal's own assessment of what it considers to be a reasonable and proportionate amount of time to spend on such preparatory work, with reference to such matters as the complexity of the proceedings, the number of witnesses and documentation required.

---

[31] S.I. 1993/3080

(2) The hourly rate is £33 and increases on 6 April each year by £1.

(3) The amount of a preparation time order shall be the product of the number of hours assessed under paragraph (1) and the rate under paragraph (2).

When a wasted costs order may be made

80.— (1) A Tribunal may make a wasted costs order against a representative in favour of any party ('the receiving party') where that party has incurred costs—
  (a) as a result of any improper, unreasonable or negligent act or omission on the part of the representative; or
  (b) which, in the light of any such act or omission occurring after they were incurred, the Tribunal considers it unreasonable to expect the receiving party to pay.
Costs so incurred are described as 'wasted costs'.

(2) 'Representative' means a party's legal or other representative or any employee of such representative, but it does not include a representative who is not acting in pursuit of profit with regard to the proceedings. A person acting on a contingency or conditional fee arrangement is considered to be acting in pursuit of profit.

(3) A wasted costs order may be made in favour of a party whether or not that party is legally represented and may also be made in favour of a representative's own client. A wasted costs order may not be made against a representative where that representative is representing a party in his or her capacity as an employee of that party.

Effect of a wasted costs order

81. A wasted costs order may order the representative to pay the whole or part of any wasted costs of the receiving party, or disallow any wasted costs otherwise payable to the representative, including an order that the representative repay to its client any costs which have already been paid. The amount to be paid, disallowed or repaid must in each case be specified in the order.

Procedure

82. A wasted costs order may be made by the Tribunal on its own initiative or on the application of any party. A party may apply for a wasted costs order at any stage up to 28 days after the date on which the judgment finally determining the proceedings as against that party was sent to the parties. No such order shall be made unless the representative has had a reasonable opportunity to make representations (in writing or at a hearing, as the Tribunal may order) in response to the application or proposal. The Tribunal shall inform the representative's client in writing of any proceedings under this rule and of any order made against the representative.

Allowances

83. Where the Tribunal makes a costs, preparation time, or wasted costs order, it may also make an order that the paying party (or, where a wasted costs order is made, the representative) pay to the Secretary of State, in whole or in part, any allowances (other than allowances paid to members of the Tribunal) paid by the Secretary of State under

section 5(2) or (3) of the Employment Tribunals Act[32] to any person for the purposes of, or in connection with, that person's attendance at the Tribunal.

Ability to pay

84. In deciding whether to make a costs, preparation time, or wasted costs order, and if so in what amount, the Tribunal may have regard to the paying party's (or, where a wasted costs order is made, the representative's) ability to pay.

Delivery of Documents

Delivery to the Tribunal

85.— (1) Subject to paragraph (2), documents may be delivered to the Tribunal—
  (a) by post;
  (b) by direct delivery to the appropriate tribunal office (including delivery by a courier or messenger service); or
  (c) by electronic communication.

(2) A claim form may only be delivered in accordance with the practice direction made under regulation 11 which supplements rule 8.

(3) The Tribunal shall notify the parties following the presentation of the claim of the address of the tribunal office dealing with the case (including any fax or email or other electronic address) and all documents shall be delivered to either the postal or the electronic address so notified. The Tribunal may from time to time notify the parties of any change of address, or that a particular form of communication should or should not be used, and any documents shall be delivered in accordance with that notification.

Delivery to parties

86.— (1) Documents may be delivered to a party (whether by the Tribunal or by another party)—
  (a) by post;
  (b) by direct delivery to that party's address (including delivery by a courier or messenger service);
  (c) by electronic communication; or
  (d) by being handed personally to that party, if an individual and if no representative has been named in the claim form or response; or to any individual representative named in the claim form or response; or, on the occasion of a hearing, to any person identified by the party as representing that party at that hearing.

(2) For the purposes of sub-paragraphs (a) to (c) of paragraph (1), the document shall be delivered to the address given in the claim form or response (which shall be the address of the party's representative, if one is named) or to a different address as notified in writing by the party in question.

---

[32] Section 5(2) was amended by the Equality Act 2010 (c. 15), Schedule 26, Part I, paragraphs 27 and 28.

(3) If a party has given both a postal address and one or more electronic addresses, any of them may be used unless the party has indicated in writing that a particular address should or should not be used.

Delivery to non-parties

87. Subject to the special cases which are the subject of rule 88, documents shall be sent to non-parties at any address for service which they may have notified and otherwise at any known address or place of business in the United Kingdom or, if the party is a corporate body, at its registered or principal office in the United Kingdom or, if permitted by the President, at an address outside the United Kingdom.

Special cases

88. Addresses for serving the Secretary of State, the Law Officers, and the Counsel General to the Welsh Assembly Government, in cases where they are not parties, shall be issued by practice direction.

Substituted service

89. Where no address for service in accordance with the above rules is known or it appears that service at any such address is unlikely to come to the attention of the addressee, the President, Vice President or a Regional Employment Judge may order that there shall be substituted service in such manner as appears appropriate.

Date of delivery

90. Where a document has been delivered in accordance with rule 85 or 86, it shall, unless the contrary is proved, be taken to have been received by the addressee—
- (a) if sent by post, on the day on which it would be delivered in the ordinary course of post;
- (b) if sent by means of electronic communication, on the day of transmission;
- (c) if delivered directly or personally, on the day of delivery.

Irregular service

91. A Tribunal may treat any document as delivered to a person, notwithstanding any non-compliance with rules 86 to 88, if satisfied that the document in question, or its substance, has in fact come to the attention of that person.

Correspondence with the Tribunal: copying to other parties

92. Where a party sends a communication to the Tribunal (except an application under rule 32) it shall send a copy to all other parties, and state that it has done so (by use of 'cc' or otherwise). The Tribunal may order a departure from this rule where it considers it in the interests of justice to do so.

Miscellaneous

ACAS

93.— (1) Where proceedings concern an enactment which provides for conciliation, the Tribunal shall—
  (a) send a copy of the claim form and the response to an ACAS conciliation officer; and
  (b) inform the parties that the services of an ACAS conciliation officer are available to them.

(2) Subject to rules 50 and 94, a representative of ACAS may attend any preliminary hearing.

National security proceedings

94.— (1) Where in relation to particular Crown employment proceedings a Minister considers that it would be expedient in the interests of national security, the Minister may direct a Tribunal to—
  (a) conduct all or part of the proceedings in private;
  (b) exclude a person from all or part of the proceedings;
  (c) take steps to conceal the identity of a witness in the proceedings.

(2) Where the Tribunal considers it expedient in the interests of national security, it may order—
  (a) in relation to particular proceedings (including Crown employment proceedings), anything which can be required to be done under paragraph (1);
  (b) a person not to disclose any document (or the contents of any document), where provided for the purposes of the proceedings, to any other person (save for any specified person).
       Any order made must be kept under review by the Tribunal.

(3) Where the Tribunal considers that it may be necessary to make an order under paragraph (2) in relation to particular proceedings (including Crown employment proceedings), the Tribunal may consider any material provided by a party (or where a Minister is not a party, by a Minister) without providing that material to any other person. Such material shall be used by the Tribunal solely for the purposes of deciding whether to make that order (unless that material is subsequently used as evidence in the proceedings by a party).

(4) Where a Minister considers that it would be appropriate for the Tribunal to make an order under paragraph (2), the Minister may make an application for such an order.

(5) Where a Minister has made an application under paragraph (4), the Tribunal may order—
  (a) in relation to the part of the proceedings preceding the outcome of the application, anything which can be required to be done under paragraph (1);
  (b) a person not to disclose any document (or the contents of any document) to any other person (save for any specified person), where provided for the purposes of the proceedings preceding the outcome of the application.

(6) Where a Minister has made an application under paragraph (4) for an order to exclude any person from all or part of the proceedings, the Tribunal shall not send a copy of the response to that person, pending the decision on the application.

(7) If before the expiry of the time limit in rule 16 a Minister makes a direction under paragraph (1) or makes an application under paragraph (4), the Minister may apply for an extension of the time limit in rule 16.

(8) A direction under paragraph (1) or an application under paragraph (4) may be made irrespective of whether or not the Minister is a party.

(9) Where the Tribunal decides not to make an order under paragraph (2), rule 6 of Schedule 2 shall apply to the reasons given by the Tribunal under rule 62 for that decision, save that the reasons will not be entered on the Register.

(10) The Tribunal must ensure that in exercising its functions, information is not disclosed contrary to the interests of national security.

Interim relief proceedings

95. When a Tribunal hears an application for interim relief (or for its variation or revocation) under section 161 or section 165 of the Trade Union and Labour Relations (Consolidation) Act 1992[33] or under section 128 or section 131 of the Employment Rights Act 1996,[34] rules 53 to 56 apply to the hearing and the Tribunal shall not hear oral evidence unless it directs otherwise.

Proceedings involving the National Insurance Fund

96. The Secretary of State shall be entitled to appear and be heard at any hearing in relation to proceedings which may involve a payment out of the National Insurance Fund and shall be treated as a party for the purposes of these Rules.

Collective agreements

97. Where a claim includes a complaint under section 146(1) of the Equality Act relating to a term of a collective agreement, the following persons, whether or not identified in the claim, shall be regarded as the persons against whom a remedy is claimed and shall be treated as respondents for the purposes of these Rules—

(a) the claimant's employer (or prospective employer); and

(b) every organisation of employers and organisation of workers, and every association of or representative of such organisations, which, if the terms were to be varied voluntarily, would be likely, in the opinion of an Employment Judge, to negotiate the variation.

An organisation or association shall not be treated as a respondent if the Judge, having made such enquiries of the claimant and such other enquiries as the Judge thinks fit, is of the opinion that it is not reasonably practicable to identify the organisation or association.

---

[33] 1992 c. 52. Section 161 was amended by the Employment Relations Act 2004 (c. 24), Schedule 1, paragraph 12. Section 165 was amended by the Employment Rights (Dispute Resolution) Act 1998 (c. 8), section 1(2).

[34] 1996 c. 17. Section 128 was amended by S.I. 2010/493. Section 131 was amended by the Employment Rights (Dispute Resolution) Act 1998 (c. 8), section 1(2).

Devolution issues

98.— (1) Where a devolution issue arises, the Tribunal shall as soon as practicable send notice of that fact and a copy of the claim form and response to the Advocate General for Scotland and the Lord Advocate, where it is a Scottish devolution issue, or to the Attorney General and the Counsel General to the Welsh Assembly Government, where it is a Welsh devolution issue, unless they are a party to the proceedings.

(2) A person to whom notice is sent may be treated as a party to the proceedings, so far as the proceedings relate to the devolution issue, if that person sends notice to the Tribunal within 14 days of receiving a notice under paragraph (1).

(3) Any notices sent under paragraph (1) or (2) must at the same time be sent to the parties.

(4) 'Devolution issue' has the meaning given to it in paragraph 1 of Schedule 6 to the Scotland Act 1998[35] (for the purposes of a Scottish devolution issue), and in paragraph 1 of Schedule 9 to the Government of Wales Act 2006[36] (for the purposes of a Welsh devolution issue).

Transfer of proceedings between Scotland and England & Wales

99.— (1) The President (England and Wales) or a Regional Employment Judge may at any time, on their own initiative or on the application of a party, with the consent of the President (Scotland), transfer to a tribunal office in Scotland any proceedings started in England and Wales which could (in accordance with rule 8(3)) have been started in Scotland and which in that person's opinion would more conveniently be determined there.

(2) The President (Scotland) or the Vice President may at any time, on their own initiative or on the application of a party, with the consent of the President (England and Wales), transfer to a tribunal office in England and Wales any proceedings started in Scotland which could (in accordance with rule 8(2)) have been started in England and Wales and in that person's opinion would more conveniently be determined there.

References to the Court of Justice of the European Union

100. Where a Tribunal decides to refer a question to the Court of Justice of the European wUnion for a preliminary ruling under Article 267 of the Treaty on the Functioning of the European Union,[37] a copy of that decision shall be sent to the registrar of that court.

---

[35] 1998 c. 46.
[36] 2006 c. 32.
[37] OJC 83, 30.03.10 p.47.

Transfer of proceedings from a court

101. Where proceedings are referred to a Tribunal by a court, these Rules apply as if the proceedings had been presented by the claimant.

Vexatious litigants

102. The Tribunal may provide any information or documents requested by the Attorney General, the Solicitor General or the Lord Advocate for the purpose of preparing an application or considering whether to make an application under section 42 of the Senior Courts Act 1981,[38] section 1 of the Vexatious Actions (Scotland) Act 1898[39] or section 33 of the Employment Tribunals Act.

Information to the Commission for Equality and Human Rights

103. The Tribunal shall send to the Commission for Equality and Human Rights copies of all judgments and written reasons relating to complaints under section 120, 127 or 146 of the Equality Act. That obligation shall not apply in any proceedings where a Minister of the Crown has given a direction, or a Tribunal has made an order, under rule 94; and either the Security Service, the Secret Intelligence Service or the Government Communications Headquarters is a party to the proceedings.

Application of this Schedule to levy appeals

104. For the purposes of a levy appeal, references in this Schedule to a claim or claimant shall be read as references to a levy appeal or to an appellant in a levy appeal respectively.

Application of this Schedule to appeals against improvement and prohibition notices

105.— (1) A person ('the appellant') may appeal an improvement notice or a prohibition notice by presenting a claim to a tribunal office—
   (a) before the end of the period of 21 days beginning with the date of the service on the appellant of the notice which is the subject of the appeal; or
   (b) within such further period as the Tribunal considers reasonable where it is satisfied that it was not reasonably practicable for an appeal to be presented within that time.
(2) For the purposes of an appeal against an improvement notice or a prohibition notice, this Schedule shall be treated as modified in the following ways—
   (a) references to a claim or claimant shall be read as references to an appeal or to an appellant in an appeal respectively;
   (b) references to a respondent shall be read as references to the inspector appointed under section 19(1) of the Health and Safety Act who issued the notice which is the subject of the appeal.

---

[38] 1981 c. 54.
[39] 1898 c. 35.

221

Application of this Schedule to appeals against unlawful act notices

106. For the purposes of an appeal against an unlawful act notice, this Schedule shall be treated as modified in the following ways—

(a) references in this Schedule to a claim or claimant shall be read as references to a notice of appeal or to an appellant in an appeal against an unlawful act notice respectively;

(b) references to a respondent shall be read as references to the Commission for Equality and Human Rights.

SCHEDULE 2 REGULATION 13(2)

THE EMPLOYMENT TRIBUNALS (NATIONAL SECURITY) RULES OF PROCEDURE

Application of Schedule 2

1.— (1) This Schedule applies to proceedings in relation to which a direction is given, or order is made, under rule 94 and modifies the rules in Schedule 1 in relation to such proceedings.

(2) References in this Schedule to rule numbers are to those in Schedule 1.

(3) The definitions in rule 1 apply to terms in this Schedule and in this Schedule—

'excluded person' means, in relation to any proceedings, a person who has been excluded from all or part of the proceedings by virtue of a direction under rule 94(1)(b) or an order under rule 94(2)(a) (read with rule 94(1)(b)).

Serving of documents

2. The Tribunal shall not send a copy of the response to any excluded person.

Witness orders and disclosure of documents

3.— (1) Where a person or their representative has been excluded under rule 94 from all or part of the proceedings and a Tribunal is considering whether to make an order under rule 31 or 32, a Minister (whether or not he is a party to the proceedings) may make an application to the Tribunal objecting to that order. If such an order has been made, the Minister may make an application to vary or set aside the order.

(2) The Tribunal shall hear and determine the Minister's application in private and the Minister shall be entitled to address the Tribunal.

Special advocate

4.— (1) The Tribunal shall inform the relevant Law Officer if a party becomes an excluded person. For the purposes of this rule, 'relevant Law Officer' means, in relation to England and Wales, the Attorney General, and, in relation to Scotland, the Advocate General.

(2) The relevant Law Officer may appoint a special advocate to represent the interests of a person in respect of those parts of the proceedings from which—

(a) a person's representative is excluded;

(b) a person and their representative are excluded;

(c) a person is excluded and is unrepresented.

(3) A special advocate shall be a person who has a right of audience in relation to any class of proceedings in any part of the Senior Courts or all proceedings in county courts or magistrates' courts, or shall be an advocate or a solicitor admitted in Scotland.

(4) An excluded person (where that person is a party) may make a statement to the Tribunal before the commencement of the proceedings or the relevant part of the proceedings.

(5) The special advocate may communicate, directly or indirectly, with an excluded person at any time before receiving material from a Minister in relation to which the Minister states an objection to disclosure to the excluded person ('closed material').

(6) After receiving closed material, the special advocate must not communicate with any person about any matter connected with the proceedings, except in accordance with paragraph (7) or (9) or an order of the Tribunal.

(7) The special advocate may communicate about the proceedings with—

(a) the Tribunal;

(b) the Minister, or their representative;

(c) the relevant Law Officer, or their representative;

(d) any other person, except for an excluded person or his representative, with whom it is necessary for administrative purposes to communicate about matters not connected with the substance of the proceedings.

(8) The special advocate may apply for an order from the Tribunal to authorise communication with an excluded person or with any other person and if such an application is made—

(a) the Tribunal must notify the Minister of the request; and

(b) the Minister may, within a period specified by the Tribunal, present to the Tribunal and serve on the special advocate notice of any objection to the proposed communication.

(9) After the special advocate has received closed material, an excluded person may only communicate with the special advocate in writing and the special advocate must not reply to the communication, except that the special advocate may send a written acknowledgment of receipt to the legal representative.

(10) References in these Regulations and Schedules 1 and 2 to a party shall include any special advocate appointed in particular proceedings, save that the references to 'party' or 'parties' in rules 3, 6(c), 22, 26, 34, 36(2), 36(3), the first reference in rule 37, 38, 39, 40, 41, 45, 47, 64, 74 to 84, 86, 96 and 98(3) shall not include the special advocate.

Hearings

5.— (1) Subject to any order under rule 50 or any direction or order under rule 94, any hearing shall take place in public, and any party may attend and participate in the hearing.

(2) A member of the Administrative Justice and Tribunals Council shall not be entitled to attend any hearing conducted in private.

Reasons in national security proceedings

6.— (1) The Tribunal shall send a copy of the written reasons given under rule 62 to the Minister and allow 42 days for the Minister to make a direction under paragraph (3) below before sending them to any party or entering them onto the Register.

(2) If the Tribunal considers it expedient in the interests of national security, it may by order take steps to keep secret all or part of the written reasons.

(3) If the Minister considers it expedient in the interests of national security, the Minister may direct that the written reasons—

(a) shall not be disclosed to specified persons and require the Tribunal to prepare a further document which sets out the reasons for the decision, but omits specified information ('the edited reasons');

(b) shall not be disclosed to specified persons and that no further document setting out the reasons for the decision should be prepared.

(4) Where the Minister has directed the Tribunal to prepare edited reasons, the Employment Judge shall initial each omission.

(5) Where a direction has been made under paragraph (3)(a), the Tribunal shall—

(a) send the edited reasons to the specified persons;

(b) send the edited reasons and the written reasons to the relevant persons listed in paragraph (7); and

(c) where the written reasons relate to a judgment, enter the edited reasons on the Register but not enter the written reasons on the Register.

(6) Where a direction has been made under paragraph (3)(b), the Tribunal shall send the written reasons to the relevant persons listed in paragraph (7), but not enter the written reasons on the Register.

(7) The relevant persons are–

(a) the respondent or the respondent's representative, provided that they were not specified in the direction made under paragraph (3);

(b) the claimant or the claimant's representative, provided that they were not specified in the direction made under paragraph (3);

(c) any special advocate appointed in the proceedings; and

(d) where the proceedings were referred to the Tribunal by a court, to that court.

(8) Where written reasons or edited reasons are corrected under rule 69, the Tribunal shall send a copy of the corrected reasons to the same persons who had been sent the reasons.

SCHEDULE 3 REGULATION 13(2)

THE EMPLOYMENT TRIBUNALS (EQUAL VALUE)
RULES OF PROCEDURE

Application of Schedule 3

1.— (1) This Schedule applies to proceedings involving an equal value claim and modifies the rules in Schedule 1 in relation to such proceedings.

(2) The definitions in rule 1 of Schedule 1 apply to terms in this Schedule and in this Schedule—

> 'comparator' means the person of the opposite sex to the claimant in relation to whom the claimant alleges that his or her work is of equal value;
> 'equal value claim' means a claim relating to a breach of a sex equality clause or rule within the meaning of the Equality Act in a case involving work within section 65(1)(c) of that Act;
> 'the facts relating to the question' has the meaning in rule 6(1)(a);
> 'independent expert' means a member of the panel of independent experts mentioned in section 131(8) of the Equality Act;
> 'the question' means whether the claimant's work is of equal value to that of the comparator; and
> 'report' means a report required by a Tribunal to be prepared in accordance with section 131(2) of the Equality Act.

(3) A reference in this Schedule to a rule, is a reference to a rule in this Schedule unless otherwise provided.

(4) A reference in this Schedule to 'these rules' is a reference to the rules in Schedules 1 and 3 unless otherwise provided.

General power to manage proceedings

2.— (1) The Tribunal may (subject to rules 3(1) and 6(1)) order—
- (a) that no new facts shall be admitted in evidence by the Tribunal unless they have been disclosed to all other parties in writing before a date specified by the Tribunal (unless it was not reasonably practicable for a party to have done so);
- (b) the parties to send copies of documents or provide information to the independent expert;
- (c) the respondent to grant the independent expert access to the respondent's premises during a period specified in the order to allow the independent expert to conduct interviews with persons identified as relevant by the independent expert;
- (d) when more than one expert is to give evidence in the proceedings, that those experts present to the Tribunal a joint statement of matters which are agreed between them and matters on which they disagree.

(2) In managing the proceedings, the Tribunal shall have regard to the indicative timetable in the Annex to this Schedule.

Conduct of stage 1 equal value hearing

3.— (1) Where there is a dispute as to whether one person's work is of equal value to another's (equal value being construed in accordance with section 65(6) of the Equality

Act), the Tribunal shall conduct a hearing, which shall be referred to as a 'stage 1 equal value hearing', and at that hearing shall—

(a) strike out the claim (or the relevant part of it) if in accordance with section 131(6) of the Equality Act the Tribunal must determine that the work of the claimant and the comparator are not of equal value;

(b) determine the question or require an independent expert to prepare a report on the question;

(c) if the Tribunal has decided to require an independent expert to prepare a report on the question, fix a date for a further hearing, which shall be referred to as a 'stage 2 equal value hearing'; and

(d) if the Tribunal has not decided to require an independent expert to prepare a report on the question, fix a date for the final hearing.

(2) Before a claim or part is struck out under sub-paragraph (1)(a), the Tribunal shall send notice to the claimant and allow the claimant to make representations to the Tribunal as to whether the evaluation contained in the study in question falls within paragraph (a) or (b) of section 131(6) of the Equality Act. The Tribunal shall not be required to send a notice under this paragraph if the claimant has been given an opportunity to make such representations orally to the Tribunal.

(3) The Tribunal may, on the application of a party, hear evidence and submissions on the issue contained in section 69 of the Equality Act before determining whether to require an independent expert to prepare a report under paragraph (1)(b).

(4) The Tribunal shall give the parties reasonable notice of the date of the stage 1 equal value hearing and the notice shall specify the matters that are to be, or may be, considered at the hearing and give notice of the standard orders in rule 4.

Standard orders for stage 1 equal value hearing

4.— (1) At a stage 1 equal value hearing a Tribunal shall, unless it considers it inappropriate to do so, order that—

(a) before the end of the period of 14 days the claimant shall—

(i) disclose in writing to the respondent the name of any comparator, or, if the claimant is not able to name the comparator, disclose information which enables the respondent to identify the comparator; and

(ii) identify to the respondent in writing the period in relation to which the claimant considers that the claimant's work and that of the comparator are to be compared;

(b) before the end of the period of 28 days—

(i) where the claimant has not disclosed the name of the comparator to the respondent under sub-paragraph (a) and the respondent has been provided with sufficient detail to be able to identify the comparator, the respondent shall disclose in writing the name of the comparator to the claimant;

(ii) the parties shall provide each other with written job descriptions for the claimant and any comparator;

(iii) the parties shall identify to each other in writing the facts which they consider to be relevant to the question;

(c) the respondent shall grant access to the respondent's premises during a period specified in the order to allow the claimant and his or her representative to interview any comparator;

(d) the parties shall before the end of the period of 56 days present to the Tribunal an agreed written statement specifying—
   (i)   job descriptions for the claimant and any comparator;
   (ii) the facts which both parties consider are relevant to the question;
   (iii) the facts on which the parties disagree (as to the fact or as to the relevance to the question) and a summary of their reasons for disagreeing;
(e) the parties shall, at least 56 days before the final hearing, disclose to each other, to any independent or other expert and to the Tribunal written statements of any facts on which they intend to rely in evidence at the final hearing; and
(f) the parties shall, at least 28 days before the final hearing, present to the Tribunal a statement of facts and issues on which the parties are in agreement, a statement of facts and issues on which the parties disagree and a summary of their reasons for disagreeing.
(2) The Tribunal may add to, vary or omit any of the standard orders in paragraph (1).

Involvement of independent expert in fact finding

5. Where the Tribunal has decided to require an independent expert to prepare a report on the question, it may at any stage of the proceedings, on its own initiative or on the application of a party, order the independent expert to assist the Tribunal in establishing the facts on which the independent expert may rely in preparing the report.

Conduct of stage 2 equal value hearing

6.— (1) Any stage 2 equal value hearing shall be conducted by a full tribunal and at the hearing the Tribunal shall—
(a) make a determination of facts on which the parties cannot agree which relate to the question and shall require the independent expert to prepare the report on the basis of facts which have (at any stage of the proceedings) either been agreed between the parties or determined by the Tribunal (referred to as 'the facts relating to the question'); and
(b) fix a date for the final hearing.
(2) Subject to paragraph (3), the facts relating to the question shall, in relation to the question, be the only facts on which the Tribunal shall rely at the final hearing.
(3) At any stage of the proceedings the independent expert may make an application to the Tribunal for some or all of the facts relating to the question to be amended, supplemented or omitted.
(4) The Tribunal shall give the parties reasonable notice of the date of the stage 2 equal value hearing and the notice shall draw the attention of the parties to this rule and give notice of the standard orders in rule 7.

Standard orders for stage 2 equal value hearing

7.— (1) At a stage 2 equal value hearing a Tribunal shall, unless it considers it inappropriate to do so, order that—
(a) by a specified date the independent expert shall prepare his report on the question and shall (subject to rule 13) send copies of it to the parties and to the Tribunal; and

(b) the independent expert shall prepare his report on the question on the basis only of the facts relating to the question.

(2) The Tribunal may add to, vary or omit any of the standard orders in paragraph (1).

Final hearing

8.— (1) Where an independent expert has prepared a report, unless the Tribunal determines that the report is not based on the facts relating to the question, the report of the independent expert shall be admitted in evidence.

(2) If the Tribunal does not admit the report of an independent expert in accordance with paragraph (1), it may determine the question itself or require another independent expert to prepare a report on the question.

(3) The Tribunal may refuse to admit evidence of facts or hear submissions on issues which have not been disclosed to the other party as required by these rules or any order (unless it was not reasonably practicable for a party to have done so).

Duties and powers of the independent expert

9.— (1) When a Tribunal makes an order under rule 3(1)(b) or 5, it shall inform that independent expert of the duties and powers under this rule.

(2) The independent expert shall have a duty to the Tribunal to—

(a) assist it in furthering the overriding objective set out in rule 2 of Schedule 1;

(b) comply with the requirements of these rules and any orders made by the Tribunal;

(c) keep the Tribunal informed of any delay in complying with any order (with the exception of minor or insignificant delays in compliance);

(d) comply with any timetable imposed by the Tribunal in so far as this is reasonably practicable;

(e) when requested, inform the Tribunal of progress in the preparation of the report;

(f) prepare a report on the question based on the facts relating to the question and (subject to rule 13) send it to the Tribunal and the parties; and

(g) attend hearings.

(3) The independent expert may make an application for any order or for a hearing to be held as if he were a party to the proceedings.

(4) At any stage of the proceedings the Tribunal may, after giving the independent expert the opportunity to make representations, withdraw the requirement on the independent expert to prepare a report. If it does so, the Tribunal may itself determine the question, or it may require a different independent expert to prepare the report.

(5) When paragraph (4) applies the independent expert who is no longer required to prepare the report shall provide the Tribunal with all documentation and work in progress relating to the proceedings by a specified date. Such documentation and work in progress must be in a form which the Tribunal is able to use and may be used in relation to those proceedings by the Tribunal or by another independent expert.

Use of expert evidence

10.— (1) The Tribunal shall restrict expert evidence to that which it considers is reasonably required to resolve the proceedings.

(2) An expert shall have a duty to assist the Tribunal on matters within the expert's expertise. This duty overrides any obligation to the person from whom the expert has received instructions or by whom the expert is paid.

(3) No party may call an expert or put in evidence an expert's report without the permission of the Tribunal. No expert report shall be put in evidence unless it has been disclosed to all other parties and any independent expert at least 28 days before the final hearing.

(4) In proceedings in which an independent expert has been required to prepare a report on the question, the Tribunal shall not admit evidence of another expert on the question unless such evidence is based on the facts relating to the question. Unless the Tribunal considers it inappropriate to do so, any such expert report shall be disclosed to all parties and to the Tribunal on the same date on which the independent expert is required to send his report to the parties and to the tribunal.

(5) If an expert (other than an independent expert) does not comply with these rules or an order made by the Tribunal, the Tribunal may order that the evidence of that expert shall not be admitted.

(6) Where two or more parties wish to submit expert evidence on a particular issue, the Tribunal may order that the evidence on that issue is to be given by one joint expert only and if the parties wishing to instruct the joint expert cannot agree an expert, the Tribunal may select an expert.

Written questions to experts (including independent experts)

11.— (1) When an expert has prepared a report, a party or any other expert involved in the proceedings may put written questions about the report to the expert who has prepared the report.

(2) Unless the Tribunal agrees otherwise, written questions under paragraph (1)—

(a) may be put once only;

(b) must be put within 28 days of the date on which the parties were sent the report;

(c) must be for the purpose only of clarifying the factual basis of the report; and

(d) must be copied to all other parties and experts involved in the proceedings at the same time as they are sent to the expert who prepared the report.

(3) An expert shall answer written questions within 28 days of receipt and the answers shall be treated as part of the expert's report.

(4) Where a party has put a written question to an expert instructed by another party and the expert does not answer that question within 28 days, the Tribunal may order that the party instructing that expert may not rely on the evidence of that expert.

Procedural matters

12.— (1) Where an independent expert has been required to prepare a report, the Tribunal shall send that expert notice of any hearing, application, order or judgment in the proceedings as if the independent expert were a party to those proceedings and when these rules or an order requires a party to provide information to another party, such information shall also be provided to the independent expert.

(2) There may be more than one stage 1 or stage 2 equal value hearing in any case.

(3) Any power conferred on an Employment Judge by Schedule 1 may (subject to the provisions of this Schedule) in an equal value claim be carried out by a full tribunal or an Employment Judge.

National security proceedings

13. Where in an equal value claim a direction is given, or order is made, under rule 94 of Schedule 1—
  (a) any independent expert appointed shall send a copy of any report and any responses to written questions to the Tribunal only; and
  (b) before the Tribunal sends the parties a copy of a report or answers which have been received from an independent expert, it shall follow the procedure set out in rule 6 of Schedule 2 as if that rule referred to the independent expert's report or answers (as the case may be) instead of written reasons, except that the independent expert's report or answers shall not be entered on the Register.

ANNEX
THE INDICATIVE TIMETABLE

Claims not involving an independent expert	*Claims involving an independent expert*
Claim	Claim
⇩	⇩
28 days	28 days
⇩	⇩
Response	Response
⇩	⇩
3 weeks	3 weeks
⇩	⇩
Stage 1 equal value hearing	Stage 1 equal value hearing
⇩	⇩
⇩	10 weeks
⇩	⇩
⇩	Stage 2 equal value hearing
⇩	⇩
⇩	8 weeks
18 weeks	⇩
⇩	Independent expert's report
⇩	⇩
⇩	4 weeks
⇩	⇩
⇩	written questions
⇩	⇩
⇩	8 weeks
⇩	⇩
⇩	⇩
⇩	⇩
Hearing	Hearing
Total 25 week	Total 37 weeks.

EXPLANATORY NOTE

(This note is not part of the Regulations)

These Regulations replace the Employment Tribunals (Constitution and Rules of Procedure) Regulations 2004 ('the 2004 Regulations'). The rules of procedure in Schedules 1 to 3 replace the existing rules of procedure in the Employment Tribunals set out in Schedules 1 to 6 to the 2004 Regulations.

Regulations 4 to 6 provide for the establishment of Employment Tribunals and the appointment of the Presidents, the Vice President and Regional Employment Judges, and regulation 7 sets out the responsibilities of those office holders.

Regulations 8 and 9 detail who shall sit to determine proceedings in the Employment Tribunals and regulation 10 make special provision for the composition of Employment Tribunals when dealing with national security proceedings.

Regulation 11 gives each President power to make practice directions in relation to the area (either Scotland or England and Wales) for which the President is responsible.

Regulation 12 delegates to the Secretary of State the power to prescribe forms to be used by claimants and respondents in proceedings before an Employment Tribunal and regulation 12(2) lists the proceedings in which a prescribed form need not be used.

Regulation 13 provides that Schedule 1 to the Regulations is to apply to all proceedings before an Employment Tribunal. However, Schedule 1 is modified by Schedules 2 and 3 in relation to the proceedings to which those Schedules apply.

Regulation 14 makes provision for the maintenance of a register of judgments and written reasons issued by an Employment Tribunal.

Regulation 15 makes transitional provision in relation to the presentation of a response which contains an employer's contract claim and in relation to proceedings which were presented before 29th July 2013 and in respect of which Schedule 3, 4 or 5 of the 2004 Regulations applied. Subject to those transitional provisions, these Regulations apply to all proceedings before the Employment Tribunals.

Schedule 1 sets out the rules of procedure for claims before the Employment Tribunals. Rule 1 sets out the definitions relevant to those rules.

Rule 2 provides that the overriding objective of the rules is to enable the Employment Tribunals to deal with cases fairly and justly.

Rules 4 and 5 contain provisions on the calculation of time and extending and shortening time limits.

Rule 7 provides for the publication by the Presidents of guidance on the exercise of powers in the rules.

Rule 8 sets out the requirements for the presentation of a claim in the Employment Tribunals and rule 10 provides that a claim shall be rejected by an Employment Tribunal if a prescribed form is not used or certain information is not contained in the claim.

Rule 11 provides that, if any enactment requires a claim to be accompanied by a fee or an application for a remission from that fee and a claim is presented without such a fee or application, then that claim shall be rejected.

Rule 12 provides that an Employment Judge may reject a claim if the Employment Tribunals do not have jurisdiction to consider it, or it is in a form which cannot sensibly be responded to or is otherwise an abuse of process.

Rule 13 provides for the reconsideration of a rejection made under rule 10 or 12.

Rule 16 provides that a respondent has 28 days from the date that the copy of the claim was sent by an Employment Tribunal in which to present a response.

Rule 17 provides that a response shall be rejected if a prescribed form is not used or certain information is not contained in the response and rule 18 provides that a response shall be rejected if it is presented late.

Rule 19 provides for the reconsideration of a rejection made under rule 17 or 18.

Rule 20 allows a respondent to make an application for an extension of time for presenting the response to a claim.

Rule 21 sets out how an Employment Tribunal will determine a claim if no response is presented or the respondent does not contest a claim.

Rules 23 to 25 set out the process for presenting, and responding to, an employer's contract claim.

Rule 26 provides for an initial consideration of the claim and response. Rules 27 and 28 set out the process for the dismissal of all, or part, of the claim or response, if at this stage the Tribunal considers that the claim, response, or the part in question, has no reasonable prospect of success.

Rules 29 to 40 set out the Employment Tribunals' case management and other powers and the procedure for making applications for case management orders.

Rule 29 sets out the Employment Tribunals' general power to manage proceedings.

Rule 30 sets out the procedure for making applications for case management orders.

Rule 36 introduces a lead case mechanism, which enables an Employment Tribunal to identify claims giving rise to common or related issues of fact and law, specify one or more of those claims as a lead claim, and stay (in Scotland sist) the other claims. The related cases shall be bound by decisions in the lead case on the related issues, although a party may apply for such a decision not to apply to a related case.

Rule 37 provides the Employment Tribunals with the power to strike out all or part of a claim or response if one the specified grounds applies.

Rule 38 provides that an unless order may specify that all or part of a claim or response shall be struck out if the order is not complied with by a specified date.

Rule 39 provides that where an Employment Tribunal considers that a specific allegation or argument in a claim or response has little reasonable prospect of success it can order the relevant party to pay a deposit of up to £1,000 as a condition of continuing to advance that allegation or argument.

Rule 40 sets out the consequences which will follow if a party fails to pay any fee required under any enactment.

Rules 41 to 50 set out the rules common to all kinds of hearings, including rules on written representations (rule 42), witnesses (rule 43) and timetabling (rule 45).

Rule 50 provides that an Employment Tribunal may make an order to prevent or restrict disclosure of any aspect of proceedings so far as necessary in the interests of justice. Paragraph (3) lists examples of orders which may be made under this rule. Any person with a legitimate interest may, if he or she did not have opportunity to make representations before the order was made, apply for such an order to be revoked or discharged.

Rules 51 and 52 set out the procedure for withdrawal of a claim and provide for dismissal following withdrawal.

Rules 53 to 56 set out the scope of, and procedure for, preliminary hearings. Rules 57 to 59 set out the scope of, and procedure for, final hearings.

Rules 60 and 61 concern decisions made by an Employment Tribunal and rule 62 concerns reasons given by an Employment Tribunal.

Rule 65 sets out when a judgment or order takes effect and rule 66 sets out the time for compliance with a judgment or order which requires the payment of money.

Rules 70 to 73 set out the procedure for reconsideration by an Employment Tribunal of a judgment.

Rules 74 to 84 describe the circumstances in which a costs (in Scotland, expenses), preparation time, or wasted costs order may be made.

Rules 85 to 91 concern the requirements on delivery of documents to an Employment Tribunal, parties and non-parties.

Rule 92 introduces a new requirement on parties to copy all communications which they send to an Employment Tribunal to all other parties.

Rule 99 provides that proceedings may be transferred between Scotland and England and Wales.

Rule 104 modifies the application of the rest of Schedule 1 in relation to levy appeals under the Industrial Training Act 1982 (modifications for such proceedings appeared in Schedule 3 to the 2004 Regulations).

Rule 105 modifies the application of the rest of Schedule 1 in relation to appeals against an improvement or prohibition notice under the Health and Safety at Work etc. Act 1974 (modifications for such proceedings appeared in Schedule 4 to the 2004 Regulations).

Rule 106 modifies the application of the rest of Schedule 1 in relation to appeals against an unlawful act notice under the Equality Act 2006 (modifications for such proceedings appeared in Schedule 5 to the 2004 Regulations).

Schedule 2 modifies the application of Schedule 1 in relation to proceedings in which a direction is given, or an order is made, under rule 94 (national security proceedings) of Schedule 1.

Schedule 3 modifies the application of Schedule 1 in relation to proceedings involving an equal value claim (as defined in rule 1 of Schedule 3).

APPENDIX 2

2013 No. 1893
TRIBUNALS AND INQUIRIES
Employment Tribunals and Employment Appeal Tribunal Fees Order 2013

Made   28th July 2013
Coming into force   29th July 2013

The Lord Chancellor makes the following Order with the consent of the Treasury in exercise of the powers conferred by sections 42(1)(d) and (2) and 49(3) of the Tribunals, Courts and Enforcement Act 2007.[1]

The Lord Chancellor has consulted the Senior President of Tribunals and the Administrative Justice and Tribunals Council in accordance with section 42(5) before making this Order.

In accordance with section 49(5), a draft of this Order was laid before and has been approved by a resolution of each House of Parliament.

PART 1
GENERAL

Citation and commencement

1. This Order may be cited as the Employment Tribunals and the Employment Appeal Tribunal Fees Order 2013 and shall come into force on the day after the date on which it is made.

Interpretation

2. In this Order—

'the 2007 Act' means the Tribunals, Courts and Enforcement Act 2007;
'appellant' means a person who appeals to the Employment Appeal Tribunal against a decision of an employment tribunal;
'claim' means any proceedings brought before an employment tribunal and includes an appeal, application, complaint, reference or question, and 'claimant' shall be construed accordingly;

---

[1] 2007 c. 15.

'claim form' means the form by means of which a person presents a claim;
'employer's contract claim' means a claim brought by an employer in accordance with articles 4 and 8 of the Employment Tribunals Extension of Jurisdiction (England and Wales) Order 1994[2] or articles 4 and 8 of the Employment Tribunals Extension of Jurisdiction (Scotland) Order 1994;[3]
'fee group' means—

    (a) in relation to the payment of the issue fee, the group of persons named as claimants in the claim form at the time the claim was presented;

    (b) subject to article 12(2), in relation to the payment of a hearing fee, the group of persons each of whom—

        (i) were named as claimants in the claim form at the time the claim was presented; and

        (ii) are named as claimants in the notification of the listing of the final hearing.

'final hearing' means the first hearing at which an employment tribunal will determine liability, remedy or costs;
'notice of appeal' means the notice referred to in rule 3(1)(a) of the Employment Appeal Tribunal Rules 1993;[4] and
'single claimant' means a claimant who is the only claimant named in the claim form.

Matters in relation to which fees are payable

3. Fees are payable in respect of any claim presented to an employment tribunal, or an appeal to the Employment Appeal Tribunal, as provided for in this Order.

PART 2
FEES IN EMPLOYMENT TRIBUNALS

Fee charging occasions

1.— (1) A fee is payable by a single claimant or a fee group—

    (a) when a claim form is presented to an employment tribunal ('the issue fee'); and

    (b) on a date specified in a notice accompanying the notification of the listing of a final hearing of the claim ('the hearing fee').

(2) A fee is payable by the party making an application listed in column 1 of Schedule 1 on a date specified by the Lord Chancellor in a notice following the making of the application.

---

  [2] S.I. 1994/1623, as amended by section 1(2) of the Employment Rights (Dispute Resolution) Act 1998 (c. 8), S.I. 2004/752 and S.I. 2011/1133.
  [3] S.I. 1994/1624, as amended by section 1(2) of the Employment Rights (Dispute Resolution) Act 1998 (c. 8), S.I. 2004/752 and S.I. 2011/1133.
  [4] S.I. 1993/2854 as amended by S.I. 1996/3216, section 1(2) of the Employment Rights (Dispute Resolution) Act 1998 (c. 8), S.I. 2001/1128, S.I. 2004/2526, S.I. 2004/3426, S.I. 2005/1871, section 59(5) of, and paragraph 5 of Part 3 of Schedule 11 to, the Constitutional Reform Act 2005 (c. 4), and S.I. 2010/1088.

(3) A fee of £600 is payable by the respondent on a date specified in a notice accompanying a notification of listing for judicial mediation.

Fees payable

5. Table 1 in Schedule 2 has effect for the purpose of defining expressions used in Table 2 in that Schedule.

6. The issue fee and hearing fee payable by a single claimant in respect of a claim listed in Table 2 in Schedule 2 ('a type A claim') is the amount specified in column 2 of Table 3 in Schedule 2.

7. The issue fee and hearing fee payable by a single claimant in respect of any claim other than one listed in Table 2 in Schedule 2 ('a type B claim') is the amount specified in column 3 of Table 3 in Schedule 2.

8. Subject to articles 9 and 10, the issue fee and hearing fee payable by a fee group is the amount calculated by reference to Table 4 in Schedule 2.

9. Subject to article 10, where, on the date on which a fee is payable in accordance with article 4, the claim form contains—

(a) one or more type A claim and one or more type B claim, the total amount of the fees payable in respect of all the claims is the fee specified in respect of a type B claim; or

(b) more than one claim of the same type, then the total amount of the fees payable in respect of all the claims is the amount specified in Table 3 or, in the case of a fee group, Table 4 in Schedule 2 for that type of claim.

10. Any fee payable by a fee group under article 8 or 9—

(a) must not exceed an amount equal to the sum of the fees which the members of the fee group would have been liable to pay as single claimants; and

(b) where one or more members of the group is entitled to remission in accordance with Schedule 3, must not exceed an amount equal to the sum of the fees which the members of the fee group would be liable to pay as single claimants, taking into account any remission which would have been granted to individual members of the group if they were single claimants.

11.— (1) The fee payable in relation to an application listed in column 1 of Schedule 1, irrespective of the number of claims or of claimants named in the application is the amount specified in the relevant part of column 2 of Schedule 1.

(2) Where an application referred to in paragraph (1) is made in respect of one or more type A claims and one or more type B claims, the amount of the fee payable in respect of the application is the amount specified in column 2 of Schedule 1 in respect of a type B claim.

Fee group—failure to pay fee

12.— (1) Where a fee payable by a fee group remains unpaid after the date specified in accordance with article 4, a member of that fee group may, before the date on which the claim to which the fee relates is liable to be struck out for non payment, notify the Lord Chancellor of that member's decision no longer to be part of the group.

(2) Where a notice is received by the Lord Chancellor before the date on which the claim is liable to be struck out, the member of the fee group who has given the notification shall be treated as a single claimant for the purposes of the claim to which the notice referred to in paragraph (1) relates.

PART 3
FEES IN THE EMPLOYMENT APPEAL TRIBUNAL

Fees payable

13. A fee of £400 is payable by an appellant on the date specified in a notice issued by the Lord Chancellor, following the receipt by the Employment Appeal Tribunal of a notice of appeal.

14. A fee of £1200 is payable by an appellant on the date specified in a notice issued by the Lord Chancellor, following a direction by the Employment Appeal Tribunal that a matter proceed to an oral hearing at which the appeal is to be finally disposed of.

PART 4
TRANSITIONAL ARRANGEMENTS, REMISSION ETC

Transitional arrangements

15. No fee is payable in respect of a claim where the claim form was presented before the date this Order comes into force.

16. No fee is payable in respect of proceedings in the Employment Appeal Tribunal where a notice of appeal was received by that Tribunal before the date on which this Order comes into force.

Remission provisions

17.— (1) Schedule 3 applies for the purposes of determining whether a person is entitled to a remission or part remission of any fee otherwise payable under this Order.

(2) Where an application for remission is made by a member of a fee group, Schedule 3 is to have effect for the purposes of determining whether or not the member of the group would be entitled to remission (whether wholly or in part) if that person was a single claimant.

18. The Lord Chancellor may disregard an application for remission by a member of a fee group if the amount of the fee payable by the fee group would not be altered in consequence of the application being granted.

International obligations

19. Where by any Convention, treaty or other instrument entered into by Her Majesty with any foreign power it is provided that no fee is required to be paid in respect of any proceedings, the fees specified in this Order are not payable in respect of those proceedings.

Signed by authority of the Lord Chancellor

Helen Grant
Parliamentary Under Secretary of State
Ministry of Justice
28th July 2013

We consent,

Robert Goodwill
Desmond Swayne
Two of the Lords Commissioners of Her Majesty's Treasury
17th July 2013

SCHEDULE 1 ARTICLES 4 AND 11
EMPLOYMENT TRIBUNALS—OTHER FEES

Fee(s) payable by applicant

Column 1	Column 2	
Type of application	*Type A claim*	*Type B claim*
Reconsideration of a default judgment	£100	£100
Reconsideration of a judgment following a final hearing	£100	£350
Dismissal following withdrawal	£60	£60
An employer's contract claim made by way of application as part of the response to the employee's contract claim	£160	–

SCHEDULE 2 ARTICLES 4 TO 9

EMPLOYMENT TRIBUNALS—ISSUE AND HEARING FEE

Table 1 Abbreviations used in Table 2 in this Schedule

CAR	Civil Aviation (Working Time) Regulations 2004[5]
CCBR	Companies (Cross-Border Mergers) Regulations 2007[6]
CEC	Colleges of Education (Compensation) Regulations 1975[7]
COMAH	Control of Major Accident Hazards Regulations 1999[8]
EA 2006	Equality Act 2006[9]
EA 2010	Equality Act 2010[10]
EAA	Employment Agencies Act 1973[11]
ECSR	European Cooperative Society (Involvement of Employees) Regulations 2006[12]
EJOs	Employment Tribunals Extension of Jurisdiction (England and Wales) Order 1994[13]Employment Tribunals Extension of Jurisdiction (Scotland) Order 1994[14]
EOR	Ecclesiastical Offices (Terms of Service) Regulations 2009[15]
ELLR	European Public Limited-Liability Company (Employee Involvement) (Great Britain) Regulations 2009[16]
ERA	Employment Rights Act 1996[17]
ETA	Employment Tribunals Act 1996[18]

---

[5] S.I. 2004/756 as amended by S.I. 2008/960 and S.I. 2010/1226.

[6] S.I. 2007/2974 as amended by S.I. 2008/583, S.I. 2009/3348, S.I. 2010/93, S.I. 2011/1606; S.I. 2009/317 and SI 2011/245.

[7] S.I. 1975/1092 as amended by S.I. 1981/1088 and section 1(2) of the Employment Rights (Dispute Resolution) Act 1998 (c. 8).

[8] S.I. 1999/743 as amended by section 328(7) of the Greater London Authority Act 1999 (c. 29), S.I. 2002/2469, S.I. 2005/1088, S.I. 2008/960, S.I. 2008/1087 and S.I. 2009/1595.

[9] 2006 c. 3.

[10] 2010 c. 15.

[11] 1973 c. 35.

[12] S.I. 2006/2059 as amended by S.I. 2009/3348 and S.I. 2010/93.

[13] S.I. 1994/1623 as amended by section 1(2) of the Employment Rights (Dispute Resolution) Act 1998 (c. 8), S.I. 2004/752 and S.I S.I. 2011/1133.

[14] S.I. 1994.1624, as amended by section 1(2) of the Employment Rights (Dispute Resolution) Act 1998 (c. 8), S.I. 2004/752 and S.I 2011/1133.

[15] S.I. 2009/2108 as amended by S.I. 2010/2407 and S.I. 2010/2848.

[16] S.I. 2009/2401 as amended by S.I. 2010/93.

[17] 1996 c. 18.

[18] 1996 c. 17.

Table 1 (*Continued*)

FVR	Fishing Vessels (Working Time: Sea-fishermen) Regulations 2004[19]
HSCE	Health and Safety (Consultation with Employees) Regulations 1996[20]
HSWA	Health and Safety at Work etc Act 1974[21]
ICR	Information and Consultation of Employees Regulations 2004[22]
ITA	Industrial Training Act 1982[23]
MSR	Merchant Shipping (Working Time: Inland Waterways) Regulations 2003[24]
NMWA	National Minimum Wage Act 1998[25]
OPR	Occupational and Personal Pension Schemes (Consultation by Employers and Miscellaneous Amendment) Regulations 2006[26]
OPS(CO)R	Occupational Pension Schemes (Contracting-Out) Regulations 1996[27]
OPS(DI)R	Occupational Pensions Schemes (Disclosure of Information) Regulations 1996[28]
PSA	Pension Schemes Act 1993[29]
REACHER	REACH Enforcement Regulations 2008[30]
RTR	Road Transport (Working Time) Regulations 2005[31]
SRSC	Safety Representatives and Safety Committees Regulations 1977[32]

[19] 2004/1713 as amended by S.I. 2009/3348.

[20] S.I. 1996/1513 as amended by section 1(2) of the Employment Rights (Dispute Resolution) Act 1998 (c. 8), S.I. 1999/3242 and S.S.I. 2006/457.

[21] 1974 c. 37.

[22] S.I. 2004/3426 as amended by S.I. 2006/514, S.I. 2006/2405, S.I. 2009/3348 and S.I. 2010/93.

[23] 1982 c. 10.

[24] S.I. 2003/3049 as amended by S.I. 2006/3223 and S.I. 2009/3348.

[25] 1998 c. 39.

[26] S.I. 2006/349 as amended by S.I. 2006/778, S.I. 2007/814, S.I. 2007/3014, S.I. 2009/615, S.I. 2009/3348, S.I. 2010/499, S.I. 2011/672 and S.I. 2012/692.

[27] S.I. 1996/1172 as amended by S.I. 1996/1577, S.I. 1997/786, S.I. 1997/819, S.I. 1997/3038, S.I. 1998/1397, section 1(2) of the Employment Rights (Dispute Resolution) Act 1998 (c. 8), S.I. 1999/3198, S.I. 2000/2975, S.I. 2001/943, S.I. 2002/681, S.I. 2005/706, S.I. 2005/2050, S.I. 2005/3377, S.I. 2006/744, S.I. 2006/778, S.I. 2006/1337, S.I. 2007/60, S.I. 2007/814, S.I. 2007/834, S.I. 2007/1154, S.I. 2007/3014, S.I. 2008/2301, S.I. 2009/598, S.I. 2009/615, S.I. 2009/846, S.I. 2009/2930, S.I. 2010/499, S.I. 2011/1245, S.I. 2011/1246, S.I. 2011/1294, S.I. 2012/542, S.I. 2012/1817; modified by S.I. 1996/1977 and S.I. 2012/687.

[28] S.I. 1996/1655 as amended by S.I. 1997/786, S.I. 1997/3038, section 1(2) of the Employment Rights (Dispute Resolution) Act 1998 (c. 8), S.I. 1999/3198, S.I. 2000/1403, S.I. 2000/2691, S.I. 2002/459, S.I. 2002/1383, S.I. 2005/704, S.I. 2005/706, S.I. 2005/2877, S.I. 2005/3377, section 50(1) of the Commissioners for Revenue and Customs Act 2005 (c. 11), S.I. 2006/467, S.I. 2006/1733, S.I. 2007/60, S.I. 2007/814, S.I. 2008/649, S.I. 2008/2301, S.I. 2009/598, S.I. 2009/615, S.I. 2009/1906, S.I. 2010/2659, S.I. 2011/1245, S.I. 2011/1246, S.I. 2012/1811, S.I. 2012/1817 and modified by S.I. 2011/673.

[29] 1993 c. 48.

[30] S.I. 2008/2852 as amended by S.I. 2009/716, S.I. 2010/1513, S.I. 2011/3058 and S.I. 2012/632.

[31] S.I. 2005/639 as amended by S.I. 2007/853 and S.I. 2012/991.

[32] S.I. 1977/500 as amended by S.I. 1992/2051, S.I. 1996/1513, section 1(2) of the Employment Rights (Dispute Resolution) Act 1998 (c. 8), S.I. 1999/860, S.I. 1999/2024, S.I. 1999/3242, S.I. 2005/1541, S.I. 2006/594, S.I. 2008/960, S.I. 2012/199 and S.I. 2006/457.

Table 1 (*Continued*)

TULR(C)A	Trade Union and Labour Relations (Consolidation) Act 1992[33]
TUPE	Transfer of Undertakings (Protection of Employment) Regulations 2006[34]
WTR	Working Time Regulations 1998[35]

Table 2 Type A claims

Column 1 *Description of claim*	Column 2 *Provision identifying the rights of the claimant*	Column 3 *Provision conferring jurisdiction on tribunal*
Application by the Secretary of State to prohibit a person from running an Employment Agency	Sections 3A EAA[36]	Sections 3A EAA
Application by a person subject to a prohibition order to vary or set it aside	Section 3C EAA	Section 3C EAA
Appeal against improvement or prohibition notice	Section 24 HSWA[37]	Section 24 HSWA
Appeal against assessment of training levy	Section 12 ITA[38]	Section 12 ITA
Complaint of deduction of unauthorised subscriptions	Section 68 TULR(C)A[39]	Section 68A TULR(C)A[40]

---

[33] 1992 c. 52.

[34] S.I. 2006/246 as amended by S.R. 2006/177, S.I. 2009/592, S.I. 2010/93; modified by section 2 of and paragraph 2 of Schedule 2 to the Ordnance Factories and Military Services Act 1984 (c. 59), section 1(4) to (9) of the Dockyard Services Act 1986 (c. 52), section 2 of the Atomic Weapons Establishment Act 1991 (c. 41) and by section 9 of the Export and Investment Guarantees Act 1991 (c. 67).

[35] S.I. 1998/1833 as amended by S.I. 1999/3242, S.I. 1999/3372, S.I. 2001/3256, S.I. 2002/3128, S.I. 2003/1684, S.I. 2003/3049, S.I. 2004/1713, S.I. 2004/2516, S.I. 2005/2241, S.I. 2006/99, S.I. 2006/557, S.I. 2006/594, S.I. 2006/2389, S.I. 2007/2079, S.I. 2008/960, S.I. 2008/1660, S.I. 2008/1696, S.I. 2009/1567, S.I. 2009/2766, S.I. 2009/3348 and S.I. 2011/1133.

[36] 1973 c. 35; sections 3A and 3C were inserted by section 35 of, and paragraph 1(3) of Schedule 10 to, the Deregulation and Contracting Out Act 1994 (c. 40) which was amended by section 1(2) of the Employment Rights (Dispute Resolution) Act 1998 (c. 8).

[37] 1974 c. 37; section 24 amended by section 1(2) of the Employment Rights (Dispute Resolution) Act 1998 (c. 8).

[38] 1982 c. 10; section 12 was amended by section 22(4) of, and paragraph 11 of Schedule 4 to, the Employment Act 1989 (c. 8) and sections 25(6) and 29 of, and paragraphs 1 and 4 of Schedule 1 to, the Further Education and Training Act 2007(c. 25)and section 1(2) of the Employment Rights (Dispute Resolution) Act 1998 (c. 8).

[39] 1992 c. 52; section 68 was substituted first by section 15 of the Trade Union Reform and Employment Rights Act 1993 (c. 19) which was then substituted by article 2(1) of S.I. 1998/1529.

[40] Section 68A was inserted by section 15 of the Trade Union Reform and Employment Rights Act 1993 (c. 19) and amended by section 1(2) of the Employment Rights (Dispute Resolution) Act 1998 (c. 8), S.I. 1998/1529 and section 240 of, and paragraph 56(1) and (4) of Schedule 1 to, the Employment Rights Act 1996 (c. 18).

Table 2 (*Continued*)

Column 1 Description of claim	Column 2 Provision identifying the rights of the claimant	Column 3 Provision conferring jurisdiction on tribunal
Complaint relating to failure to deduct or refuse to deduct an amount to a political fund	Section 86 TULR(C)A	Section 87 TULR(C)A[41]
Complaint that an employer has failed to permit time off for carrying out trade union duties	Section 168 TULR(C)A[42]	Section 168 TULR(C)A
Complaint that an employer has failed to permit time off for union learning representatives	Section 168A TULR(C)A[43]	Section 168A TULR(C)A
Complaint that an employer has failed to pay for time off for union learning representatives	Section 169 TULR(C)A[44]	Section 169 TULR(C)A
Complaint that an employer has failed to permit time off for trade union activities	Section 170 TULR(C)A[45]	Section 170 TULR(C)A
Complaint that employer has failed, wholly or in part, to pay remuneration under a protective award	Section 190 TULR(C)A[46]	Section 192 TULR(C)A[47]
Complaint that the Secretary of State has not paid, or has paid less than, the amount of relevant contributions which should have been paid into a pension scheme	Section 124 PSA[48]	Section 126 PSA
Breach of contract, except where the employer's contract claim is made made by way of application as part of the employer's response to the employee's contract claim (as to which, see instead article 4 and Schedule 1 to this Order)	Section 3 ETA[49]	Articles 3 and 4 of each of the EJOs

[41] Section 87 was substituted by section 6 of the Employment Rights (Dispute Resolution) Act 1998 (c. 8).

[42] Section 168 was amended by S.I. 1995/1925, S.I. 2006/246 and section 1(2) of the of the Employment Rights (Dispute Resolution) Act 1998 (c. 8).

[43] Section 168A was inserted by section 43 of the Employment Act 2002 (c. 10).

[44] Section 169 was amended by section 43 of the Employment Act 2002 (c. 10) and section 1(2) of the of the Employment Rights (Dispute Resolution) Act 1998 (c. 8).

[45] Section 170 was amended by section 43 of the Employment Act 2002 (c. 10) and section 1(2) of the of the Employment Rights (Dispute Resolution) Act 1998 (c. 8).

[46] Section 190 was amended by section 1(2) of the of the Employment Rights (Dispute Resolution) Act 1998 (c. 8), sections 34 and 51 of, and Schedule 10 to, the Trade Union Reform and Employment Rights Act 1993 (c. 19) and by section 240 of, and paragraph 56(1) and (14) of Schedule 1 to, the Employment Rights Act 1996 (c. 18).

[47] Section 192 was amended by section 1(2) of the of the Employment Rights (Dispute Resolution) Act 1998 (c. 8) and by S.I. 1998/1658.

[48] 1993 c. 48; section 124 was amended by section 90 of the Pensions Act 1995 (c. 26), section 240 of, and paragraph 61(1) and (3) of Schedule 1 to, the Employment Rights Act 1996 (c. 18) and by section 319(1) of, and paragraphs 9 and 20 of Schedule 12 to the Pensions Act 2004 (c. 35).

[49] 1996 c. 18; section 3 was amended by sections 35, 36 and 54 of, and Schedule 8 to, the Employment Act 2002 (c. 10).

Table 2 (*Continued*)

Column 1 Description of claim	Column 2 Provision identifying the rights of the claimant	Column 3 Provision conferring jurisdiction on tribunal
Reference to determine what particulars ought to be included in a statement of employment particulars or changes to particulars	Sections 1 and 4 ERA	Section 11 ERA[50]
Reference to determine what particulars ought to be included in an itemised pay statement	Section 8 ERA	Section 11 ERA
Complaint of unauthorised deductions from wages	Section 13 ERA	Section 23 ERA[51]
Complaint that employer has received unauthorised payments	Section 15 ERA	Section 23 ERA
Complaint that employer has failed to pay guaranteed payment	Section 28 ERA	Section 34 ERA[52]
Complaint that employer has failed to permit time off for public duties	Section 50 ERA[53]	Section 51 ERA(54)[54]
Complaint that employer has refused to permit, or has failed to pay for, time off to look for work or arrange training	Sections 52 and 53 ERA	Section 54 ERA[55]
Complaint that employer has refused to allow, or has failed to pay for, time off for ante-natal care	Sections 55[56], 56, 57ZA and 57ZB[57] ERA	Sections 57[58] and 57ZC[59] ERA

---

[50] 1996 c. 18; section 11 was amended by section 1(2) of the of the Employment Rights (Dispute Resolution) Act 1998 (c. 8) and by S.I. 2011/1133.

[51] Section 23 was amended by sections 1(2) and 15 of, and paragraph 18 of Schedule 1 to, the Employment Rights (Dispute Resolution) Act 1998 (c. 8) and by S.I. 2011/1133.

[52] Section 34 was amended by section 1(2) of the of the Employment Rights (Dispute Resolution) Act 1998 (c. 8) and by S.I. 2011/1133.

[53] Section 50 was amended by section 134(1) of, and paragraph 88 of Schedule 9 to, the Police Act 1997 (c. 50), S.I. 2000/90, S.I. 2000/1737, S.I. 2000/2463, section 60(2) of the Standards in Scotland's Schools etc Act 2000 (c. 6), S.I. 2001/2237, S.I. 2002/808, S.I. 2002/2469, section 34 of, and paragraphs 99 and 100 of Schedule 4 to, the Health and Social Care (Community Health and Standards) Act 2003 (c. 43), sections 59 and 174 of, and paragraphs 84 and 86 of Schedule 4 to, the Serious Organised Crime and Police Act 2005 (c. 15), section 2 of, and paragraphs 177 and 179 of Schedule 1 to, the National Health Service (Consequential Provisions) Act 2006 (c. 43), section 52 of, and paragraph 31 of Schedule 14 and Part 1(B) of Schedule 15 to, the Police and Justice Act 2006 (c. 48), S.I. 2007/961, S.I. 2007/1837 section 39 of, and paragraph 8 of Schedule 3 to, the Offender Management Act 2007 (c. 21), S.I. 2010/1080,S.I. 2010/1158, S.I. 2011/2581, section 99 of, and paragraph 219 of Schedule 16 to, the Police Reform and Social Responsibility Act 2011 (c. 13), section 11 of, and paragraph 24 of Schedule 2 to the Education Act 2011 (c. 21) and sections 55, 179, 249 and 277 of, and paragraphs 72 and 74 of Schedule 5, paragraphs 68 and 69 of Schedule 14, paragraph 6 of Schedule 17, paragraph 6 of Schedule 19 to, the Health and Social Care Act 2012 (c. 7).

[54] Section 51 was amended by section 1(2) of the of the Employment Rights (Dispute Resolution) Act 1998 (c. 8) and by S.I. 2011/1133.

[55] Section 54 was amended by section 1(2) of the of the Employment Rights (Dispute Resolution) Act 1998 (c. 8) and by S.I. 2011/1133.

[56] Section 55 was amended by S.I. 2002/53 and S.I. 2004/1771.

[57] Sections 57ZA and 57ZB were inserted by S.I. 2010/93.

[58] Section 57 was amended by section 1(2) of the of the Employment Rights (Dispute Resolution) Act 1998 (c. 8) and by S.I. 2011/1133.

[59] Section 57ZC was inserted by S.I. 2010/93.

Table 2 (*Continued*)

Column 1 *Description of claim*	Column 2 *Provision identifying the rights of the claimant*	Column 3 *Provision conferring jurisdiction on tribunal*
Complaint that employer has refused to allow time off for dependants	Section 57A ERA[60]	Section 57B ERA[61]
Complaint that employer has failed to allow, or to pay for, time off for trustee of pension scheme	Sections 58[62] and 59 ERA	Section 60 ERA[63]
Complaint that employer has failed to allow, or to pay for, time off for employee representative	Sections 61[64] and 62 ERA	Section 63 ERA[65]
Complaint that employer has failed to allow, or to pay for, time off for young people in Wales and Scotland	Section 63A[66] and 63B[67] ERA	Section 63C ERA[68]
Complaint that employer has failed to pay for time off on medical or maternity grounds	Sections 64[69], 68[70] and 68C[71] ERA	Sections 70[72] and 70A[73] ERA
Complaint that employer has failed to allow time of for studies or training or the refusal is based on incorrect facts	Section 63D to 63H ERA[74]	Section 63I ERA[75]

[60] Section 57A was inserted by section 8 of, and Part II of Schedule 4 to, the Employment Relations Act 1999 (c. 26) and amended by section 261 of, and paragraph 151 of Schedule 27 to, the Civil Partnership Act 2004 (c. 33).

[61] Section 57B was inserted by section 8 of, and Part II of Schedule 4 to, the Employment Relations Act 1999 (c. 26) amended by S.I. 2011/133.

[62] Section 58 was amended by section 18 of, and paragraph 19 of Schedule 2 to, the Welfare Reform and Pensions Act 1999 (c. 30), section 320 of, and Part 1 of Schedule 13 to, the Pensions Act 2004 (c. 35) and section 44 of, and paragraph 12 of Schedule 3 to, the Teaching and Higher Education Act 1998 (c. 30).

[63] Section 60 was amended by section 1(2) of the of the Employment Rights (Dispute Resolution) Act 1998 (c. 8).

[64] Section 61 was amended by S.I. 1999/1925 and S.I. 2006/246.

[65] Section 63 was amended by section 1(2) of the of the Employment Rights (Dispute Resolution) Act 1998 (c. 8) and S.I. 2011/1133.

[66] Section 63A was inserted by section 32 of the Teaching and Higher Education Act 1998 (c. 30) and amended by section 39 of the Education and Skills Act 2008 (c. 25) and by section 149 of, and paragraphs 1 and 50 of Schedule 9 to the Learning and Skills Act 2000 (c. 21).

[67] Section 63B was inserted by section 33 of the Teaching and Higher Education Act 1998 (c. 30).

[68] Section 63C was inserted by section 33 of the Teaching and Higher Education Act 1998 (c. 30) and amended by S.I. 2011/1133.

[69] Section 64 was amended by S.I. 1999/3232.

[70] Section 68 was modified in its application by S.I. 2003/1964 and S.I. 2006/1073.

[71] Section 68C was inserted by S.I. 2010/93.

[72] Section 70 was amended by section 1(2) of the of the Employment Rights (Dispute Resolution) Act 1998 (c. 8) and S.I. 2011/1133. It has also been modified in its application by S.I. 2003/1964 and S.I. 2006/1073.

[73] Section 70A was inserted by S.I. 2010/93.

[74] Sections 63D to 63H were inserted by section 40 of the Apprenticeships, Skills, Children and Learning Act 2009 (c. 22).

[75] Section 63I was inserted by section 40 of the Apprenticeships, Skills, Children and Learning Act 2009 (c. 22) and amended by S.I. 2011/1133.

Table 2 (*Continued*)

Column 1 *Description of claim*	Column 2 *Provision identifying the rights of the claimant*	Column 3 *Provision conferring jurisdiction on tribunal*
Complaint that employer has unreasonably failed to provide a written statement of reasons for dismissal or the particulars are inadequate or untrue	Section 92 ERA[76]	Section 93 ERA[77]
Reference in respect of a right to redundancy payment	Section 135 ERA	Sections 163[78] and 177[79] ERA
Reference related to payment out of National Insurance Fund	Section 166 ERA[80]	Section 170 ERA
References related to payments equivalent to redundancy payments	Sections 167, 168 and 177 ERA	Section 177 ERA
Complaint that the Secretary of State has failed to make any, or insufficient, payment of out the National Insurance Fund	Section 182 ERA	Section 188 ERA[81]
Appeal against a notice of underpayment	Section 19C NMWA[82]	Section 19C NMWA
Appeal against a notice issued by the Commission for Equality and Human Rights where the notice relates to an unlawful act	Section 21 EA 2006[83]	Section 21 EA 2006
Complaint that prospective employer made enquiries about disability or health	Section 60 EA 2010	Section 120 EA 2010
Application in relation to the effect of a non-discrimination rule in an occupational pension scheme	Section 61 EA 2010	Section 120 EA 2010
Complaint in relation to a breach of a sex equality clause	Section 66 EA 2010	Section 127 EA 2010
Complaint in relation to a breach of, or application in relation to the effect of, a sex equality rule in an occupational pension scheme	Section 67 EA 2010	Section 127 EA 2010

[76] Section 92 was substituted in part by S.I. 2002/2034 and amended by section 9 of, and paragraphs 5 and 12 of Schedule 4 to, the Employment Relations Act 1999 (c. 26), sections 53 and57 of, and paragraph 28 of Schedule 1 and paragraphs 24 and 31 of Schedule 7 to, the Education Act 2002 (c. 32) and S.I. 2012/989. It has also been modified in its application by S.I. 2003/1964 and S.I. 2006/1073.

[77] Section 93 was amended by section 1(2) of the of the Employment Rights (Dispute Resolution) Act 1998 (c. 8). It has also been modified in its application by S.I. 2003/1964 and S.I. 2006/1073.

[78] Section 163 was amended by section 1(2) of the of the Employment Rights (Dispute Resolution) Act 1998 (c. 8) and by section 7 of the Employment Act 2008 (c. 24).

[79] Section 177 was amended by section 1(2) of the of the Employment Rights (Dispute Resolution) Act 1998 (c. 8).

[80] Section 170 was amended by section 1(2) of the of the Employment Rights (Dispute Resolution) Act 1998 (c. 8).

[81] Section 188 was amended by section 1(2) of the Employment Rights (Dispute Resolution) Act 1998 (c. 8).

[82] 1998 c. 39; section 19C inserted by section 46 of the Employment Relations Act 2004 (c. 24) and substituted by section 9 of the Employment Act 2008 (c. 24).

[83] 2006 c. 3; section 21 amended by section 211(1) of, and paragraphs 61 and 67 of Schedule 26 to the Equality Act 2010 (c. 15) (as amended by S.I. 2010/2279).

Table 2 (*Continued*)

Column 1 *Description of claim*	Column 2 *Provision identifying the rights of the claimant*	Column 3 *Provision conferring jurisdiction on tribunal*
Complaint in relation to a breach of a maternity equality clause	Section 73 EA 2010	Section 127 EA 2010
Complaint in relation to a breach of, or application in relation to the effect of, a maternity equality rule in an occupational pension scheme	Section 75 EA 2010	Section 127 EA 2010
Complaint in relation to terms prohibiting discussions about pay	Section 77 EA 2010	Section 120 EA 2010
Complaint that a term in a collective agreement is void or unenforceable	Section 145 EA 2010	Section 146 EA 2010
Appeal of decision of compensating authority	Regulation 42 CEC	Regulation 42 CEC
Complaint that employer has failed to pay for remunerated time off for safety representative	Regulation 4(2) of, and Schedule 2 to, the SRSC	Regulation 11 SRSC
Reference that there has been a failure to consult with employee representatives about contracting out of pension scheme	Regulation 4 OPS(CO)R and regulation 9 of OPS(DI)R	Regulation 4 OPS(CO)R and regulation 9 of OPS(DI)R
Complaint that employer has failed to pay for time off to carry out Safety Representative duties or undertake training	Regulation 7 of, and Schedule 1 to, the HSCE	Schedule 2 to the HSCE
Complaint that employer has refused to allow annual leave, compensation, payment, compensatory rest	Regulations 13, 13A,14, 16, 24, 24A, 27 and 27A WTR	Regulation 30 WTR
Appeal against improvement or prohibition notice	Paragraph 6 of Schedule 3 to WTR	Paragraph 6 of Schedule 3 to WTR
Appeal against improvement or prohibition notice	Regulation 18 COMAH	Regulation 18 COMAH
Complaint in relation to refusal of annual leave or to make payment	Regulation 11 MSR	Regulation 18 MSR
Complaint in relation to refusal to provide paid annual leave	Regulation 4 CAR	Regulation 18 CAR
Complaint in relation to failure to provide free health assessments	Regulation 5 CAR	Regulation 18 CAR
Complaint in relation to refusal of annual leave or to make payment	Regulation 11 FVR	Regulation 19 FVR
Complaint that employer has refused to allow or failed to pay for time off for information and consultation or negotiating representatives	Regulations 27 and 28 ICR	Regulation 29 ICR
Appeal against improvement notice	Paragraph 6(2) of Schedule 2 to the RTR	Paragraph 6(2) of Schedule 2 to the RTR
Complaint in relation to failure of employer to inform or consult	Regulation 13 TUPE	Regulation 15 TUPE
Complaint that employer has failed to allow, or pay for, time off for functions as employee representative	Paragraphs 2 and 3 of the Schedule to OPR	Paragraph 4 of the Schedule to OPR

Table 2 (*Continued*)

Column 1 *Description of claim*	Column 2 *Provision identifying the rights of the claimant*	Column 3 *Provision conferring jurisdiction on tribunal*
Complaint that employer has failed to allow, or pay for, time off for members of special negotiating body	Regulations 28 and 29 ECSR	Regulation 30 ECSR
Complaint that employer has failed to allow, or pay for, time off for members of special negotiating body	Regulations 43 and 44 CCBR	Regulation 45 CCBR
Appeal against notice from Health and Safety Executive or a local authority	Regulation 21 and Part 2 of Schedule 8 to REACHER	Regulation 21 and Part 2 of Schedule 8 to REACHER
Reference to determine what particulars ought to be included in an itemised statement of stipend	Regulation 6 EOR	Regulation 9 EOR
Reference to determine what particulars ought to be included in a statement of particulars or changes to particulars	Regulations 3 and 6 EOR	Regulation 9 EOR
Complaint that employer has failed to allow, or pay for, time off for members of special negotiating body	Regulations 26 and 27 ELLR	Regulation 28 ELLR.

Table 3 Amount of fee—claim made by a single claimant

Column 1	Column 2	Column 3
Fee type	Type A claim	Type B claim
1. Issue fee	£160	£250
2. Hearing fee	£230	£950

Table 4 Amount of fee—fee group

Part A—Type A claim

Column 1	Column 2		
Type of fee	Number of claimants/amount of fee		
	2-10	11-200	Over 200
Issue fee	£320	£640	£960
Hearing fee	£460	£920	£1380

Part B—type B claim

Column 1	Column 2		
Type of fee	Number of claimants/amount of fee		
	2-10	11-200	Over 200
Issue fee	£500	£1,000	£1,500
Hearing fee	£1900	£3,800	£5,700

SCHEDULE 3 ARTICLE 17
REMISSIONS AND PART REMISSIONS

Interpretation

1.— (1) In this Schedule—

'child' means a child or young person in respect of whom a party is entitled to receive child benefit in accordance with section 141, and regulations made under section 142, of the Social Security Contributions and Benefits Act 1992;[84]

'child care costs' has the meaning given in Part 3 of the Criminal Legal Aid (Financial Resources) Regulations 2013;[85]

'couple' has the meaning given in section 3(5A) of the Tax Credits Act 2002;[86]

'disposable monthly income' has the meaning given in paragraph 5;

'excluded benefits' means—

(a) any of the following benefits payable under the Social Security Contributions and Benefits Act 1992—
   (i)   attendance allowance paid under section 64;
   (ii) severe disablement allowance;
   (iii) carer's allowance;
   (iv) disability living allowance;
   (v)   constant attendance allowance paid under section 104 as an increase to a disablement pension;
   (vi) council tax benefit;
   (vii) any payment made out of the social fund;
   (viii) housing benefit;

(b) any direct payment made under the Community Care, Services for Carers and Children's Services (Direct Payments) (England) Regulations 2009,[87] the Community Care, Services for Carers and Children's Services (Direct Payments) (Wales) Regulations 2011;[88] or section 12B(1) of the Social Work (Scotland) Act 1968;[89]

(c) a back to work bonus payable under section 26 of the Jobseekers Act 1995;[90]

---

[84] 1992 c. 4.

[85] S.I. 2013/471.

[86] 2002 c. 21. Section 3(5A) was inserted by paragraph 144 of Schedule 24 to the Civil Partnership Act 2004 (c. 33).

[87] S.I. 2009/1887.

[88] S.I. 2011/831.

[89] 1968 c. 49; section 12B was inserted by section 4 of the Community Care (Direct Payments) Act 1996 (c. 30). Subsection (1) was amended by section 7 of the Community Care and Health (Scotland) Act 2002 (asp 5) and section 70 of the Regulation of Care (Scotland) Act 2001 (asp 8).

[90] 1995 c. 18. Section 26 has been amended but none of those amendments are relevant to this Order.

(d) any exceptionally severe disablement allowance paid under the Personal Injuries (Civilians) Scheme 1983;[91]

(e) any pension paid under the Naval, Military and Air Forces etc. (Disablement and Death) Service Pension Order 2006;[92]

(f) any payment made from the Independent Living Funds; and

(g) any financial support paid under an agreement for the care of a foster child;

'gross annual income' means total annual income, for the 12 months preceding the application for remission or part remission, from all sources other than receipt of any of the excluded benefits;

'gross monthly income' means total monthly income, for the month in which the application for remission or part remission is made, from all sources other than receipt of any of the excluded benefits;

'the Independent Living Funds' means any payment made from the funds listed at regulation 20(2)(b) of the Criminal Legal Aid (Financial Resources) Regulations 2013;

'partner' means a person with whom the party lives as a couple and includes a person with whom the party is not currently living but from whom the party is not living separate and apart;

'party' means the individual who would, but for this Schedule, be liable to pay the fee required under this Order.

(2) Paragraphs 2, 3 and 4 do not apply to a party for whom civil legal services, for which a certificate has been issued under the Civil Legal Aid (Procedure) Regulations 2012,[93] have been made available under arrangements made for the purposes of Part 1 of the Legal Aid, Sentencing and Punishment of Offenders Act 2012[94] for the purposes of the proceedings.

Full remission of fees—qualifying benefits

2.— (1) No fee is payable under this Order if, at the time when a fee would otherwise be payable, the party is in receipt of a qualifying benefit.

(2) The following are qualifying benefits for the purposes of sub-paragraph (1)—

(a) income support under the Social Security Contributions and Benefits Act 1992;

(b) working tax credit, provided that no child tax credit is being paid to the party;

(c) income-based jobseeker's allowance under the Jobseekers Act 1995;

(d) guarantee credit under the State Pension Credit Act 2002;[95] and

(e) income-related employment and support allowance under the Welfare Reform Act 2007.[96]

---

[91] S.I. 1983/686 as amended by S.I. 1983/1164, S.I. 1983/1540, S.I. 1984/1289, S.I. 1984/1675, S.I. 1985/1313, S.I. 1986/628, S.I. 1987/191, S.I. 1988/367, S.I. 1988/2260, section 123 of, and paragraph 3 of Schedule 8 to, the Criminal Justice Act 1988 (c. 33), S.I. 1989/415, S.I. 1990/1300, S.I. 1991/708, S.I. 1992/702, S.I. 1992/3226, S.I. 1993/480, S.I. 1994/715, S.I. 1994/2021, S.I. 1995/445, S.I. 1997/812, S.I. 1999/262, S.I. 2001/420, S.I. 2002/672, S.I. 2004/717, S.I. 2005/655, S.I. 2005/3031, S.I. 2006/765, S.I. 2007/646, S.I. 2008/592, S.I. 2008/2683, S.I. 2009/438, S.I. 2010/283, S.I. 2010/1172, S.I. 2011/811, S.I. 2011/1740, S.I. 2012/670 and modified by S.I. 2005/3137.

[92] S.I. 2006/606 amended S.I. 2006/1455, S.I. 2007/909, S.I. 2008/679, S.I. 2008/2683, S.I. 2009/706, S.I. 2010/240, S.I. 2011/235, S.I. 2011/1740 and S.I. 2012/359.

[93] S.I. 2012/3098.

[94] 2012 c. 10.

[95] 2002 c. 16.

[96] 2007 c. 5.

Full remission of fees—gross annual income

3.— (1) No fee is payable under this Order if, at the time when the fee would otherwise be payable, the party has the number of children specified in column 1 of the following table and—
- (a) if the party is single, the gross annual income of the party does not exceed the amount set out in the appropriate row of column 2; or
- (b) if the party is one of a couple, the gross annual income of the couple does not exceed the amount set out in the appropriate row of column 3.

Column 1 Number of children of party	Column 2 Single	Column 3 Couple
no children	£13,000	£18,000
1 child	£15,930	£20,930
2 children	£18,860	£23,860
3 children	£21,790	£26,790
4 children	£24,720	£29,720

(2) If the party has more than 4 children then the relevant amount of gross annual income is the amount specified in the table for 4 children plus the sum of £2,930 for each additional child.

Full and part remission of fees—disposable monthly income

1.— (1) No fee is payable under this Order if, at the time when the fee would otherwise be payable, the disposable monthly income of the party is £50 or less.
(2) The maximum amount of fee payable is—
- (a) if the disposable monthly income of the party is more than £50 but does not exceed £210, an amount equal to one-quarter of every £10 of the party's disposable monthly income up to a maximum of £50; and
- (b) if the disposable monthly income is more than £210, an amount equal to £50 plus one-half of every £10 over £200 of the party's disposable monthly income.

(3) Where the fee that would otherwise be payable under this Order is greater than the maximum fee which a party is required to pay as calculated in sub-paragraph (2), the fee will be remitted to the amount payable under that sub-paragraph.

Disposable monthly income

5.— (1) A party's disposable monthly income is the gross monthly income of the party for the month in which the fee becomes payable ('the period') less the deductions referred to in sub-paragraphs (2) and (3).
(2) There are to be deducted from the gross monthly income—
- (a) income tax paid or payable in respect of the period;
- (b) any contributions estimated to have been paid under Part 1 of the Social Security Contributions and Benefits Act 1992 in respect of the period;

 (c) either—
  (i) monthly rent or monthly payment in respect of a mortgage debt or hereditable security, payable in respect of the only or main dwelling of the party, less any housing benefit paid under the Social Security Contributions and Benefits Act 1992; or
  (ii) the monthly cost of the living accommodation of the party;
 (d) any child care costs paid or payable in respect of the period;
 (e) if the party is making bona fide payments for the maintenance of a child who is not a member of the household of the party, the amount of such payments paid or payable in respect of the period; and
 (f) any amount paid or payable by the party, in respect of the period, in pursuance of a court order.

(3) There will be deducted from the gross monthly income an amount representing the cost of living expenses in respect of the period being—
 (a) £315; plus
 (b) £244 for each child of the party; plus
 (c) £159, if the party has a partner.

Resources of partners

6.— (1) For the purpose of determining whether a party is entitled to the remission or part remission of a fee in accordance with this Schedule, the income of a partner, if any, is to be included as income of the party.

(2) The receipt by a partner of a qualifying benefit does not entitle a party to remission of a fee.

Application for remission or part remission of fees

7.— (1) A party is only relieved by paragraphs 2 to 4 of liability to pay a fee if that party makes an application for remission in accordance with this paragraph.

(2) An application for remission or part remission of a fee must be made to the Lord Chancellor at the time when the fee would otherwise be payable.

(3) Where a claim for full remission of fees is made, the party must provide documentary evidence of, as the case may be—
 (a) entitlement to a qualifying benefit; or
 (b) gross annual income and, if applicable, the children included for the purposes of paragraph 3.

(4) Where a claim for full or part remission of fees under paragraph 4 is made, the party must provide documentary evidence of—
 (a) such of the party's gross monthly income as is derived from—
  (i) employment;
  (ii) rental or other income received from persons living with the party by reason of their residence in the party's home;
  (iii) a pension; or
  (iv) a state benefit, not being an excluded benefit; and
 (b) any expenditure being deducted from the gross monthly income in accordance with paragraph 5(2).

Remission in exceptional circumstances

8. A fee specified in this Order may be reduced or remitted where the Lord Chancellor is satisfied there are exceptional circumstances which justify doing so.

Time for payment following remission application

9.— (1) Where a person applies for remission on or before the date on which a fee is payable, the date for payment of the fee specified in article 4 is disapplied.

(2) Where the Lord Chancellor refuses remission or grants part remission of a fee, the amount of the fee which remains unremitted must be paid within such period as may be notified in writing by the Lord Chancellor to the party or the fee group (as the case may be).

Refunds

10.— (1) Subject to sub-paragraph (3), where a party has not provided the documentary evidence required by paragraph 7 and a fee has been paid at a time when, under paragraph 2, 3 or 4, it was not payable, the fee must be refunded if documentary evidence relating to the time when the fee became payable is provided at a later date.

(2) Subject to sub-paragraph (3), where a fee has been paid at a time where the Lord Chancellor, if all the circumstances had been known, would have reduced or remitted the fee under paragraph 8, the fee or the amount by which the fee would have been reduced, as the case may be, must be refunded.

(3) No refund shall be made under this paragraph unless the party who paid the fee applies within 6 months of paying the fee.

(4) The Lord Chancellor may extend the period of 6 months mentioned in sub-paragraph (3) if the Lord Chancellor considers that there is a good reason for an application being made after the end of the period of 6 months.

EXPLANATORY NOTE

(This note is not part of the Order)

This Order introduces fees for claims made to an employment tribunal and appeals to the Employment Appeal Tribunal.

Part 2 makes provision for fees to be payable when a claim is presented to an employment tribunal and following notification of listing for the final hearing. The amount of the fee depends upon the type of the claim and the number of claimants. Different fees apply to single claimants and to groups of claimants, called 'fee groups'. 'Type A claims' are listed in Table 2 of Schedule 2 to the Order. All other claims are called 'Type B claims', for the purposes of calculating the amount of the fee payable. The amount of the fees payable by single claimants are listed in Table 3 of Schedule 2 and the amount payable by fee groups of different sizes are listed in Table 4 of Schedule 2.

Fees are also payable in an employment tribunal by the party making an application of the type mentioned in Schedule 1 to this Order and a fee of £600 is payable by a respondent when the parties agree to judicial mediation.

In addition, article 12 allows a claimant in an employment tribunal to opt out of a fee group and continue as a single claimant if the fee group they were previously included in has failed to pay the appropriate fee and might be struck out for non-payment of that fee.

Part 3 deals with fees in the Employment Appeal Tribunal. A fee of £400 is payable by an appellant following receipt of a notice of appeal by the Employment Appeal Tribunal. A fee of £1200 is payable by an appellant following notification of a direction by the Employment Appeal Tribunal for an oral hearing to dispose finally of proceedings.

Part 4 makes transitional arrangements and provides for fee remission in some circumstances.

APPENDIX 3

Practice Directions

EMPLOYMENT TRIBUNALS (ENGLAND & WALES)

Presidential Practice Direction—Presentation of Claims

1. This Presidential Practice Direction, which sets out the methods by which a completed form may be presented, is made in accordance with the provisions of Regulation 11 of the Employment Tribunals (Constitution & Rules Procedure) Regulations 2013. The Practice Direction has effect on and from 29 July 2013.

2. Rule 8 (1) of Schedule 1 of the Employment Tribunals (Constitution and Rules of Procedure) Regulations 2013 ('the Rules') is in the following terms:

   'Presenting the claim

   8.— (1) A claim shall be started by presenting a completed claim form (using a prescribed form) in accordance with any practice direction made under regulation 11 which supplements this rule.'

3. For the purpose of this Presidential Practice Direction 'claims' are defined by Rule 1 of the Rules as any proceedings before an Employment Tribunal making a complaint. A 'complaint' is also clarified as anything that is referred to as a claim, complaint, reference, application or appeal in any enactment which confers jurisdiction on the Tribunal.

4. **Methods of starting a claim**

   A completed claim form may be presented to an Employment Tribunal in England & Wales:

   Online by using the online form submission service provided by Her Majesty's Courts and Tribunals Service, accessible at www.employmenttribunals.service.gov.uk;

   By post to: **Employment Tribunal Central Office (England & Wales), PO Box 10218, Leicester, LE1 8EG.**

   A claim may also be presented in person to an Employment Tribunal Office listed in the schedule to this Practice Direction. If a claim is so presented, it must be so within tribunal business hours (9am to 4pm, Monday to Friday, not including public holidays or weekends).

5. The Tribunal shall reject a claim if it is not accompanied by the appropriate fee or a remission application (Rule 11).

David Latham
President, Employment Tribunals (England and Wales)
Dated: 29 July 2013

Additional Information for the Assistance of Individuals who wish to present claims

The following information does not form part of this Practice Direction but is provided for the assistance of those who wish to present claims (hereafter 'claimants').

1. If a claim is rejected for not being accompanied by the relevant fee or admission application (see item 5 above) for the purposes of the time limit which applies to presentation of the claim, time will continue to run.

2. Guidance on methods of payment is available at http://www.justice.gov.uk/ tribunals/employment/claims.

3. The speediest and most efficient method of presenting a claim will normally be by using the online submission service. The online system will assist in calculating the fee which is due, will ensure that a claimant does remember to pay or apply for remission (since it will not allow the claim to be submitted otherwise) and will reach the fee processing centre very quickly. It also leaves no room for doubt about when the claim was presented since this is recorded electronically. That may be important if the claim is being presented close to the end of the limitation period. An electronic version of the claim form can be found at www.employmenttribunals.service.gov.uk.

Schedule

Region	Address
Birmingham	13th Floor Centre City Tower 7 Hill Street Birmingham B5 4UU
East Anglia	Huntingdon Law Courts and Tribunals Centre Walden Road Huntingdon Cambridgeshire PO29 3DW
East Midlands	3rd Floor Byron House 2A Maid Marian Way Nottingham NG1 6HS
Leeds	4th Floor City Exchange 11 Albion Street Leeds LS1 4ES
London Central	Victory House 30–34 Kingsway London WC2B 6EX

EMPLOYMENT TRIBUNALS (SCOTLAND)

Presidential Practice Direction—Presentation of Claims

Rule 8 (1) of the Employment Tribunals Rules of Procedure (as set out in Schedule 1 of the Employment Tribunals (Constitution and Rules of Procedure Regulations 2013) is in the following terms:

'Presenting the claim

8.— (1) A claim shall be started by presenting a completed claim form (using a pre-scribed form) in accordance with any practice direction made under regulation 11 which supplements this rule.'

This Presidential Practice Direction, which sets out the methods by which a completed claim form may be presented, is made in accordance with the powers set out in Regulation 11 of the Employment Tribunals (Constitution and Rules of Procedure) Regulations 2013. The Practice Direction has effect from 29 July 2013.

Methods of presenting a completed claim form

A completed claim form may be presented to an Employment Tribunal in Scotland:

1. Online by using the online form submission service provided by Her Majesty's Courts and Tribunals Service, accessible at www.employmenttribunals.service.gov.uk;

2. By post to **Employment Tribunals Central Office (Scotland), PO Box 27105, GLASGOW, G2 9JR.**

A claim may also be presented, in the alternative, by hand to an Employment Tribunal Office listed in the schedule to this Practice Direction. If a claim is so presented, it must be done within tribunal business hours (9am to 4pm, Monday to Friday, not including public holidays or weekends).

Whichever method of presentation is used, the claim form must be accompanied by the relevant fee or a remission application.[1]

Shona Simon
President, Employment Tribunals (Scotland)
Dated: 29 July 2013

---

[1] Information about the fees payable for making a claim can be found at http://hmctsformfinder. justice.gov.uk/HMCTS/FormFinder.do (search for leaflet/form number 'T435' if you are mak-ing a claim as an individual; or 'T436' if you are making a claim as part of a group of claimants. Information on the remission scheme which applies can be found at http://hmctsformfinder.justice. gov.uk/HMCTS/FormFinder.do (Search for leaflet/form number 'T438'). In both cases paper copies of the relevant booklet are available on request from the Employment Tribunal Office in Glasgow (contact details available in attached schedule).

Additional Information for the Assistance of Individuals who wish to present claims

The following information does not form part of the Practice Direction but is provided for the assistance of individuals who wish to present claims (hereafter 'claimants').

1. If a claim is not accompanied by a fee or a remission application then it will be legally rejected. If this happens then, for the purposes of the time limit which applies to presentation of the claim, time will continue to run. If the claim was first presented close to the time limit then this could mean the claim is time barred if a claimant chooses to resubmit the claim with the fee or remission application.

2. Guidance on methods of payment is available at http://www.justice.gov.uk/tribunals/employment/claims. Claimants should note that cash cannot be accepted at a local Employment Tribunal Office. If you are only able to pay by cash then further information on what you should do is available by telephoning +44 (0)845 795 9775.

3. The speediest and most efficient method of presenting a claim will normally be by using the online submission service. The online system will assist in calculating the fee which is due, will ensure that a claimant does remember to pay or apply for remission (since it will not allow the claim to be submitted otherwise) and will reach the fee processing centre very quickly. It also leaves no room for doubt about when the claim was presented since this is recorded electronically; that may be important if the claim is being presented close to the end of the limitation period. An electronic version of the claim form can be found at www.employmenttribunals.service.gov.uk.

Schedule

Office	Address
Aberdeen	Mezzanine Floor Atholl House 84–88 Guild Street Aberdeen AB11 6LT
Dundee	Ground Floor Block C Caledonian House Greenmarket Dundee DD1 4QB
Edinburgh	54–56 Melville Street Edinburgh EH3 7HF
Glasgow	Eagle Building 215 Bothwell Street Glasgow G2 7TS Telephone: 0141 204 0730

Index